7: PERSPECTIVES IN CRITICISM

PERSPECTIVES IN CRITICISM

7:

Leonard Cabell Pronko

The World
of Jean Anouilh

UNIVERSITY OF CALIFORNIA PRESS
Berkeley and Los Angeles
1961

University of California Press
Berkeley and Los Angeles, California
Cambridge University Press
London, England

LIBRARY OF CONGRESS CATALOG CARD NO. 61-6778
Printed in the United States of America
Designed by Ward Ritchie

To My Mother and Grandmother

Acknowledgments

IT IS A PLEASURE to express here my gratitude to Professor Panos Morphos of Tulane University for his guidance and encouragement during the writing of this book. I wish also to thank Professors Charles Silin, William Woods, Concha Zardoya, and Aline Taylor, who read the manuscript and offered many valuable suggestions. I owe a special debt of gratitude to Miss Marie-Jeanne Lefèvre, who spent many hours checking my translations and gave me the benefit of her keen intelligence and fine intuition. I am also greatly indebted to La Table Ronde of Paris for their kind permission to quote from the works of Anouilh.

L.C.P.

Pomona College
Claremont, California

Contents

Illustrations

Introduction

JEAN ANOUILH is generally recognized to be one of the leading and most representative playwrights of the generation that began writing shortly before the Second World War. At the age of fifty he has produced almost thirty plays, some of them of considerable value in themselves, all of them interesting for the picture they present of man's condition, and for the dramatic values that they embody. The principal purpose of this study is to examine these two aspects of Anouilh's plays: the dramatic themes and their expression. They are not, as one might suspect, mutually exclusive. As in the classics, the structure, the characters, and the style are so closely bound up with the themes that it is impossible to discuss one without the others.

The first part of the book, entitled "Dramatic Themes," deals with the major preoccupations of Anouilh: man's predicament, love, money, and the social classes. Upon even a cursory examination of Anouilh's plays, these questions stand out as being those of most constant interest. The human predicament involves the relationship of individuals to themselves, to each other, to God or some indefinite omnipotence, and to their past. The love theme is treated with a notable absence of "moonlight and roses." Both love and the questions of money and social caste are related to the theme of man's fate, and are, to a degree, an illustration of it.

The second part of this study, entitled "Dramatic Values," stresses the way in which Anouilh has handled themes that bear a more direct relation to his dramatic art: the theater as life and life as theater, the meaning of realism in the theater, the function of the characters, and the use of myth.

When a dramatist has put himself so passionately into his plays as has Anouilh, biographical details are of little importance except as a corroboration of what we have found in the works, and in telling us the reasons for the existence of certain characters or themes. This is particularly true in Anouilh's instance, because we know so little of his life, and his plays give us a truer picture of the man than can any of the factual data that we are able to gather. Extremely retiring, Jean Anouilh is seldom seen in public except at the *première* of one of his plays. Writing to Hubert Gignoux in answer to a request for biographical details, Anouilh said:

> I have no biography, and I am very glad of it. I was born in Bordeaux on the 23rd of June, 1910. I came to Paris when I was young and attended the Colbert Primary School and later Chaptal College. A year and a half at the Law Faculty in Paris, then two years in an advertising firm, where I learned to be ingenious and exact, lessons that for me took the place of studies in literature. After my play *L'Hermine* was produced I decided to live only by writing for the theatre, and a little for films. It was folly, but I did right to make that decision. I have managed never to touch journalism, and in films all I have on my conscience are one or two cheap farces and a few unsigned and now forgotten romantic melodramas. The rest is my life, and for as long as it pleases Heaven for it to be my private business, I shall keep the details to myself.[1]

Apart from this skeletal information, we know that one of his relatives was director of the Casino at Arcachon, not far from Bordeaux, and Anouilh's mother played in the orchestra. For three months in 1919 he spent every evening listening to the operettas at the Casino. If this did not mark the incipience of his interest in the theater, it at least provided him with the background for more than one play, and an experience with theater people which was to serve him later in his creation of characters.[2]

By that time he was already writing plays in imitation of Edmond Rostand. His first long play, which remains unpublished, was written at the age of sixteen.

During his two years in the advertising business Anouilh supplemented his income by writing publicity scripts and comic gags for the films. At this time he met Monelle Valentin, whom he was later to marry, and subsequently divorce. It was she who created on the stage many of the roles of his young heroines, including that of Antigone.

At the age of nineteen, Anouilh wrote *Mandarine*, his earliest play to be produced, although it did not see the footlights until three years later in 1933. Of this play, which remains unpublished, Edward Owen Marsh says:

> Like so many of his later plays this first effort was about the hypocrisy men are prepared to countenance for the sake of money. An innocent young girl, with a missionary passion for the redemption of sinners, wastes her pure love on trying to save a smooth gigolo whom his unsavoury friends have nicknamed "Mandarine." The play did not hang together and though the critics saw in it signs of skill in handling characters and dialogue they were not very impressed.[3]

In 1931 Anouilh became secretary of Louis Jouvet's company, which brought him into direct contact with the world of the theater. Jouvet, however, showed little interest in Anouilh's talents as a dramatist, although he was kind enough to lend the young man the stage furniture from his production of Giraudoux's *Siegfried* when Anouilh was married and could not afford to furnish an apartment.

It was at the recommendation of Pierre Fresnay that Paulette Pax produced at the Théâtre de l'Oeuvre his first serious play, *L'hermine* (*The Ermine*), in April, 1932.[4] Although it ran for a bare thirty-seven performances, it was considered to reflect a real dramatic temperament. The next three years, spent in comparative poverty, witnessed the writing of *Jézabel, Le bal des voleurs* (*Thieves' Carnival*), and *La sauvage* (*Restless Heart*), none of which received production until a later date. It was only in 1935 that another of Anouilh's plays was produced, this time *Y avait un prisonnier* (*Once Was a Prisoner*) at the Théâtre des Ambassadeurs. The play was relatively successful and the film rights were bought by Hollywood, which fact assured Anouilh's financial position at least. He continued to support himself by writing film scenarios, including those of *Caroline Chérie, Cavalcade d'Amour, Monsieur Vincent, Anna Karénine,* and *Deux Sous de Violettes.*

In 1937 *Le voyageur sans bagage* (*Traveller Without Luggage*) was produced with both artistic and financial success, and in the following years one of Anouilh's plays was produced almost every season. *Le bal des voleurs, La sauvage,* and *Le rendez-vous de Senlis* (*Dinner with the Family*) in 1938, *Léocadia* (*Time Remembered*) in 1939, *Eurydice* (*Legend of Lovers* in the United States, *Point of Departure* in England) in 1941, *Antigone* in 1944 with frequent revivals thereafter, *Roméo et Jeannette* (*Fading Mansions*) in 1946, *L'invitation au château* (*Ring Round the Moon*) in 1947, *Ardèle* (*Cry of the Peacock*) and *Cécile* in 1949, *La répétition* (*The Rehearsal*) in 1950, *Colombe* (played in English as *Mademoiselle Colombe*) in 1951,

La valse des toréadors (*Waltz of the Toreadors*) in 1952, *L'alouette* (*The Lark*) in 1953, *Ornifle* in 1955, *Pauvre Bitos* (*Poor Bitos*) in 1956, *L'hurluberlu* (*The Fighting Cock* in the United States*) early in 1959, and *Becket ou L'honneur de Dieu* (*Becket or the Honor of God*) in the 1959–60 season. Most of these plays have been gathered together in various collections under the titles of *Pièces noires* (*Black Plays*), *Pièces roses* (*Rose Plays*), *Nouvelles pièces noires* (*New Black Plays*), *Pièces brillantes* (*Brilliant Plays*), and *Pièces grinçantes* (*Grating Plays*).

It was *Antigone* that firmly established Anouilh's popularity in France, for it appeared during the German Occupation and served as a rallying point for the disheartened French, who could see their own struggle reflected in the conflict between the uncompromising attitude of Antigone and the expediency of Créon. They identified Antigone with the spirit of freedom, and Créon with the Vichy government, and not even the threat of air raids could keep them away from the theater. A quarrel soon broke out between those who maintained that Anouilh had shown too much sympathy for Créon's viewpoint and was therefore in sympathy with the Vichy government, and those who asserted that the author was clearly on the side of his heroine. However, it seems doubtful that Anouilh had intended his play to have the political meaning that was found in it. Madame Béatrix Dussane notes that during the entire Occupation Anouilh remained "immersed in his work, declaring that he cared nothing for politics." [5]

Several years before the outbreak of the Second World War the themes and conflicts of *Antigone* were already established as part of Anouilh's dramatic universe, and it seems sensible, in view of his professed apolitical attitudes, to assume they reflect personal preoccupations and are an outgrowth of the conditions that marked his early life. This does not imply that Anouilh knows nothing of the intricacies of French politics. In his later plays he makes pointed political references, which apparently not only amuse and excite his audience, but on at least one occasion—at the opening of *Pauvre Bitos*—led to a near riot. This play, it might be noted, has not been released by the author for foreign presentation, since it deals, at least in part, with resistance and collaboration, and Anouilh does not feel that the dirty linen of the French should be washed in public—at any rate, not before a non-French public. *L'hurluberlu* contains allusions that might be applied to De Gaulle, and *Becket* gives passing mention to collaboration and resistance. But such political implications are only of incidental interest, and add little to the real and lasting meaning of Anouilh's plays, which are concerned with a more fundamental struggle.

Today Anouilh is a firmly established dramatist whose every *première* is eagerly awaited. In spite of success, he is rarely seen in public, and assiduously refuses to grant interviews. When his plays are in rehearsal, however, he is ever-present, and when he forgets his "charming Bordeaux shyness of manner"[6] he can become bitingly sarcastic. During rehearsals of *Colombe*, four actors resigned from the company. It is pleasant to be able to add that the leading actors in the recent production of *Becket*, which Anouilh directed along with Roland Piétri, considered the author to be not only a skillful director but an agreeable one as well.[7] His acting ability has also been commented upon by those who have had the good fortune to hear him read his plays, and Louise de Vilmorin says he is the most extraordinary actor she has ever known.[8] Anouilh and Monelle Valentin seem to have passed some of their talent on to their daughter Catherine, for she has already appeared in several plays, including *Ornifle* in 1955.

Anouilh has been generous and discerning in his appreciation of new dramatists. When *En attendant Godot* (*Waiting for Godot*) was presented in 1953, he published a letter in *Arts* praising Beckett's play and affirming its importance. Three years later, a letter in *Le Figaro* contributed greatly to the success of Ionesco's *Les chaises* (*The Chairs*) in its revival at the Studio des Champs-Elysées. His encouragement of these authors, however, has not prevented him from introducing a spirited parody of the avant-garde theater in the second act of *L'hurluberlu.*

It is only since the war that Anouilh has become known abroad. His plays have been produced throughout Europe, and in the United States with a certain success. It is noteworthy, however, that Anouilh's success in this country nowhere nearly matches that which he enjoys on the Continent. This may perhaps be ascribed to several factors. In the first place, Anouilh's basic pessimism runs against the grain of the optimism that is typical, if not of all, of at least the majority of people who form the commodity theater audience in the United States.[9] Second, the situations he presents are sometimes typically French, and therefore strike no responsive chord in an American audience. The cuckold theme and the *ménage à trois* are, after all, timeworn traditions in French literature, whereas in Anouilh's opinion they "remain an enigma to the American audience, and therefore cannot reach and touch them."[10] Third, as Anouilh himself has pointed out, "there has been a certain incomprehension with regard to my plays produced in the States. They have been weighed in the balance of realism, and found wanting, whereas they are not realistic, but a poetic and imaginative interpretation of reality."[11] The Broadway theaters usually present plays cast more or less in the realist's forms, and cater to an audience that prefers to have its thinking done for it. Anouilh's plays, often realistic in some respects, require a certain amount of thought on the part of the beholder. Moreover, that thought may lead us to discover things about ourselves which we would prefer not to know. Last, the American translators, or rather adapters, of Anouilh's plays have seldom done them justice, and have frequently wrought fundamental changes in the works.

In the past few years, particularly with the advent of Off-Broadway theater in New York, the American public has waked up to some of the interesting serious and avant-garde drama being written in Europe. Today Anouilh's popularity here seems on the increase. His first real success in the United States was with the Cherry Lane Theater production of *Thieves' Carnival* during the 1954–55 season. This production won the Antoinette Perry Award and received a citation from the Cultural Division of the French Embassy.

Before 1954, only five Anouilh plays had been seen in New York, none of them running for more than sixty-eight performances. Even Katharine Cornell's impressive *Antigone* had only sixty-four performances in 1945–46. *Ardèle,* under the title of *The Cry of the Peacock,* folded after two nights in 1949, but it was revived in a new, more faithful adaptation (that of Lucienne Hill) in 1957 and enjoyed a happier fate. *Legend of Lovers* closed in 1951 after twenty-two performances and its revival in 1960 was no more fortunate.

The successful run of *Thieves' Carnival* was followed in 1955–56 by the triumphant performance of Julie Harris in *The Lark; Waltz of the Toreadors* in 1956–57; and *Time Remembered* in 1957–58. *The Fighting Cock* folded quickly in 1960, and at the time of writing plans are announced for a production of *Becket or the Honor of God* in 1960–61.

Until recently, London was more aware of French theatrical life than was New York. *Ring Round the Moon,* Christopher Fry's adaptation of *L'invitation au château,* had revealed Anouilh to English audiences, who before 1950 had given only cool receptions to *Antigone* and *Roméo et Jeannette (Fading Mansions).* Since 1950, however, his plays have been produced frequently in London with considerable success.

To date, a number of articles on the theater of Anouilh have appeared. Four books are concerned exclusively with this subject. One, Hubert Gignoux's *Jean Anouilh* (1946), includes discussion of only one or two plays beyond those designated as *Pièces roses* and *Pièces noires. A la Rencontre de Jean Anouilh* by Jean Didier (1946) is a slim volume, inaccurate in details, which amounts to little more than an article. The most exhaustive study of Anouilh's theater is found in Edward Owen Marsh's *Jean Anouilh, Poet of Pierrot and Pantaloon* (1953); it is a work of popularization dwelling at length upon the plot of each play. It contains an excellent Introduction and Conclusion, is clearly written, well-organized, and well-conceived. Mr. Marsh has, as he himself tells us, preferred to stay on general grounds. Robert de Luppé's short study, *Jean Anouilh* (1959), investigates several important themes in Anouilh's theater, but it is not exhaustive. It is of particular interest for its discussion of the more recent plays and for a valuable bibliography. There still exists, however, a need for more detailed studies of the important aspects of Anouilh's theater, and for a synthesis of his work to date. The present book is an attempt to satisfy in part that need by dealing with the major themes and the dramatic world they reveal.

Part One: Dramatic Themes

1

Man's Predicament

THE MAJOR serious dramatists of the French Occupation and the period following it—a Sartre, a Camus,
or an Anouilh, for example—are concerned primarily
with man and his place in the universe. Instead of a
theater of character, France has today a theater dealing
with the human predicament. The dramatist does not
present a personage for our scrutiny; we are not expected to delight in the development of character, in
the skillful revelation of various traits, or in the use of
realistic psychological detail. Rather is our attention
centered upon the characters as representative of man
today, his situation in the world and in the universe, and
his relation to other men and to his destiny. The serious
contemporary playwright is interested in the entire human condition, and his emphasis is not upon the individual, but upon man. This theater seeks "to explore
the state of man in its entirety and to present to the
modern man a portrait of himself, his problems, his
hopes and his struggles."[1] One of the achievements of
the modern writers has been to allow us to see the
plight of mankind in that of the characters.

Anouilh's view of life and man's place in the universe
has remained essentially unchanged throughout his career. The later plays clarify and elaborate upon ideas
presented in the early ones. To be sure, there is a certain
development and a shift in focus as the author matures.

3

But it is noteworthy that Anouilh's basic concepts are present from the beginning and have not changed fundamentally in the course of almost thirty years. If this has led to some degree of repetition, it is to be regretted, but that very repetition tends to give a certain unity to Anouilh's theater. He has developed what we might call a personal mythology, composed of characters, situations, and language which are peculiar to his world and reflect effectively his view of life.

The development of Anouilh's themes makes it possible to divide the plays into several periods, based upon fundamental similarities among the plays of the various groups.

THE FIRST GROUP: MAN AGAINST HIS PAST (1931–1939)

The Pièces Noires

The plays of the first group—those written during the thirties—stress the plight of man trying to escape from his past, sometimes succeeding but more often than not, failing. In *L'hermine* (1931), the earliest play that Anouilh has allowed to be published, the protagonist, Frantz, thinks at first he has been successful, but discovers that it is impossible to escape his past. Frantz is in love with Monime, the niece of the Duchesse de Granat, but it is impossible for him to marry her. He is too poor, and the Duchess would never consent to her niece's marriage with the son of her late physician. She has raised Frantz, but she feels no real love for him, and treats him as a social inferior. As far as the Duchess is concerned, there can be no question of any relationship between Monime and Frantz. The young man's only hope lies in obtaining a large sum of money from a wealthy American business man, Mr. Bentz, which will enable him to make a fortune for himself and elope with Monime. But Bentz refuses him the loan, and Frantz, in desperation, decides to murder the Duchess.

4

He carries out his plan, and successfully avoids suspicion. But when Monime, who had never agreed to his fantastic plan in the first place, accuses him of killing for money and tells him she can never love him now, Frantz gives himself up.

This desperate young man, so reminiscent of a Julien Sorel or a Raskolnikov, maintains that he is seeking an absolute purity in a world where compromise is the rule. Unfortunately, Frantz identifies purity with money, and this obscures the facts, for money in itself is one of the most patent symbols of compromise. We begin to wonder whether Frantz is sincere in his desire for purity, or whether that desire is merely a rationalization of his desire for money and security. He protests that his life with Monime must remain untouched by the dirt and cares that poverty carries with it and which ultimately would destroy their feeling for each other. Unlike the later heroes of Anouilh, Frantz is seeking happiness. He has not yet learned that he must refuse happiness, and that happiness is incompatible with the heroic temperament which constantly questions and seeks a perfection not to be found in life.

L'hermine seems to represent a stage in Anouilh's development when he had not clearly thought out the ideas he wished to express. There is a confusion of motives and action, which leads to a weak and sometimes awkward presentation of Frantz's case.

The mediocre people, the placid bourgeois, the Sartrean *salaud*, are cruelly satirized throughout the theater of Anouilh. They are the people who are not profoundly affected by anything, because they live only on the surface, they are frozen into attitudes, have accepted the rules of the game, and have ceased to think. Monime is such a person, to a certain extent, for she is willing to make concessions. The other characters of *L'hermine*—the Duchess and Frantz's friends Philippe and Florentine—are even more clearly presented as people of this type. But the satire does not attain all its bitterness in this first play. In fact, the whole of *L'hermine* appears as a light and somewhat confused sketch of themes that take on greater relief in later plays. Here the contrast between the two types of people—what Anouilh subsequently denotes as the two "races"—is not so great as it later becomes. It is implicit, but not made so evident as in *La sauvage* or *Eurydice,* for example, where it is formulated relevantly and convincingly.

The real drama of *L'hermine,* as in every one of Anouilh's serious plays, lies in the conflict between the hero's inner world and the exterior world he faces. The latter imposes upon him certain conditions that he feels are diametrically opposed to the person he considers himself to be. For Frantz in particular, these conditions are opposed to what he believes to be his happiness.

In *Jézabel* (1932) this conflict becomes more complex. Marc feels that his real self is vastly different from the world in which he has lived, and yet, because that world is his past, clinging forever to him, he cannot escape it, and to be completely honest he must accept it also as a part of him. This play, which has never been produced, is melodramatic and lugubrious throughout. It is the story of a poverty-stricken young man, Marc, who is in love with Jacqueline, a rich young woman. It is once again the pattern of Frantz and Monime. But Marc is not seeking his happiness. On the contrary, he has fled from Jacqueline and her group of friends; he can never become one of them, for he has discovered that his mother (the Jezabel) has taken as her lover the chauffeur of Jacqueline's father. The mother is a pitiful creature, clinging tenaciously to the last remnant of her youth, dyeing her hair, wearing garish clothes, and pitilessly trying to destroy the memory of the pure girl she once was. She is completely degenerate and given to drunkenness and debauchery, getting no pleasure from her lovers, but caught in the habit of the life she has been leading. Her feverish search for love serves as a mask to reality, for she is afraid of the truth. She

6

prefers to let things go as they are without seeking the answers:

> *The Mother.* I'm willing to become an old woman, but not an old woman living alone in a house with her ideas. . . . Don't look any further. Don't ask yourself anything more. . . . What do you want to find out that will make us both suffer?
>
> *Marc.* The truth! And I'll find out what it is, even if it's the most horrible truth. . . .
>
> *The Mother.* Marc, don't! Marc, you're young, you're good. . . . Be happy, and let me end quietly, without asking me anything more. What's the use now? Tell me, what's the use?[2]

Marc's father is little better. His wife describes him thus: "He always thought he was infallible. He would preach at everyone about everything. He, who couldn't do anything. . . . The stupid fool!"[3] A feeble drunkard, he is interested in money and women.

The mother, we discover, is in urgent need of money to clear her lover who has stolen from his employer, so that he will not abandon her for another woman who might provide him with the money. She begs her husband to give her the necessary money, but he refuses. When he brings home some mushrooms, she purposely fails to pick out the poisonous ones and serves them to her husband, who dies. But Marc receives his father's money and refuses to give it to his mother. She discovers that her chauffeur has fled. In the last act, after Marc has decided to leave home to free himself forever from this horrible past, his mother and Georgette the maid, who has been his mistress, attempt to keep him with them. Jacqueline appears in a last vain attempt to persuade Marc and his mother to leave their surroundings and start life anew with her: "It's shameful to say it, but you'd see how easy a little money makes everything. Marc loves me, I love him, and we'll both love you."[4] But Marc realizes this is impossible: he too is one of the damned, as are all the members of the household. He cannot accept salvation in the form of Jacqueline because he realizes he is part of his family, even though he may be, as Jacqueline points out, of another race. The burden of his mother's crime should not weigh upon him. He was ignorant of it, and yet he confesses to Jacqueline that it was he who committed the murder. He is part of his mother and therefore as responsible as she. Moreover, he desired his father's death, and in claiming that he is the murderer he recognizes his moral guilt.

Marc realizes he is trapped in the net of his own past and the past of his family, without hope of escape. His wish is, "to become, at last, an orphan. An orphan without memories."[5] But such an escape is impossible in real life, for Marc is not only the total of his innate characteristics and urges, which are of the good race and would seem to destine him for the world of Jacqueline, but he is also the victim of his environment. The social and financial *ambiance* in which he was raised, the material and moral misery of his family, their position in society, and their actions, all form part of Marc's past, and hence of his present. This unfortunate past, given the sensitivity and heroic temperament of Marc, causes an acute awareness of his misery, both material and spiritual, imbues him with shame, anxiety, and a feeling that he does not deserve or cannot attain a better fate. Unlike Frantz, Marc understands that happiness is impossible for his kind, and hence he refuses the grace offered by Jacqueline.

Speaking of *Jézabel*, Gabriel Marcel astutely remarks:

> Here we can already see confronting each other the two worlds that will always face each other in Anouilh: the sordid world of sinners and the polished world of the virtuous which Jacqueline alone represents here. If there is a drama, it is because Marc, who by his aspirations belongs to the

8

world of virtuous people, is tied by his very fibers to the world of the debauched.[6]

The problem is a moral one: in spite of his inner purity Marc feels neither the strength nor the right to deny this abject world that is also a part of him. Although he does not explicitly deny his past, he does refuse the easy solution of finding a cheap kind of happiness in forgetfulness with his mother and Georgette. When he leaves home at the end of the play, it is the promise of happiness, which on the lips of his mother has the sounds of compromise and vulgarity, that breaks him loose. Rather than lose himself in the easy, slovenly, everyday pattern of life to which his family has accustomed him, Marc is determined to find his own life. His escape from the past is an indication that he is seeking now to free himself—to become at last that orphan which he desired to be—but there is no evidence that he will succeed. Indeed, if we accept the view adopted by Anouilh in his next *pièce noire, La sauvage,* we must conclude that Marc cannot succeed and remain true to himself at the same time.

The struggle between the individual and his past constitutes the major theme of *La sauvage* (1934) also. Thérèse is the daughter of a second-rate café orchestra director, whose wife, with her husband's begrudging consent, has become the mistress of the orchestra's pianist. Thérèse is in love with Florent, a rich young man, a successful composer to whom everything comes easily, who has never suffered a day in his life, safe within his walls of money, and gifted with the graces of talent, easy success, and happiness. At first Thérèse looks forward to a successful marriage with Florent, for she is young, idealistic, and optimistic. But gradually she discovers that her love for Florent is affected by the attitudes of others toward that love. Her parents are interested in wringing money out of their future son-in-law; Thérèse's best friend advises her to get the most out of him while she can. With horror, Thérèse realizes that she is as much a part of this milieu as are her parents and friends, in spite of the fact that she too, like Marc, by her aspirations belongs to a better world than they. But for her to deny them would be an act of dishonesty inconsistent with her inner purity. In an impressive scene at the end of the first act, after desperately attempting to display contempt for the coins that Florent throws away when he tells her that money need not come between them, she throws herself to the ground and starts to pick them up: "On my knees, on my knees. I must pick them up on my knees in order not to lie. I belong to that race."[7] Thérèse, like Marc, is not free to repudiate her past. She must be true to herself. And she can do this in the vicious milieu of her past better than in the virtuous one represented by Florent and his family. In *La sauvage* the characters of the two worlds are brought into relief by the contrast: the world of Thérèse and her family, poverty-stricken, suffering, vulgar, and miserable; and the world of Florent—like that of Jacqueline—bright and smiling, successful, happy, incapable of understanding or feeling the misery of those about them. The rich have been spared the blows of life and have received freely the gift of happiness, but with it is coupled a superficiality of awareness, for they cannot understand anything outside their own circle of life, and this circle has been extremely narrow. The poor, on the other hand, are keenly aware of suffering even when they themselves are happy. But they cannot understand the rich. The two worlds are forever separated.

Not all the poor are sensitive enough, the play suggests, to perceive their complete misery. They are aware of their material misery at times, but completely oblivious to their spiritual misery. An improvement in their material condition would blind them to the continuing wretchedness of their moral condition. Unlike the others, Thérèse is aware of the discordance between her soul and her life, and in the new and unfamiliar setting of Florent's home she endeavors to find her own reality. After an attempt to make the compromise required by society and by happiness, she discovers she can be true to herself only by returning to the milieu she had hoped to reject, for happiness—"filthy happiness"—entails a loss of purity and requires living on the surface—becoming impregnable to the reality of life, which is suffering. Thérèse tries to become indifferent, but she cannot. She realizes, "there will always be a lost dog somewhere to keep me from being happy . . ."[8] She must leave Florent, and go out, "to knock around in the world."[9]

Y avait un prisonnier (1934) is the story of a man, Ludovic, who has just returned from fifteen years imprisonment for fraud. Emerging from his confinement, with what his family and friends call leftist ideas, Ludovic is shocked by the artificiality and hypocrisy of life as he sees it being lived—life as he, too, would have lived it had he not been imprisoned. In a scene of pathetic irony, Ludovic inquires of his best friend Marcellin what he has done during the past fifteen years. After a vain effort to think of something he has done, Marcellin is forced to admit:

> *Marcellin.* It goes by faster than you think, and each day is like the next. . . .
> *Ludovic.* But is the life of free men nothing more than words? . . . But you certainly must have made other trips, I imagine, without taking a step. Trips deep into a living being, or deep into a crowd . . . You've been living free in the midst of other men; that could mean a trip each day, couldn't it? . . . Not a love, not a hate? Not an enthusiasm for an idea or for a person?
> *Marcellin.* This kind of life may seem mediocre to you, but I'm satisfied with it myself. I consider that I've spent my time happily, but honestly too, without hurting anyone.[10]

Ludovic realizes that this facile, shallow life would have been his own, and he would have resembled Marcellin like a brother, if he had not been isolated from the compromising influence of society. Rather than return to such superficiality, which is being imposed upon him by his family, Ludovic runs away, and with him he takes his mute friend of prison-days, La Brebis, a symbol of the childhood and spontaneity toward which Ludovic is fleeing and upon which he now wishes to build his life.

Ludovic's past, which he succeeds in escaping, for the time being at any rate, is not the same lurid past as that of Marc and Thérèse. On the contrary, it corresponds superficially to the virtuous world of a Jacqueline or Florent, but it is corrupt beneath, and just as shallow as the world of the complacent rich in the three earlier plays. Ludovic does not escape from one world into another, as Thérèse vainly tried to do, but from his corrupt past into the golden age of childhood, where he may be free and outspoken, unhampered by social conventions and the necessary lies. Ludovic is fortunate, for he is able to resolve the conflict between the claims of his inner self of compulsion and those of society by fleeing the latter.

Gaston, in *Le voyageur sans bagage* (1936), is in a more fortunate position than most people, for he is unhampered by any memories of the past. He is free to choose, as very few are free. A victim of amnesia during the First World War, he has been confined to an institution for eighteen years, but finally the Duchesse Dupont-Dufort, aunt of one of his doctors, has taken it upon herself to discover his real identity by introducing him into the homes of various families who claim him as theirs. The first home, that of the Renaud family, proves to be the correct one, and slowly Gaston begins to recognize himself as the son of Mme Renaud. Positive proof by means of a scar is given him by his brother's wife, who had been his mistress; but by now

Gaston has discovered that the person he was eighteen years ago is so different morally from the person he feels himself to be today that his youth inspires him with horror. He decides to destroy the Jacques Renaud who seduced the maids, stole his brother's wife, and injured for life his best friend, and to become a new person starting again from the state of purity represented by childhood. For it is not accidental that from among all those who claim him, the one person whom Gaston finally chooses to be his only relative is a child. "Leave me alone with my family," he says to the others as the curtain falls. "We must confront our memories."[11]

In rejecting his past, Gaston refuses moral identification with a person who is different from what he considers to be his present *moi*. His action is a refusal to accept the responsibility for what he was in the past, because he now feels completely divorced from that person. It is questionable whether Gaston's solution is a valid one, for in a few years, or even sooner, he will have created a past for himself, and he being what he is, and life being what it is, any past threatens to become heavy on his hands. Moreover, the situation created in the play is so artificial that one is forced to think how impossible it is in reality to escape both one's own self, with one's weaknesses and innate vicious impulses, and the superimposed past of one's life. The fanciful, happy ending that Anouilh contrives is less a plausible reality than the wishful thinking of humanity in its pathetic effort to change the self and the past which seem to be invested with the inexorability of tragic necessity. After all, *Le voyageur sans bagage* is included in the *Pièces noires*, and although its escapist ending may appear to be a happy one, its implications are pessimistic. Indeed, one may go so far as to doubt that Gaston is a changed person at all, and see in his desire for freedom and his refusal of responsibility the same willfulness that was so obnoxious in the child of his past. We may be justified in wondering whether that undesirable child may not wake within him at any time to prove that what he had considered his present and more real self is but another side of the same person whose inverse is still as evil as the person he thinks he has murdered and thereby escaped.

The Pièces Roses

In *Le bal des voleurs* (1932), *Le rendez-vous de Senlis* (1937), and *Léocadia* (1939), all *Pièces roses*, we see one or more of the protagonists escaping, to some degree at least, from the past and also from the present. But their only means of escape is flight into a world of fancy created in each instance by the characters involved, or made possible by the circumstances. The *Pièces roses* in themselves neither assure us that one can successfully escape from reality for any length of time, nor do they tell us the contrary: that man cannot escape. However, when placed beside the *Pièces noires*, with which they are contemporaneous, the fugacity of such a solution becomes apparent, for we can see that the dreams in which the characters lose themselves are not a valid answer to the problems with which we have seen them confronted in the *Pièces noires*. One might even wonder whether Anouilh has not sought to satirize in these "rosy" plays those facile writers of entertainment who treat the problems of life in a superficial way.

Le bal des voleurs (1932), which belongs to the same year as *Jézabel*, is at an opposite pole to that gloomy play: it is almost completely gay; touched only fleetingly and infrequently with flecks of black. The dark moments are those in which Lady Hurf becomes aware of her solitude, bored "as an old carpet," and doubly alone—not only separated from others, but now a stranger to the real person she was as a child. Her happiness lies only on the surface—it is a role being played, as Anouilh tells us happiness must always be. She is one of the few people in Anouilh's theater who, although recognizing the falseness of happiness and the absurdity of life, accept them calmly.

14

The romantic tale involved in *Le bal des voleurs* is only a tale of escape. Juliette plays the game of love with all her youth and spontaneity, and Gustave, the robber with whom she falls in love, is in the end prevailed upon, we feel, to assume a false identity so that he may be accepted as Juliette's fiancé.

Le voyageur sans bagage and *Le rendez-vous de Senlis* (1937) form a point of contact between the *Pièces noires* and the *Pièces roses*. Both begin in a light vein and soon become serious, and both end with the protagonist believing he has created a new past and future. Georges in *Le rendez-vous de Senlis* is a young man who married a shrew for her money, at the insistence of his parents and a friend, who are now living off the wealthy woman. In the meantime Georges has met and fallen in love with a young girl, Isabelle. As the play opens, Georges is preparing to receive her. He has rented a house in the country, has hired actor and actress to play the roles of his parents, and has dinner and a maître d'hôtel sent over from a catering establishment. All this is necessary because Georges has fabricated for Isabelle's benefit an entire "ideal" family and past to conform to his dreams. But Georges is called away suddenly, because his wife is threatening suicide, and Isabelle arrives amidst the consternation of the actor and actress who are no longer certain whether or not they are to play their roles. In the second act we see the situation in Georges' home: we become aware of his liaison with the wife of his friend Robert, and of the completely selfish motives of Robert's friendship. In the third and fourth acts the ideal and the real worlds come into contact, and the latter threatens surely to destroy the former. But through faith in the power of love and of their dream, Georges and Isabelle are able to reject completely the unpleasant reality of Georges' past, and the two of them go in to dinner with the "ideal" father and mother. Meanwhile the ideal parents have long since ceased playing the roles Georges had planned for them: Georges' flight into his dream, far from being complete, is a caricature of his dreams. He still has not changed his past, but only deludes himself in believing he has freed himself from it. There still remains the same question that we saw arise at the end of *Le voyageur sans bagage:* How long can this dream, even in its form of caricature, endure against reality?

In *Léocadia* (1939), Albert, a prince, lives in a dream world inhabited by all the people and decorated with all the backgrounds he knew for three happy days he spent with the extravagant actress Léocadia. After only three days together, Léocadia had accidentally strangled herself, following a passionate discussion on music, by knotting her scarf too enthusiastically about her neck. Since her death, Prince Albert has lived in a dream trying to relive his three days with her, and pampered by his aunt, the Duchess, who has arranged for all the places and people they knew in those days to be removed to the park of the chateau. The Duchess has discovered a poor modiste, Amanda, who bears a striking resemblance to Léocadia, and she has arranged for the child to come to the chateau in an attempt to divert the Prince's mind from his dream and give him a more healthy reality somewhat similar to his dream. As Amanda soon discovers, the Prince was never really in love with Léocadia: she is only the symbol of something to take the place of the emptiness that was life before he knew her.[12] For fear of discovering the truth —that there is no meaning behind it—the Prince does not seek to go beyond the symbol. Amanda succeeds in bringing him to his senses by her purity and spontaneity. To do so she must kill the image of poor Léocadia, represented by the outlandish bird that the Duchess buries in her rose bushes, for Amanda is also happiness, and happiness is always terrible.

If the characters of the *Pièces roses* are unheroic in their compromise with happiness and their refusal to accept life as it is, they at least possess the noble desire

16

for the purity of life that dares to be what it is without excuses. But they are satisfied with a happiness that Anouilh later satirizes as illusory and unworthwhile. Amanda personifies all this sham happiness and sums it up when she answers the Prince's query as to who she is by saying, "Only a young girl in a white dress buttering a slice of bread in the sun."[13]

The dramatic conflict in these plays of the first period, from *L'hermine* to *Léocadia*, is between the hero's inner image of what he most believes himself to be, and the environment and past that impose upon him a character that is at variance with his imagined "true self." The struggle for freedom ensues, and the hero inevitably returns to his former misery, or at any rate, does not deny it or forget it, for to do so would be to become untrue to a part of himself. The power of one's environment and past is so strong that it pulls apart those who under other circumstances might have had some chance for happiness together. The opposition between environments is usually made in terms of wealth and poverty. In all these plays, wealth means happiness, but a happiness at the expense of insensitivity to the suffering of others, for the wealthy have been protected from real life, and know nothing but the surfaces. This is apparent as early as in *L'hermine* where the Duchess treats both Frantz and her companion Marie-Anne as mere animals. Frantz's resentment of the rich is found again in Marc and Thérèse, both of whom know life as poor, filthy, and ugly. They are acquainted only too well with the moral as well as the material misery of life. They resent the immunity that the rich enjoy against the suffering of the world; not because they would like to have that immunity for themselves, but because it seems unfair that anyone should enjoy it at the expense of others. The calm and ease of the rich, their ability to forgive, is insulting to the poor. Marc says to Jacqueline:

I admire you with hatred. You're so beautiful and

everything is so dirty here, so poor and rotten.
. . . What goodness, what brightness in your
face! . . . Yes, I know I can tell you everything,
that you'll understand everything, and forgive
everything! . . . You're going to be admirable, as
always.[14]

This explosion that is almost certain to take place
when the rich and the poor come together is examined
thoroughly in *La sauvage*. When Thérèse realizes that
she is too different from Florent, that they can never
truly understand each other, and that she can never be
faithful to herself if she becomes part of his life, she
finally expresses all her resentment against the rich:

You don't know anything human, Florent . . .
(*She looks at him.*) Those wrinkles, what pains
drew them there? You've never had a real sorrow,
a shameful sorrow like a suppurating wound . . .
You've never hated anyone, even those who have
hurt you, anyone can see that in your eyes. . . .
How sure you are of yourself! . . . How strong
you are! . . . You're a rich man. It's worse [than
a conqueror]. A conqueror who hasn't even
fought.[15]

Florent can only smile and forgive, and shed one small
tear which is quickly forgotten, for he is so self-sufficient
that even Thérèse is not truly necessary to him.

Although the hero is not clearly defined yet in the
plays of the first period, he is established as the person
who is opposed to the compromises of life; whose first
purpose is the quest for purity through fidelity to what
he considers his truest self.[16] This purity is usually expressed in terms of childhood—that period of freedom
and spontaneity before we learned the games of pretense and hypocrisy. It is another version of the Garden
of Eden, Baudelaire's green paradise which represents
a positive value of the past. The hero would like to
cling tenaciously to the purity represented by such a
vision, and consequently he tends to reject the adult

18

world. Throughout the plays of Anouilh we hear of the hero refusing to grow up, or regretting his lost childhood. Unfortunately, this innocent paradise is not our only past. Superimposed upon it is the miserable past of man afflicted with sin, represented in most instances by the intolerable world of the poor. The hero attempts to escape from the latter and to return to the former. This is clearly illustrated in *Jézabel*, where Marc worships an old photograph of his mother as she was when he was a child—it is to this mother that he would return, and find the uncomplicated yet pure happiness of those first years. It is also illustrated by Marc's reference to that epoch when the innocence of his childhood had imposed upon the world a language of innocence in which his mother was a part: "Mother, mother, why have we lost the words of my childhood?"[17] But such a return is impossible, not only for Marc, but for everyone, and so at the end of the play the hero seeks to escape from his more recent past, represented in *Jézabel* by the family and environment. The same is true of Thérèse and Frantz: they are striving to free themselves from the postlapsarian aspect of their past. Thérèse discovers that to do so she must make a compromise with herself and accept the complacent virtue of the rich. Instead she chooses to return to the vicious atmosphere of her adolescence, which has at least the courage to be what it is. After a pathetic struggle Thérèse realizes, as do all the true heroes of this theater, that she cannot become what she is not; that even if she attempted to do so, her past forever present would plague her and she could never be happy. As a result she returns to her misery.

When the protagonist goes beyond the limits of his role, forgetting his past, as do Gaston and the characters of the *Pièces roses,* we feel he is not being true to all the aspects of his being, which includes his past as well as his aspirations in the present. The protagonists of the *Pièces roses* are not of a heroic stature.

19

They are not like those who, refusing to escape into a world of dreams, face reality as it is, at the same time denouncing it and remaining aware of its limitations.

Contrasted to the hero are the mediocre people who are satisfied to be just what they are, and are usually willing to accept life on its own terms, without questioning. A few of them, like Lady Hurf, question life, are aware of its real absurdity, and yet accept it. They are not made of the heroic stuff that resists reality. They will swallow their pride, whereas Thérèse, Marc, and Frantz cannot do so. In later plays the people who accept life with full awareness are sometimes given more heroic qualities. Créon, for example, accepts through strength rather than weakness, considering it his duty to do so. This division into several types of people is clearly defined in the next plays, but the word *race* has already been used by 1932, although its meaning at that time is not clear. In *Jézabel*, Jacqueline tells Marc, "You can't stay here another day. *You* belong to another race."[18] She means that Marc does not belong to the same degenerate group as his father and mother; her division is a moral one. Marc is set apart because he has not given in to the animal in himself, but is striving for something finer than his background would seem to permit. Jacqueline may also remember that Marc adjusted well to her group of friends, and believe that he belongs in that carefree, wealthy milieu rather than among the poor. We have already seen Thérèse of *La sauvage* cry "I belong to that race," as she throws herself to the ground to pick up the money Florent so blithely throws away. For Thérèse *race* may have two values also: she is a member of the poor class for whom money assumes great importance, and she is also a member of the heroic group of those who cannot lie but must remain true to themselves by being what they are.

Thus, the word *race* as used in Anouilh's theater, during the first period at least, is somewhat ambiguous.

It has an economic connotation of rich and poor, and a moral connotation of heroic and nonheroic, or acceptable and unacceptable, with those various classifications possessing different values depending upon which character uses them and when they are used. It would be useless to attempt to make a "racial" arrangement of the characters in the first group of plays, for at the time they were created Anouilh had not sharply set apart one group from the other in those terms. However, we can say which characters are heroic and which are not, as they conform to the heroic pattern Anouilh has established in such plays as *Jézabel* and *La sauvage*.

THE SECOND GROUP: THE REFUSAL OF REALITY (*1941–1946*)

The next four plays—the first three of which Gabriel Marcel calls the "central range"[19] of Anouilh's work—lay more stress upon the author's fundamental ideas than had his previous plays. *Eurydice* (1941), *Antigone* (1942), *Roméo et Jeannette* (1945), and *Médée* (1946) place the heroic individual in the center of the stage as he faces reality and says no to it. The feeling of death is ever-present, and every one of the heroines goes down morally victorious. The central struggle is no longer between the protagonist's past and his aspirations. It has shifted to something more universal: the inner world versus the entire outer world, which is the only one recognized by society. The revolt against the past is only part of a larger revolt, and in *Antigone* there is no past against which to revolt, for Antigone creates herself only in the present.

The first two plays of this group were written during the war, and it is possible to interpret their emphasis upon fundamentals and the presence of death as results of attitudes inspired by the war. It seems plausible, however, to consider such attributes a reflection of the natural development of an artist who, coming to maturity, is able to express himself more concisely on those issues that he considers most important. It may be, of course, that the war helped to deepen his experience and move him more determinedly in the direction in which he had already started with his first plays, leading him now to think in terms of the more fundamental, cosmic forces that determine the fate of man.

Eurydice (1941) still shows some preoccupation with the escape from a sordid past, and in this respect it belongs to Anouilh's first period. But insofar as this escape is only part of a larger refusal of the compromises of life, and insofar as *Eurydice* treats with greater emphasis and clarity the essential notions only suggested in the first group of plays—enlarging upon them and imbuing them with a new universality—it belongs to the second period.

Orphée travels with his father, a second-rate café musician, and together they earn their living by playing harp and violin in dingy restaurants. In a provincial railway station Orphée meets Eurydice, daughter of a second-rate traveling actress. The two fall in love, and it is strongly suggested that their meeting was brought about by some superhuman power. They leave together—Orphée deserting his father, and Eurydice, the troupe with which she was traveling. In a squalid hotel room in Marseilles they consummate their love. Eurydice soon realizes that Orphée has a fantastic image of her in his mind, and that she can never conform to this ideal Eurydice. Her humiliating past clings to her, and she is forced to lie to Orphée. Finally realizing that their love can never be based on the truth and cannot last, rather than destroy Orphée's idealized image of her, Eurydice flees, only to be killed in an automobile accident. Orphée is distraught, but a mysterious stranger, Monsieur Henri, who has been ever-present during the play, offers to arrange a meeting between Orphée and the dead Eurydice. It takes place in an eerie light in the railway waiting-room in which they had met, and they are surrounded by all the people they have known together. The one condition imposed upon Orphée is that he must not look upon Eurydice until dawn, or she will die forever. Orphée soon realizes that Eurydice is lying to him about her unsavory past, and the only way he can assure himself is by looking into her eyes. He understands that their love cannot go on without being contaminated by contact with life, and rather than let that happen he looks at Eurydice, and she disappears. Orphée is disconsolate at the loss, but M. Henri convinces him that it is for the best, and at his instigation Orphée goes out to meet his death, thus rejoining an ideal Eurydice in a realm where life cannot corrupt.

Eurydice shows, as does *La sauvage,* that man cannot successfully escape from his past. This theme is expressed much more clearly and forcefully in the later play. The past includes not only the persons and circumstances with which man has had dealings, but all past events—even those that seemed alien. The stranger that one happened to look at from a distance leaves an indelible imprint, because one cannot help reacting to even the most objective stimuli. When Orphée and Eurydice are alone in their hotel room, they discuss the various people whom they have seen and who have played a part in their life together:

> *Orphée.* They've gone on now, the good as well as the bad. They've done their little song and dance in your life . . . They're that way in you now, forever. (*A silence.*)
>
> *Eurydice (asks suddenly).* Then, supposing one has seen many ugly things in life, do they all remain a part of you?
>
> *Orphée.* Yes.
>
> *Eurydice.* Neatly lined up, side by side, all the dirty sights, all the people, even those we've hated, even those we've avoided? All the bad words

we've heard, you think we keep them deep inside us? And all the gestures we've made, our hands remember them still, you think?

Orphée. Yes. . . .

Eurydice. But then you can never be alone with all that around you. We're never sincere, even when we want to be with all our strength . . . If all the words are there, all the filthy outbursts of laughter, if all the hands that have touched you are still sticking to your flesh, then you can never become someone else?[20]

Later, when Orphée meets Eurydice returned from the dead, he sees her surrounded by all the people she has known, each one declaring a different truth about her:

Orphée. It's too difficult; all the people you've known are around you; all the hands that have touched you are there, clinging to you. And all the words you've spoken are on your lips . . .[21]

Once again we see the "sticky" quality of the past—man trapped in the net not only of his past actions, but also of all his past experiences. This was an important element in separating Frantz from Monime, Marc from Jacqueline, and Thérèse from Florent. Now it separates Eurydice from Orphée. But it is important to note that in this instance the two lovers come from similar backgrounds: the chasm that separates poverty from wealth does not separate Orphée from Eurydice. The past in itself is sufficient.

In *Antigone* (1942) there is no past weighing upon the heroine: she has chosen her role. As she tells her sister Ismène: "You chose life, and I death."[22] She makes the choice simply because it is her vocation, "through an intimate taste for death."[23] Créon has ordered that the body of Polynices remain unburied, and that anyone attempting to bury it be condemned to death. With full knowledge of what she is doing, Antigone goes to bury her brother, not through religious compunctions, nor for love of her brother, for she discovers from Créon

24

that the bodies of the two brothers were unrecognizable, and it is not certain which one is now buried and which one lies unburied without the walls. The burial of Polynices is only a pretext for Antigone to assert what she feels to be her real self in opposition to the compromises necessitated by life. Her action is a negative revindication of her right to refuse, of which Marcel says:

> Evidence of an important fact: the disastrous dissociation that has taken place today between liberty and the positive values to which it should normally be subordinated. . . . She [Antigone] will not accept a vile complicity with life. But let us note carefully that it is here a question of a false plenitude which is a vacuum. A liberty that is only a will to refuse can only fling itself toward death.[24]

And, indeed, Antigone goes to her death, thinking it is the only answer that one can give to life if one is to remain true to oneself. She represents the universe of childhood—the kingdom of the ideal judged through subjectively chosen values. Her revolt is gratuitous; without direction; unmotivated in terms of a past. Her action arises only from a deep-felt necessity to become what she believes to be her truest self. The substance of the conflict lies not in Antigone's opposition of god and family ties to Créon's support of the public welfare and of government, but in the opposition of Antigone as a symbol of the idealist to Créon who, while also following certain ideals, is dedicated to a realistic solution of life's dilemmas. Oreste Pucciani points out that Créon, "in accepting the responsibilities of power, is ethically bound to behave according to a given pattern,"[25] and in this respect he is no longer free. Antigone, however, is committed to no public value—only to herself and her own ideals. Selfish though this may be, she remains free to follow her ideal. Pucciani continues:

> The eloquent justification which he [Créon] gives

of his position is based on a realistic diagnosis of human problems and an assertion of certain pragmatic truths. . . . Créon's position does not exclude a certain idealism, but it is essentially different from that of Antigone. It is an idealism of earthly things, of humble happiness. . . . Antigone's point of view requires a more strict adherence to a transcendent ideal. She scorns the happiness of Créon, which appears to her to be of the essence of mediocrity.[26]

In a scene that is at once dramatically effective and philosophically suggestive, Antigone and Créon come to grips. Créon is eager to save his niece, and will make a compromise so that she may continue to live. But Antigone is dead set against any kind of compromise. She flatly refuses his offer and tells him she will return to bury the body as often as he uncovers it. Antigone acts not for her brother or for anyone else, but for herself: "For no one. For myself."[27] She at least is free to die, for she has never said yes to life: "I can still say 'no' to everything I don't like, and no one can judge me. And you, with your crown, with your guards, and all your paraphernalia, all you can do is to make me die, because you've said 'yes.' "[28] Créon explains to her that there must be some who say yes to life, who will lead the ship of government, give some organization to life, and save men from their selfishness. But Antigone will not understand; she speaks to Créon from afar—from a kingdom that Créon with his wrinkles can never enter again. This is the realm of youth, with its spontaneity and naturalness untainted by life—an ideal realm to which in childhood all men are by nature committed, and which they all eventually abandon, thereby bringing about the compromise that in Anouilh's view is an inescapable part of living and growing old. Antigone refuses the smiles, the lies, and the indifference that will buy her a rag of happiness:

You disgust me, all of you, with your happiness!

> With your life that we have to love at any price.
> You're like dogs who lick everything they find.
> And a little bit of happiness day by day, if you're
> not too exigent. But *I* want everything, right away
> —and I want it to be complete—or else I refuse! *I*
> don't want to be modest, *I* don't want to be satis-
> fied with a little piece of cake if I've been a good
> little girl. I want to be certain of everything *today*,
> and I want it to be as beautiful as when I was a
> child—or else I'd rather die.[29]

Such is the heroic attitude: the refusal of "filthy hope,"
and the search for the purity represented by the lost
paradise of childhood.

To the pleasant picture Créon would paint of life—
"It's a book that you love, a child playing at your feet,
it's a tool that you hold firmly in your hand, a bench
where you can rest in the evening, in front of your
house"[30]—Antigone opposes a more cruel reality:

> What will my happiness be? What kind of
> happy woman will little Antigone become? What
> wretched acts will she have to perform too, day
> after day, to bite off her little rag of happiness?
> Tell me, who must she lie to, who smile at? To
> whom must she sell herself? Who will she have to
> let die, pretending she doesn't see?[31]

Antigone's refusal of happiness is also her refusal of
life, for the two terms are equated. "I want to know
how I'll go about it, to be happy also," she cries out to
Créon. "You say that life is so beautiful. I want to know
how I'll go about it, to live."[32] This is no refusal of reality: it is a refusal of life itself. If such a refusal is
negative, with no positive values implied, it is because
Antigone sees life in such terms that a positive stand has
no meaning. If life is a compromise and the evil is to
wish to live, then Antigone may assert her freedom by
choosing death. Créon, bound by his commitment, can
but let her follow her inclination—he is powerless to
stop her. All those who make the compromise are no

longer free in Anouilh's world, despite the strength of their will or the power of their intellect. Créon is a giant among them, for he is keenly intelligent and has made his bargain with life while fully cognizant of what he was doing. But he also realizes that this is not the way of happiness in life, for understanding destroys the possibility of happiness: "What we need is never to know. . . . What we need is never to grow up."[33] Créon knows that from a certain viewpoint Antigone was right, just as Antigone finally realizes that Créon was right to a certain extent.[34]

If, practically speaking, Créon is right in his arguments against Antigone, that is precisely his weakness, for, in the words of Gabriel Marcel, "we are thrown into a world where being right perhaps means nothing, and where nobility could very well be on the side of those absurd, intractable beings who refuse to play the dishonorable game of a sobered existence."[35]

Only the brutal guards—mediocre in every way, completely unaware of what life is—are unaffected by what has happened: "None of this matters to them," says the Chorus at the end of the play. "It's no skin off their back. They keep on playing cards . . ."[36]

In *Roméo et Jeannette* (1945), the good bourgeois Frédéric, his middle-class mother, and his fiancée Julia arrive at Julia's home to meet her family. The house is empty and in great, and apparently typical, disorder. One by one the members of the family drift in: the cynical cuckold brother Lucien; the lazy good-for-nothing father; and, last, Julia's sister Jeannette, another child of nature who, it soon becomes apparent, is supporting the household with the money she receives for bestowing her favors upon a local nobleman. The virtuous, bourgeois visitors are shocked at the state of affairs, but they try to make the best of the family meeting. In spite of himself, Frédéric feels drawn to Jeannette. It is clear that Fate has taken an interest in them, and there can be no question of the two renouncing each other. Together they flee into the forest, where in a ruined cabin they recognize the fatality of their meeting and of their invincible love. Before long, Lucien arrives and warns them cynically that their love is bound to fail, for God is peculiarly sensitive to the odor of love and wakens in order to destroy it whenever it bothers him: "He has a nose, a terrible sense of smell, and the odor, nothing but the odor of love, he sniffs it. And he doesn't like it, he doesn't like it at all."[37] News arrives that Julia, in desperation over Frédéric's flight, has taken poison. Frédéric returns to her, leaving Jeannette to a tryst with her nobleman lover. The last act takes place a week later: Julia has been cured, and the three visitors are preparing to leave this unfavorable environment. Frédéric has decided to carry out his original plan and marry Julia. Suddenly Jeannette appears. She has just been married to her noble lover, and in the excitement of the festivities she has escaped to bid Frédéric farewell. She invites him to make their own love eternal by dying together, but Frédéric refuses, for he believes one must accept life and the concessions it requires. As he and his mother drive off with Julia, he catches sight of Jeannette standing on the shore where the tide is coming in. Spontaneously he jumps from the carriage to save her, and together they are drowned, while Lucien watches from the window and cynically comments in an aside to God: "Are you satisfied? This is just how everything was supposed to happen. I had told them you didn't like that."[38]

The conflict in *Roméo et Jeannette* is between the concepts of the virtuous bourgeois, who believe one must grow up one day and accept the fact that life is not so beautiful as one had thought as a child,[39] and the absolute refusal of Jeannette to accept life on such terms. "I don't want to grow up. I don't want to learn to say yes. Everything is too ugly,"[40] she says—reminding us of Antigone. Because of his contact with Jeannette, Frédéric is transformed, and is finally able at the end of the play to die with his beloved. Before he knew Jeannette, his world was the typical one of the mediocre race, in which everything is tagged and pigeonholed: "Ah! If only I had never known you! The world had a shape before, good or bad. The things around me had a place and a name, and everything was so simple."[41] Now that he has come into contact with the heroic race his life cannot be the same again, for he has realized its absurdity. He requires an impulsion, however, in order to make the final renunciation of life. "This horror and all these useless gestures, this grotesque adventure, is ours," he tells Jeannette, revealing that he has seen through the surface to the real absurdity of life. "We must live it," he adds. "Death is absurd also."[42] Frédéric is not basically of the heroic temperament; he would, like Créon, go on living in the face of life's meaninglessness, for to die is too cowardly, he thinks.[43] It is only by an act of grace that he realizes himself at the last moment as he runs toward Jeannette and is engulfed by death. Frédéric can act as he does because, unlike Créon, he is not responsible for a whole nation.

In *Médée* (1946), a short but highly significant play, which follows in its main outlines the story of Euripides and Seneca, it is Créon who speaks for the lesser race when he asks Médée to leave him and his people, "under this sky of reason, beside this even sea, which has nothing to do with your disordered passions and cries."[44]

Jason, tired of his life with Médée, would make the compromise; he would simply forget the absurdity that is life, as most men do, in order to be able to go on living. And he feels himself strong now, for although he is of the lesser race he has the majority on his side:

> *Médée*. Race of Abel, race of the just, race of the rich, how calmly you speak. It's good, isn't it, to have heaven on your side, and the police as well?

It's good to think at last like your father, and your father's father, like all those who have always been right. . . . Play the game, Jason, make the gesture, say yes! You're preparing a beautiful old age for yourself! . . .

Jason. Go your way. Keep turning around, tear yourself apart, beat yourself, scorn, insult, kill, refuse everything that is not yourself. As for me, I'm stopping. I'm satisfied. I accept these appearances as rigorously, as resolutely as I once refused them with you. And if I must go on fighting, it's for them that I'll fight now, humbly, with my back to that flimsy wall built by my own hands between absurd nothingness and myself. . . . And that's probably what being a man means, in the final analysis, and nothing else.

Médée. Don't doubt it, Jason. You're a man now.

Jason. Good-bye, Médée. I can't say to you: be happy . . . Be yourself.[45]

In this opposition between the husband and wife who have lived together for many years, the difference between the two races is once more made clear: the comfortable life of the man who will play the game is contrasted to the constant struggle of the woman who insists upon being herself. Médée faces the absurd nothingness of life fearlessly, whereas Jason protects himself from it by an illusion, which he hopes will bring him forgetfulness and happiness. This is what it is to become a man, Médée agrees, with telling irony. Médée's search for herself brings her to the realization that her life with Jason has also been a compromise, because she became caught in the habit of her love for him, dependent upon him, and their relationship lost its spontaneity. The only way she can fulfill herself is by giving herself to the evil that she feels is her most real self. For a moment she thinks some small indication of Jason's weakness would save her, but, like Thérèse, she would have realized that the gulf between the two races is too great to be bridged. In order to become herself she must destroy her children, which not only are a living testimony of her compromise with Jason, but represent a will to live and be happy.[46]

Her children murdered, Médée can shout to Jason, "I've found again my country and my virginity which you took from me! I am Médée at last, forever!"[47] And Jason, like another Créon, turns almost heroically toward the reëstablishment of order. But Jason is not a true hero, because, although he maintains that he must build without illusions, what he is about to construct is a world "à notre mesure"—a world for men and not for heroes—and though he may be disillusioned himself, he accepts, and he will never convince the other members of his race of the meaninglessness of their lives. The end of the play tells us this, as the nurse and the guard look forward hopefully to the little pleasures of the coming year:

> *The Nurse.* After the night comes the morning, and there's coffee to be made, and then the beds. And when you've finished sweeping up, you have a few minutes to sit in the sun before you begin peeling the vegetables. That's when it's good, if you've been able to scrounge a few pennies, to feel a wee warm drop in the pit of your stomach. . . . It's going to be a good year. There'll be sunshine and wine. . . .
>
> *The Guard.* Can't complain. There'll be enough bread again this year for everyone.[48]

In order to accept this world of petty happiness in which the "flimsy wall" of illusion gives some form to life by establishing rules and conventions, Jason rejects chaos. And Jason, who has lived with Médée and seen life through her eyes, knows that she is right. His blindness is willful, for only through blindness can he hope to achieve any kind of happiness. The world of Médée is without reason, without light or repose; it is a place of disorder and darkness in which petty men are trying to sweep out a little place for themselves. When a man of the lesser race comes into contact with the hero, or when he has a soul that enables him to understand the nothingness beneath the comedy of life, the world always loses its form and becomes complicated and uncomfortable for him. This is exactly what took place with Frédéric when he suddenly saw the world through Jeannette's eyes.

Jason pities Médée because of her solitude, for she will be alone through eternity, attached forever to herself, surrounded by a world that she can see only through herself. Jason fails to realize that all men are alone but remain unaware of their solitude because it is hidden from their view by the various illusions to which they cling.

In *Eurydice* Monsieur Henri describes for us with more clarity than we have found in the previous plays the two races into which men are divided: the mediocre or average, and the heroic:

> My friend, there are two races of men. A numerous, fecund, happy race, a fat, flabby dough, which eats its sausage, has its children, uses its tools, counts its pennies, one year like the next in spite of epidemics and wars, till old age overtakes it; people made for living, everyday people, people you can scarcely imagine as dead. Then there are the others, the noble ones, the heroes. Those that you can very easily imagine laid out, pale, with a gaping red hole in the head, one moment triumphant with a guard of honor, and the next, dangling between two policemen—the cream of the crop.[49]

The mediocre man, forever satisfied with himself, seeking to become nothing more than what he already is, clings to life, searches for happiness through the compromises that living and growing old necessitate, takes on the shell that society imposes upon us, and lives on the surface. The hero questions himself and seeks a purity superior to that found in life, almost always ending his search in death.

Among those who accept life are two characters whose strength and lucidity raise them to an almost heroic level: Créon and Jason. They take a positive stand for life, realizing at the same time that they might have refused the obligations imposed upon them. Seen through the eyes of the intransigent hero, deaf to all but his inner voices, they seem to be creatures of the mediocre race, however noble and heroic they may appear to us. Orphée, Antigone, Médée, and Jeannette all say no, not only to reality, but to life itself. If life cannot conform to their vision, then it is not worth living, for it will sully the pristine purity of their true "selves." For us, the course of Créon and Jason may seem wiser and nobler, but, from what Gabriel Marcel calls the "vacuum"[50] of their convictions, the heroic race will not admit this, for they look upon the act of living itself as a compromise. Theirs is a revolt against not only the solution given by any particular law, but against any laws whatsoever, for they reserve the right to act according to their own inner compulsions. There is a fundamental weakness in the heroic revolt of Anouilh's characters, for it is not based upon any universal criterion of what should or should not be. It may stand as a criticism of life and of a universe in which this must be so, in which perhaps there are no universal values. The chaos reflected by the revolt in a so-called vacuum is only an indication of the absurdity of man's condition. But as a practical solution to man's problems it is not valid. Perhaps this is indicative of Anouilh's belief that man's problem has no valid solution.

Life is the same for all, but only the hero and those few heroic individuals who go on living have the courage to see it as it is. Most of the weaker race mask the bitter truth with laws, codes of morality, rules, and

34

what for them amounts to any form of trickery that will avoid the real issue, for they are afraid to let their hearts or minds be touched by a profound emotion or a daring thought. They are puppets, having no real life within themselves, but they feel themselves strong, for they have the majority on their side. Moreover, they are blind to any view but their own, and when they speak of life it is always in the same shallow accents.

In *Eurydice* Orphée's father, a miserable failure in life, talks constantly of the prices of meals and the best way to take advantage of the menu by exchanging the vegetable for a second dessert and choosing a *plat garni* which includes a vegetable. This pitiful *cabotin* is well qualified to describe the superficial aspects of what he considers an adventurous life, for he has lived long and has been knocked about. But the life he describes is a hideous caricature of life as it is lived by the happy race. As Orphée lies stricken with sorrow at the death of Eurydice, his father attempts to console him by presenting himself as a typical product of life in order to convince his son of life's beauty and value. The contrast between the father's concept of himself and our own understanding of what he really is gives the scene a touch of sadly ironic humor, typical of Anouilh.

The father describes his life as a youth at the Conservatoire de Niort, where he engaged in many escapades, serenaded his sweetheart, and drank heartily: "We were young and gay. We understood what life was all about."[51] This weak and ineffectual man advises practicing Swedish gymnastics to keep fit, and confides, without realizing the irony of what he is saying, that will power is the secret of pleasure and success. And money is their source, bringing with it prestige and honor. Not only are his ideals middle-class, but his representation of reality is falsified by his refusal to see himself as he is. His refusal even to consider his situation in the light of the truth (or his inability to do so) is a tacit acceptance of it, for he could not reject or rebel against his situation without first recognizing it for what it is.

Orphée's description of life is much more realistic and points up the monotony and hopeless absurdity of life without purpose:

> It seems to me that since mother died, I follow you to the café terraces with my violin, I watch you struggling with your check each evening. I listen to you talk about the menu and the *prix fixe*, and then I go to bed and I get up the next morning.[52]

The same contrast between the easy life of the mediocre and the hero's refusal is seen in the compromise Eurydice wishes to make in order to go on living and Orphée's unwillingness to accept life on such terms. "Accept happiness," she begs of him, and he answers as every hero must: "I cannot."[53] All the other characters in the play have accepted; Orphée is the only one with the courage to face reality and say no.

Antigone, Roméo et Jeannette, and *Médée* show the same conflict between the hero's or the heroine's aspirations and the world of compromise that they must face and in contact with which they would become sullied. Antigone, Jeannette, and Médée, like Orphée, say no to life and realize themselves victoriously in death. Their morality is one of completeness, and they must remain faithful to the inner self by answering spontaneously the imperious demands of the "savage" individual. Contrasted to them are the mediocre who consent to play the game, and who seek happiness by hiding the truth of life's absurdity from themselves. Lacking the necessary intelligence to perceive any facet of the truth, they simply vegetate, saying, like Monsieur Delachaume in *Le rendez-vous de Senlis:* "Money and love: what else can you ask for? Life is simple after all, for God's sake!"[54] In varying degrees this simple, pleasant picture of life is opposed to the nothingness that the hero sees behind the illusion.

L'alouette, written in 1953, actually belongs to this central period of Anouilh's theater, for in it we see again the intransigent heroine who refuses to say yes to life. Unlike the other plays written during the third period, *L'alouette* shows us the unconquered heroine who remains true to herself. This play is thus linked in a very tangible way with the preceding group of plays; but at the same time it seems to foreshadow Anouilh's later works.

The play tells the story of the trial of Jeanne d'Arc. Hovering about the edges of the courtroom are the various people who have played parts in Jeanne's life, and during the play each of them takes the center of the stage to relive his scenes with Jeanne, for she cannot be condemned until she has played for her judges each of the climactic scenes of her life. After recanting, Jeanne realizes her error, refuses to comply with her judges' wishes, and is taken to the stake to be burned. At the last moment, Beaudricourt rushes in and stops the execution, reminding everyone that Jeanne has not played the scene of the coronation at Reims, and the agreement was that she be allowed to play every scene from her life. The play ends with a tableau of the scene in the cathedral, in which we see the true Jeanne d'Arc.

The difference between Jeanne and Antigone is that Antigone acts for herself alone, becoming almost dehumanized, whereas Jeanne has a love for the common man and is filled with the milk of human kindness so abhorred by the Inquisitor who judges her. She would lead all the simple-hearted into the kingdom of God, for she believes they are all good, as the wolves that God created innocent are good. The theme of the "Natural Man" who has faith in the native goodness of humanity remains a constant theme in Anouilh's plays. There is a difference, however. Frantz is "naturally" good, but he has no faith in man as his brother, and he can say along with Orphée, "I hate them all, one by one . . ."[55] Jeanne, imbued with love, strikes a note of

37

optimism in the blackness of Anouilh's theater. Indeed, the play ends on a joyful note—one we would not have expected from this author. The ending may appear to be contrived, but it is impressive in that what survives is not Jeanne the martyr burning for her convictions, but Jeanne as a symbol of a France that is joyous and invincible, led from time to time by a pure ideal: "that little lark singing in the sky of France, over the heads of the foot-soldiers."[56]

One must not hasten to take this for a facile optimism, for Jeanne is alone, and opposed to her is not only the power of the Church and its organization, but the thoughtless brutality of those very people whom she loves and who have come early to get good seats to watch her execution. They are the same people who would have acclaimed her triumphal entry had she taken Rouen; people with no mind of their own; those whom the grisly Inquisitor can lead. The Inquisitor represents that aspect of the Church which claims to be devoted to God alone, considers man as a despicable sinner, and admits nothing that does not conform to its own cruel dogma. This unsmiling, immovable, inhuman force is opposed to the humanity of Jeanne, and it is a formidable enemy for her, just as she is for it. The Inquisitor denies all that Jeanne stands for: youth, generosity, and human kindness are all enemies, and he who loves man cannot love God. No individual thinking is allowed, for this would upset the death-like rigidity of the established conventions. Little girls of mystic bent are given hard work to do, "and it all drowns quietly in the dishwater . . . ," or else they marry, "and at the second howling brat hanging at their skirts, we no longer have to worry about the voices they hear."[57] These are not the people the Inquisitor fears; nor does he fear the devil: "After all, he's a former angel: he belongs to us."[58] Rather is he frightened by those who are worthy of themselves, whose true God is an unconquered vision of their truest self. These are the people who will never submit to the dominion of the Idea. Inhuman, organized, abstract, and formal, the Idea is a safeguard for the mediocre.

> *The Inquisitor.* However powerful we become some day, in one shape or another, however strong the Idea becomes in the world, however hard, precise, and subtle its organization and its police become; there will always be a man to be tracked down somewhere, a man who has escaped us, whom we'll catch at last, whom we'll kill, and who will humiliate once again the Idea at the height of its power, simply because he will say "no" without lowering his eyes. (*He hisses malignantly between his teeth, looking at Jeanne.*) The insolent race![59]

Here Anouilh returns again to his idea of the two races, and Jeanne who, like Antigone, is there to say no, reminds us of the latter heroine by the absurdity of her refusal; for, as her judge, Cauchon, a more humane representative of the Church than is the Inquisitor, points out, she is not an infidel—they all worship the same God and Jeanne acknowledges the Church. But, she insists, "when something is black, I can't say it's white, that's all."[60]

Not only is the Inquisitor a strong adversary for Jeanne, but with his unbending determination and desire for an absolute but empty perfection, he suggests certain aspects of the heroine which might be turned against her. He is, in some respects, a caricature of heroic intransigence, and seems to announce the anti-hero that we shall see later in *Pauvre Bitos* (1956). Bitos, too, condemns those who will not conform to his pattern of perfection, and says, "We must do away with men as much as possible."[61]

If Jeanne gives in momentarily to the exhortations of Cauchon, it is because she is sincerely convinced of her duty to do so, by the image of Christ's suffering for her, and by Charles' assurance that he no longer needs

her. Her temporary physical salvation affords a relief
to all: to the Inquisitor because man has said yes; to
Cauchon because he abhors seeing Jeanne suffer and
believes in the efficacy of the Mother Church; to the
queens and Agnès Sorel because it is so unpleasant to
suffer and so pleasant to live; and to Charles because it
is inconvenient to have people devoted to one, for it
creates obligations.

But Jeanne soon realizes she was wrong. To remain
true to herself she must die, or she will no longer be
Jeanne, for unless she accepts her death she cannot relive the scene at Reims, which represents the true, the
eternal Jeanne d'Arc. Warwick tries to dissuade her by
telling her that time will arrange everything. But this is
precisely what Jeanne refuses:

> But I don't want things to work out . . . I don't
> want to live your time . . . Can you see Jeanne
> having lived, and things having worked out?
> Jeanne freed perhaps, vegetating at the French
> court on a small pension? . . . Jeanne accepting
> everything, Jeanne with a tummy. Jeanne become
> an epicure . . . Can you imagine Jeanne in make-
> up, wearing a hennin, stumbling over her train,
> pampering her little dog, or with a man at her
> heels? Who knows: even Jeanne married?[62]

We are reminded of Antigone refusing to grow old and
become someone who is not her real self, or Jeannette
consummating her love with Frédéric in death before
time covers them with falsehood.

Warwick cannot understand Jeanne's decision. In explanation, she adds, "there's nothing to be done, we just
don't belong to the same race."[63]

THE THIRD GROUP: THE COMPROMISE WITH LIFE
(1947–1956)

The third group of plays includes all those written since
Médée, with the exception of *L'alouette* (1953) and
Anouilh's last play, *Becket ou L'honneur de Dieu*

(1959). The volume ironically entitled *Pièces brillantes* contains *L'invitation au château* (1947), *Cécile ou L'école des pères* (1949), *La répétition ou L'amour puni* (1950), and *Colombe* (1950). Four other plays— *Ardèle ou La marguerite* (1948), *La valse des toréadors* (1951), *Ornifle ou Le courant d'air* (1955), and *Pauvre Bitos ou Le dîner de têtes* (1956)—have been gathered together under the title *Pièces grinçantes*. *L'hurluberlu* is published separately but belongs in spirit to the last collection. The only brilliance in these plays is the superficial one given by the witty dialogue, the colorful or gaudy costumes, and the hollow histrionics of the frivolous characters who take the stage; but beneath this superficial brightness we feel the grating disillusion that is fundamental to Anouilh.

The playwright's interest is no longer centered on the heroic personage as he encounters life with its compromises. He now directs his attention to the mediocre people who have accepted life. Sometimes, as in *La répétition,* he shows what a change is effected in the life of a member of the lower race when the real world is revealed to him by a member of the heroic race. Most often, however, the unheroic claims the center of the stage. Rather than contrasting those who accept life with those who refuse it, these "brilliant" plays and "grating" plays oppose the innocent and sincere to the, sometimes unwittingly, wicked and cruel. The pathetic struggles of the few good characters, almost lost midst the others, give rise to a deep feeling of despair in their behalf, for we realize that the cards are stacked against them. This pessimistic attitude constitutes a profound criticism of the adult characters who have lost the purity of childhood. Those who, like Général Saintpé, retain some memory of that realm, are surrounded still by a faint aura of tarnished nobility. In *Ornifle* and *Bitos* we see an almost complete inversion of the once-heroic character.

The complicated intrigue of *L'invitation au château*

41

(1947), in which once again a poor young girl comes into a wealthy milieu, proves nothing, for all ends happily as the hands of the author pull the strings of his puppets to arrange the cheerful denouement. Isabelle, at the instigation of Horace, comes to a ball at the chateau in order to win Frédéric, Horace's twin brother, away from Diane, the cruel, unloving woman of whom he is enamored. In the course of the play Isabelle falls in love with Horace, who is as cold and incapable of love as Diane. All turns out well when Frédéric realizes that he really loves Isabelle, and she, that Frédéric is the one she is in love with, since he is a physical replica of Horace, but with more appealing moral qualities. Unlike Thérèse, Isabelle does not refuse happiness, for this is not a *pièce noire,* and the dream is allowed to dominate.

Many of the stock characters of the earlier plays are found in *L'invitation au château:* the wealthy Madame Desmermortes who, like Lady Hurf of *Le bal des voleurs,* is as bored "as an old carpet,"[64] and who engages in a bit of fantastic intrigue to amuse herself; Isabelle's mother partakes of both the good-for-nothing fathers who believe the artist should be allowed all liberties and the mothers who would take advantage of their daughters and sell them to the highest bidder.

According to the mediocre people who dominate this play, life is a game, and the only thing we can do is to play it. This brings them a small amount of consolation for the solitude that is man's lot.[65] Isabelle, sincere and pure, refuses to play the game: "It's bad to think only of playing."[66] But the game Horace plays is one of his own devising, up to a certain point at least. Horace has accepted life, but he is one of those brilliant cynics who know exactly what they have done. Possessing the acuity to perceive the good, he lacks that intransigent desire for utter purity which characterizes the good man. Unlike Créon, Horace will not make the best of life through a well-meaning and honest evaluation, so that it will not be too disordered, but sets out to dispose of life's course so that it will fit his own selfish and wicked desires. He will be the "strong man." It is his belief that we are far too generous with destiny. For once he is going to organize things:

I find man too modest. He lets himself be led when it's almost always up to him to decide, and he's practically indomitable. Love, sickness, stupidity; he's found it convenient to call all that: fatality. As for me, I know none but death, my dear. . . . I'm not in a mood to put up with the normal order of things today . . . So much the worse for fatality![67]

This is a fine speech, and would be highly significant if we did not see that the belief in complete free will exhibited by Horace is hardly borne out by the end of the play. Horace, too, becomes caught up in the whirl of intrigue, and instead of remaining outside and in complete control, he is pushed into the waiting arms of Diane. Man's self-proclaimed freedom is a farce, the play seems to say. The play itself is a farce, and we must not take too seriously the words of its characters, for they are but puppets, every one—even those who, like Horace and Mme Desmermortes, believe themselves in control of the strings. At one point, Mme Desmermortes, watching the dancers from her wheelchair, exclaims: "Ah! how stupid this ball is . . . Look at them whirling around. They think they're having a good time, and all they're thinking of is their petty vanity and their petty affairs."[68] She seems to be standing outside the game of life for a moment; but it is only for a moment. We see later that Mme Desmermortes is not really free: "We must live with our own class, whether we like it or not,"[69] she tells Horace. And when Capulat, her highly romantic companion and reader, rhapsodizes in verse, Mme Desmermortes tells her to cease her versifying; but she is so little in possession of her freedom that she too speaks in verse:

> *Capulat.* Behold, they are now back from their
> bitter laving,
> The black and icy wave will waft them
> to their love.
> You kept your mouth closed, child, and
> perhaps he will be loving.
> *Mme Desmermortes.* Capulat! Capulat! Cease this
> infernal rhyming!
> *Capulat.* Alas, Madame, I cannot stop this
> time . . .
> These happenings have overwrought my
> soul,
> It masters me and speaks itself in rhyme!
> *Mme Desmermortes.* Then go compose [your
> verses] outside the
> winter garden![70]

Ardèle ou La marguerite (1948) shows us once again the people who live only on the surface, believing above all that appearances must be respected. Général Saintpé has called a conference of his immediate family to decide what to do about his hunchbacked sister Ardèle, who has fallen in love with the hunchbacked tutor of the General's youngest son. The tutor has been dismissed and Ardèle locked in her room. She in turn has bolted her door from the inside and refuses to eat. By accident the door is left unlocked, and at night Ardèle signals to her lover and lets him into her room, where the two commit suicide.

This play is dominated by the wicked and ugly. The General's youngest son and his sister's young daughter are grotesque caricatures of the adults and no longer evoke the purity of childhood. Ardèle herself, the symbol of pure, heroic love, does not appear, nor is she heard. The only sounds that come from her room are the two pistol shots that announce the double suicide. She has found the only way to avoid the corruption of life. The General has accepted a loveless existence with his wife, because he did not have the courage to leave

44

her; his sister the Countess and her husband Gaston have made the best of an unhappy marriage by taking lovers and pretending that all is well. The major pre-occupation of the central characters in *Ardèle* is to keep up appearances. It is for this reason that they cannot admit of a union between Ardèle and another hunch-back, for it would cause talk. Ardèle's feelings are not important. "There is something more than love," says the Countess. "There is society. There is scandal."[71] "You know very well," she adds later, "that it's only a question of keeping up appearances, of not giving people scandal to feed on."[72] Youth with its uncompro-mising character and its purity is far behind and for-gotten. Gabriel Marcel says of this play:

> The horror of life and of what we call love rises like an unbearable odor from the kind of human flower bed that Anouilh has created with cruel and diligent art. . . . Undoubtedly the fundamental obscenity of existence has rarely been denounced with such fury. But isn't this an impasse? I, person-ally, remain convinced that a truly great dramatist cannot confine himself to so negative an attitude toward life.[73]

But this negative attitude, which could easily lead to stagnation, and to which Marcel is not alone in object-ing,[74] continues to dominate in the following plays where the good race fails to justify itself in any manner. There is now no Antigone who goes victoriously to her death; in the end of *La répétition,* Lucile, the only pure personage in the play, flees and thus fades from the picture in a colorless manner. The same is true of Julien in *Colombe,* who is in the beginning a dominant person, but who in the end seeks consolation for the disap-pointments of life in a dream of the promises of the past. In *La valse des toréadors* the heroic character is absent.

La répétition (1950) tells how the Count and Count-ess prepare to present Marivaux's *La double inconstance*

45

at a party they are planning. The rehearsals of the play, whose cast includes the couple's guests, are intertwined with the scenes from the real life of the characters, and parallels are suggested between the roles each one of the people is playing and his situation in real life. The Count, Tigre, feels himself falling in love with Lucile, a governess from the orphanage on the estate, who is to play a role in the Marivaux work. The Count's wife and his mistress join forces to prevent the affair that they see about to mature. Events are manipulated so that Tigre is called away, and a friend, Héro, who lives in a drunken stupor, is assigned the task of seducing Lucile. This he accomplishes through rousing her pity, and by telling her he has been charged with this mission by Tigre himself who is tired of her. The following morning Lucile flees; Tigre sets out after her, with little hope of ever finding her; and Héro, disgusted after all with the vile role he has agreed to play, provokes a duel with the Countess' lover, who is known to be an excellent shot.

The central conflict of the play is between Tigre's old self and the self revealed to him by his contact with Lucile. For the first time in his life he has fallen in love and seen what living really means. Before, he had been content, like the other members of his circle, to think of life as one big party. But his meeting with Lucile reawakens the feeling for purity which he had in his youth. His wife even notices that he has taken on the look he had in an old photograph she had seen.[75] In contrast to the simplicity of life before, he has discovered that to live is always "complicated and degrading."[76] In a conversation with his wife toward the end of the play, Tigre describes his new feeling in contrast to his old life:

> We've lived life as though it were a ballet, set to music, with fixed steps, and gracefully. . . . I shall always think it the only intelligent way to live, to escape disorder and vulgarity. Only, . . .

46

That graceful and clear-cut line that goes from my first successful cotillion to my probable presidency at the Jockey Club in twenty years, and my funeral at the Madeleine with all Paris there in top hats, I've just realized that it would be a lovely memory for everyone else, a nice theme for an article in the *Figaro*—and nothing for me. I didn't know why I was always so gay; I was bored.[77]

But the Count is not made of heroic stuff: he will continue to accept the taint of life. Héro has accepted also; he is aware of life's true ugliness. "How ugly life is,"[78] he repeats on several occasions. But he at last, through his contact with Lucile, has the courage to die —his challenging the Countess' lover is equivalent to suicide.

Lucile may remind us of Antigone in her refusal to be reasonable, and in her refusal to play the game,[79] but we cannot help feeling that she is just what Héro calls her—"a little cardboard heroine"[80]—and that Pierre de Boisdeffre is right when he says of *La répétition* that "all these characters seem pale and faded, a softened imitation become quaint and dainty; they no longer possess that fervor and hardness which we admired in their predecessors."[81]

Colombe (1950) is anything but quaint and dainty. The characters are drawn with heavy strokes and their differences brightly highlighted. Julien, the representative of the pure race, is entirely unsympathetic, clumsy, antisocial, and sour. His saving quality is honesty with himself and with others. But, like other heroes, he makes life uncomfortable for others and he cannot understand or adapt to their weaknesses. In short, he is another Alceste. This rather unpleasantly misanthropic presentation of the heroic race has its own logic within the framework of Anouilh's general ideas as they develop from the admirable heroism of Thérèse and of Orphée, through the more even balance of Antigone and Créon, where it is suggested that there is some justification for

47

the acceptance of life. The same spirit is found in *Médée*, though perhaps not to so marked a degree. In the *Pièces brillantes* and the *Pièces grinçantes*, with the hero mostly on the periphery, we see the cruelty of those who have said yes to life, but we see in addition, and particularly in the instance of Julien, the impossibility of the hero's stand in life. His purity is still admired, but that blind obsession that was so much a part of Antigone is almost criticized in Julien.

Unfortunately, Julien has fallen in love with Colombe, a young florist-shop helper. The play opens after they have been married for two years. Julien, refusing to take advantage of his mother's influence, is about to do his military service, and he has come to ask his mother, Madame Alexandra the great tragedienne, to look after his young wife Colombe during his absence. It becomes apparent almost immediately that Colombe and Julien are members of different races. He is all intractability and seriousness; she is gaiety and facility. The paste and powder of the theater appeal to her at once, and she readily accepts its artificiality. When Julien returns on leave he discovers that Colombe has fallen into a life of compromise: she is no longer the pure young woman he loved. It becomes apparent that she was never the woman he believed her to be. The Colombe he loves exists only in his imagination. *Colombe* tells the story of what would have happened had Orphée and Eurydice consented to live. The two races confront each other in Julien and Colombe:

> *Julien.* I know your heart is good, and that you're making an effort to understand what I'm explaining to you [the corruption of the theater world]; but you're still a child, and facility lays terrible traps. . . .
> *Colombe.* But is facility so bad?
> *Julien.* Yes, Colombe.
> *Colombe.* And yet easy and pleasant things are good.

48

Julien (shouts). No, they're not good! . . .
Colombe. How complicated everything is with you,
darling. . . . And for me everything is so much
simpler . . . Everyone is nice, nothing is ugly,
and all I want is to be happy.[82]

For Julien, life is ugly. Like the earlier heroes, he desires an unconditional purity that conforms to his inner
image of himself and of Colombe. But Anouilh paints
him in so unfavorable a light—as boorish and pedantic
—that we feel Anouilh has for once failed to favor his
heroic race in its struggle with the mediocre. When
Julien describes his father—an impossible rigorous and
misanthropic individual with no sense of humor, who
committed suicide when his wife deserted him after
three weeks of marriage—he is also describing himself.
If Julien is truly his father's son, he too will kill himself
after the death of his ideal. His brother Armand, on
the other hand, is his mother's son—given to false brilliance and the easy compromise. "What do you expect,
old chap," he says to Julien, trying to excuse himself
for having seduced Colombe, "facility, temptation . . .
You know how it is!" Julien can only answer with a wild
roar, "No, I don't know how it is! I'll never know how
it is!"[83]

Armand reveals the lack of freedom of the mediocre:
"I'm weak, I know. When I enjoy something: wasting
my money at poker, drinking one too many, pinching a
pretty leg; it's useless for me to tell myself no, it's
stronger than I am, and I say yes."[84]

La Surette, Madame Alexandra's secretary and scape-
goat, is also enslaved, for he bitterly resents the bowing
and scraping required by the old actress, but he will not
assert himself. "You can be free when you want, La
Surette,"[85] Julien tells him, but La Surette is not willing
to undergo the necessary suffering and anguish: the renunciation required by true freedom.

In *La valse des toréadors* (1951) Anouilh returns to
Général Saintpé[86] and his deranged wife Amélie, and

49

by putting them in slightly different circumstances, reveals in more detail certain aspects of their lives. Some seventeen years ago, we discover, at a ball at Saumur, the then young officer Léon met a girl with whom he fell in love. For the past seventeen years he has been waiting for his wife to die so that he might marry Ghislaine. However, his fidelity to her has not interfered with his amorous activities. Ghislaine suddenly appears at the General's chateau with letters that purport to prove Amélie has been unfaithful, thus freeing the General from his duty to her. Ghislaine, who is still a virgin, becomes acquainted with the General's idealistic young secretary Gaston. They fall in love and the General, who in a melodramatic finale discovers that his secretary is his illegitimate son, is forced to agree to the marriage.

Throughout the play the General struggles pathetically to recall the young lieutenant of the days before he started cheating himself. But life has covered him with too hard a shell, and when he describes life to his young secretary, he pictures it as a long family dinner—boring like all family dinners, but necessary, with a certain established ceremony, which all agree upon for convenience's sake and to satisfy appearances: "We must of course play the game according to the rules." But once the meal is ended, the law of the jungle takes over and, unseen by the others, one seduces the maids and flirts with the kitchen help.[87] There is a place for the ideal, too, in the General's scheme of things. A distant place, to be sure: the ideal is like a buoy that we never quite lose from sight. No one ever reaches it, of course, but that is not required. Those eccentrics who do try to reach it come what may, splash everyone else and always end up drowning—dragging down with them a number of unfortunates who might otherwise have continued to paddle about.[88] The General's secretary is young and prefers trying to swim rapidly toward the buoy, even if he drowns in the attempt. The General, after a silence, admits that the boy is right: it is ignoble to grow old and to understand. He advises the youth to avoid causing others to drown, for the General has accustomed himself to everything except to hurting others. But it is one of the conditions of life, as Anouilh envisages it, that one cannot be himself without hurting others. Hence the General himself will be hurt when the young secretary steals his chaste mistress from him: the secretary has had the courage to do ill, while being true to himself—a courage that the General never had, and the lack of which explains why he is still bound to his wife whom he no longer loves. As Sartre would say, the General's life is not "authentic."

For the General, as for all adults, life is a question of respecting appearances. Any amount of cheating is permitted so long as the front is kept up. This is the picture of the General's entire life—answering every fifteen minutes to his wife's insane shouts of "Léon! Léon!" and seducing the maids when they come to make the beds in the children's rooms. It is also the meaning of the parable of the Spartan youth who stole a fox and rather than admit the theft let the fox devour his stomach. The young secretary, perplexed at first by the fable, sums up its lesson as, "when someone does something dishonorable, honor consists of never admitting it."[89] The General is dissatisfied with the answer: "Let's forget it," he says. "You'll understand when you grow up. Just remember this: it's necessary to keep up appearances."[90] For the General, for Madame Alexandra, for all the members of the mediocre race who live on the surface, for governments and institutions alike (the reference to the army's attempt to save face in the Dreyfus affair, and the blind patriotism of Déroulède is clear enough[91]), appearance is what counts.

The General is one of those of the mediocre race who have some insight into the true situation. He knows that happiness lies only on the surface—it is a role people play, some of them without realizing it is a role.

This realization gives rise to his feeling of solitude and fear: he knows that he is nothing more than a well-decorated shell, and after surveying the inner vacuum he has emerged to make a noise in order to reassure himself.[92] The noise is the game of life, the frenzied search for happiness, for love and money. The game is not particularly meaningful, but it makes one feel less alone in the dark.

Ornifle ou Le courant d'air (1955), and *Pauvre Bitos ou Le dîner de têtes* (1956) introduce a hero who is an inversion of the former heroic characters of Anouilh. Ornifle, like Général Saintpé, would have liked to "give his all," but he has discovered that life is not so made. As a young man he had been extremely idealistic, but when we meet him he is an aging Don Juan who avenges himself upon life by becoming as corrupt as possible. His adversary is God himself, and Ornifle does not hesitate to accuse his opponent of unfair play: after all, God is bound to win in the end, for the game is weighted in his favor. Ornifle wounds his wife, who accepts him as he is and tries to overlook his infidelity; he wounds his long-suffering and highly romantic secretary, Supo, who yearns to give herself to him; he wounds his friends and even his illegitimate son who suddenly arrives upon the scene planning to kill the man responsible for his illegitimate status. And at the end of the play, after attempting to seduce this young man's fiancée, Ornifle goes off to a rendezvous with a lady friend, and a moment later we learn that he has died of a heart attack. God has won, as Ornifle predicted, but sooner than the old libertine had expected.

Ornifle is what we may call an antihero, but at least he is heroic in stature because of the very nature of his struggle and the adversary that he has chosen. Poor Bitos is quite different. In him we see the continuation of the misanthropic personage represented by Julien in *Colombe*. Petty, narrow-minded, embittered by his poverty-stricken youth, Bitos has become a deputy for the

Procureur de la République after the Resistance. A man of principles, he refuses to make compromises of any kind, and condemns to death his childhood friend without blinking an eye.

The play tells how Bitos is invited to a *dîner de têtes* by some wealthy acquaintances—his enemies since *lycée* days. Each guest is to impersonate a character of the Revolution, and Bitos has been assigned the unpleasant role of Robespierre, which corresponds perfectly to his personality and to the position he occupies as judge in the community. The wealthy guests make fun of Bitos, maintaining that it is Robespierre they are addressing, and in the end Bitos realizes he has been the butt of a cruel joke. This intransigent antihero, so like Antigone in many ways, has become an object of mockery and scorn, a grotesque caricature of the heroine of 1942. Antigone may have been disturbing, but Bitos is frankly boring: a stiff and humorless personage.

The entire second act of the play takes us back to the days of the Reign of Terror, and Bitos reënacts the scenes of the life of Robespierre. In a conversation with Mirabeau he is told, "There is something dogmatic about you, something a bit pedantic, a bit stiff—let's be frank, a bit tedious—which annoys people."[93] The heroic race has fallen low indeed!

In *L'hurluberlu* (1958) we are once again in the luxurious country home of a retired general, but Ludovic reminds us more of Julien in *Colombe* than he does of Général Saintpé: he has never learned to make concessions. Twice he is compared to Molière's Alceste, for poor Ludovic is another of Anouilh's disillusioned idealists. When the parish priest asks him why he is so full of hate, he replies: "It's not hate, Father. It's pain. I've felt this pain for fifty years. It's beginning to seem like a long time. As a little boy, I had imagined things would be entirely different. I've never gotten over it."[94]

Married to a wife half his age who is unhappy and bored, the General is worried lest he lose her. So he agrees to let his daughter's boy friend, David Edward Mendigalès, produce on his estate a play for some church festival. The General, his family, and friends will all take part. In the meantime, Ludovic holds secret meetings to conspire against the government, which are the talk of the province and indeed of all France. He hopes to save his country by imposing a rigorously honest regime. As the play ends, the General's friends have all abandoned his conspiracy, leaving him alone; his wife has shown a disturbing interest in a young neighbor; and his daughter, deserted by David Edward, has run off to her mother in Brussels to find there the sympathy her father refuses her.

The subtitle of *L'hurluberlu* is "the amorous reactionary." Ludovic is reactionary not only in his politics; he is reactionary above all in his devotion to the past: "I don't want anything to change, ever!"[95] he cries. Like Antigone, he would refuse the adult world, but for the old General it is too late. His petulant behavior is comic rather than tragic, and in scene after scene he caricatures unconsciously the heroine of sixteen years earlier. But no one takes Ludovic seriously. Even the government makes no attempt to repress his revolutionary activities, for his political revolt is as ineffective as his moral revolt, and in the final analysis it is life with its cruel facility which wins. Twice the General is knocked to the ground: first by the mundane and ultramodern David Edward Mendigalès, and then by the brutal dairyman from next door. As the embittered idealist lies on his lawn among the chairs, he concludes that life— like the play they have prepared—must go on, and fortunately, in spite of everything, man can laugh at his own performance.

The antiheroic characters, and the colorless treatment usually afforded to the so-called heroic race in these later plays of Anouilh, seem to indicate a loss of faith in the efficacity of the revolt as an answer to the ugliness of life. Constant repetition of such phrases as

"How ugly life is!" strike us as presenting an enigma with no suggestion of a solution. There is no longer the violent protest against human misery: only the statement that it exists. The impasse that Gabriel Marcel saw in *Ardèle* is patent in the other plays of the postwar period. Serge Radine sees in the theater of Anouilh a gradual descent, brought about by the lack of any positive values: "Frightening expression of the despair of a man who believed he could affront the Absolute and take hold of it, and who, looking suddenly at his hands, realized that they were empty."[96] He sees the only hope for Anouilh's salvation as a dramatist in a forgetting of himself, "in order to find some great hope of collective salvation, whether it be socialist or Christian in inspiration."[97] Gabriel Marcel implies a similar conviction, but with considerably more justice directs his criticism against the lack of appreciation for human dignity to be found in the first plays of this period:

> The danger to which Anouilh's theater seems exposed is that in the last analysis pity itself tends to become mockery. We see the ultimate countenance of this work as a grimace, but a grimace cannot be the expression of a theatrical thought. Whoever disregards the nobility and grandeur of the human drama condemns himself to seeing himself one day condemned.[98]

In the plays of the first and second periods, Anouilh's heroes gave some semblance of meaning to life by making it the means through which they realized themselves, by their very refusal of it. In the plays of the third period, however, the picture is one of compromise, and the outlook seems more pessimistic than ever. We can find no hole in the fabric of an absurd universe through which to bring in some meaning. One is led to wonder whether Jaspers' criticism of the distortion of Tragic Knowledge into a Tragic World View is not applicable here:

> Wherever total lack of faith seeks to parade as

form, it finds the philosophy of nothing-but-trag-
edy well suited as a camouflage for nothingness.
Tragic grandeur is the prop whereby the arrogant
nihilist can elevate himself to the pathos of feeling
himself a hero. Where seriousness has been lost,
an experience of pseudo-seriousness is produced
by the violent stimulus of tragedy. The racial past,
the sagas, the Greek tragedy are all invoked. Yet
what had then been the reality of faith becomes
now a deliberate and dishonest substitute for nothingness. . . . Such perversion of tragic philosophy
then sets free the turmoil of dark impulses: the delight in meaningless activity, in torturing and in
being tortured, in destruction for its own sake, in
the raging hatred against one's own despised
existence.[99]

One is justified in suspecting Anouilh's heroes of
"arrogant nihilism," and in asking whether they have
not attempted to make of their lack of faith in humanity a system that overlooks those elements of man's
constitution which are capable of saving him from himself. In the last group of plays especially, the weakness
and immorality of the characters seems to point to the
conclusion that man is not worth saving.

Becket ou L'honneur de Dieu

In *Becket ou L'honneur de Dieu* (1959) Anouilh returns to the intransigent characters of his first and
second periods, but presents a more mature and positive
hero than any of the earlier ones.

Becket, a proud and independent Saxon, has become
the bosom companion of Henry II, and together the
young men revel and reign. It is the keenly intelligent
and sensitive Becket who is the real power in England,
and Henry recognizes it by making him Chancellor.
When the old Archbishop of Canterbury dies, Henry
names his friend to the post in order to have strong support in his struggle with the clergy. Becket warns him,

however, that he cannot be on God's side and the King's at the same time.

As prelate, Becket believes he has finally found his true role. Until his appointment he had been as though absent, only acting the part of playboy and Chancellor. With the vigor and zeal typical of the heroic race, he sells his fine clothes, gives his money to the poor, and sets about to defend God's honor and His Church against the King, as it had never been done before. Forced to flee, Becket seeks refuge in a French monastery, but the game of penance and prayer is too easy for him, and he returns to England to minister to his flock. Before crossing the Channel, he has a last encounter with Henry on a windswept plain in Normandy, and together they realize that they can no longer communicate, for one speaks the language of absolutes and defends the honor of God, whereas the other speaks the language of political expediency, defending the honor of the King. History takes its course, and the Archbishop is murdered before the altar of his cathedral. The play ends as it had begun, with Henry at Canterbury doing penance for the murder of Becket, for he needs to win the Saxons to his side. Now that his most fearful opponent is dead, he can proclaim his royal will "to defend henceforth the honor of God and the memory of our friend."[100]

Although Becket recalls Antigone in his intractable attitude before the King, he strikes us at once as being more mature and more logical. For Becket is not revolting in a vacuum, and he is not reduced to admitting that he is acting for himself. He is defending a positive value—the honor of God—and he stands for "the unwritten law which always bends the heads of kings at last."[101] It is that same unwritten law that gives Sophocles' Antigone such strength and authority.

Henry, on the other hand, has none of the dignity or weight of Créon. He is a weak, pathetic, and brutal figure, dependent upon Becket for his decisions, and lost without the friendship that had meant so much to him. The honor of the King, like the honor of the Pope, and that of the priests, monks, and soldiers who bandy the word about thoughtlessly, is a pitiable thing—a hollow mockery that masks political or financial opportunism. For Becket, honor represents an absolute which cannot be defiled. In his early exploits with Henry, as a young debauchee, we see that Becket is already a man of honor, even though the word at that time has no meaning for him. His morality is an aesthetic one, and if he refuses to lie or to give in to the pattern of expediency set by the King, it is because he considers such behavior inelegant. Generous and kind, yet proud, aloof, and reserved, Becket can give himself to no one, for he has not yet found anything that will satisfy him entirely. As the first act closes, he whispers to the sleeping King, "As long as Becket must improvise his honor, he will serve you. And if some day he finds it . . . But where is Becket's honor?"[102]

The answer is quickly given, and once he has accepted the role of Archbishop, Becket plays it to the hilt, for he had warned the King in no uncertain terms: "I love at least one thing, my lord, and of that I'm sure. To do well what I have to do."[103]

In the impressive scene on the plains of Normandy, Henry attempts to dissuade Becket from his decision to excommunicate several Norman barons, by employing an image we have already heard on Créon's lips: that of the ship of state which must be directed by someone at the helm. Ironically enough, it is Becket who had suggested the metaphor in an earlier argument with the clergy when the young man was still on Henry's side. And now it is Becket who supplies the answer: someone must defend the absurd wind that blows against the ship—and God with it. There is a stalemate in the discussion as Becket, in language at first highly reminiscent of Antigone's, describes his position to the King:

58

Becket. I'm not here to convince you. I'm only here to say no.

The King. But you've got to be logical, Becket!

Becket. No. That's not necessary, my king. We just have to do what we've been charged to do—absurdly, to the bitter end.

The King. And, I thought I knew you once. . . . "Absurdly." That's a word that doesn't sound like you.

Becket. Perhaps not. I'm no longer myself.

The King (snickers). You've been touched by grace?

Becket (gravely). Not by the grace you're thinking of. I'm not worthy.

The King. Then you've become a good Saxon again, in spite of your father's worthy collaborationist sentiments?

Becket. Not even that.

The King. Then what?

Becket. It's simply that I felt myself entrusted with something for the first time, in that empty cathedral somewhere in France, where you ordered me to take up this burden. I was a man without honor. And suddenly I had one: the one that I would never have imagined could become mine—the honor of God. An incomprehensible and fragile honor, like a persecuted child king.[104]

What begins as the same absolute negation of Antigone ends here on an affirmative note as Becket evokes the ideal he has chosen to defend. But there is something that does not ring true in all this, and Becket suggests what it is when he answers Henry's question, "Have you begun to love God?" After a pause, the Archbishop replies gently, "I've begun to love the honor of God."[105] It is clear enough that Thomas doubts the existence of the God whose honor he assumed in that empty cathedral somewhere in France. If he has great faith, it is a faith in himself and in the image he has created of his best self. His prayers and apostrophes to God only reflect the perfectionism of the aesthetic moralist who is playing his role to the fingertips. Louis of France touches the heart of the matter when he explains: "Becket has a protective tenderness for the King. But the only thing in the world he loves is the idea of his honor which he has forged for himself."[106]

This sounds curiously like the total lack of faith parading as form, of which Jaspers speaks. We begin to suspect that Becket is more like Antigone than is at first apparent. Although he may lack her childish arrogance, he may very well share her "nihilism," for God's honor turns out to be another way of expressing the heroic desire for an impossible absolute.

But Becket's "no" is not spoken against life; unlike Antigone's, it does not represent the will to refuse. It has a more positive side: it is spoken against compromise, and in favor of a value (God, the Church) which, however incomprehensible it may be as an absolute, does have a meaning in human terms. In this sense, Becket is more profoundly human than Antigone or Jeannette. He does not go toward death with their eagerness, scorning "filthy hope" and happiness. He accepts death because it is a necessary part of his role.

We must not conclude that Anouilh has found a more optimistic solution to the conflicting exigencies of the hero and of life, for the last scene of the play suggests that such men as Becket scarcely affect the mediocrities who destroy them. As the curtain falls we are left with a disillusioned picture of hypocrisy and compromise which reminds us of the depressing world of *Colombe* or *Ornifle*. Several years earlier Anouilh had paused in his portrait of the world empty of heroes to tell the story of Jeanne d'Arc. *Becket* may be another momentary reversion to this heroic world. It is interesting to note, however, that both *Becket* and *L'alouette* indicate a more positive outlook than the earlier heroic dramas. Whether Anouilh is on the threshold of a new period we cannot say on the evidence of a single play. As yet he has not suggested any practical solution to the problems posed by life as it is revealed in his theater. But it is not the function of the dramatist to supply us with answers. It is enough if he presents his picture of the human predicament in a dramatically effective way. Philosophers and prophets may propose solutions. Anouilh has been content to show us the various roles man is condemned to play in his unfriendly universe.

Destiny and God

Who, or what, is responsible for designating the role a man will play?

In the plays of the first group there is no mention of God, and destiny is conceived of only in a vague and uncertain way. It is a power that depends upon man to accomplish things. In *La sauvage* it is suggested that God is completely indifferent to man. Hartman tells Thérèse that she, perhaps, is like a God to the scullery maid who every evening risks losing her job in order to steal into the garden and catch sight of Thérèse. But Thérèse is unaware of her. That scullery maid may in turn keep chained in the courtyard a dog for whom she is a god, and to whom she pays no attention. The problem is not gone into any further than this before *Eurydice*. That man is alone is certain, for all the protagonists from Frantz to Ornifle complain of solitude.

Those whom Anouilh has presented as the heroic men in the plays of the first period find life absurd. God does not appear to exist for them; and if there is no God and man is alone, the hero must be obedient to nothing but what he believes to be his real self. He can follow no laws or codes set down by society, for that would result in a rigidity and lack of spontaneity which the heroic soul constantly rejects. "Don't try to fool yourself with honesty and morality,"[107] Frantz tells Monime (*L'hermine*) somewhat ironically, for he is at the same time duping himself with high-sounding words and

61

heroic attitudes. The only moral order that exists for Anouilh's hero is the inner one he imposes upon himself, and the only reason he behaves the way he does is to satisfy his inner voice. When asked why he has done a certain thing, the hero is usually reduced to admitting that it was "for myself," or what is equivalent for the outside world—"For nothing."[108]

During this first period there seems to exist some confusion in Anouilh's concepts of destiny, fate, and God, and their relationship to the free will of man. Destiny, when mentioned at all, is conceived of as a vague and indifferent power, seemingly working within a deterministic system. God is absent.

With *Eurydice*, however, and the beginning of the second period, destiny suddenly comes to the fore, in the person of Monsieur Henri who is destiny incarnate and who is present at every crucial moment of the play, directing the fates of men in a less deterministic and more personal way. Even when he is absent he is only in the next room. He may seem to be preoccupied with his thoughts, but Orphée is sure that he sees what is going on in the little railway station where the "fated" meeting of the lovers takes place. Such a meeting, in a railway station where there is constant coming and going, might have impressed us as pure chance, had not Monsieur Henri been there to tell us that destiny is always responsible: "These brief instants when one surprises destiny placing his pawns are disturbing, aren't they?"[109]

When Orphée wishes to take upon himself the responsibility for the loss of Eurydice, Monsieur Henri accuses him of pride: "What a strange compulsion to put a possessive pronoun before each one of your puppet strings."[110] This is more than a suggestion that man is devoid of free will and nothing more than a pawn in the hands of destiny. Monsieur Henri makes it clear that each of our acts, whether we perceive it or not, is ruled by a power that is omnipresent. That man may influence that power is also suggested, but not firmly stated. If Monsieur Henri represents destiny, and Orphée is able to wring from him an exception to natural law, then this is an indication that man is not entirely bereft of control. "What difference did my suffering make to you?" asks Orphée. Monsieur Henri responds:

> I don't know. It's the first time. Something foreign began to weaken in me. And if you continued to weep and suffer, it would have bled like a wound . . . I was just leaving the hotel. I put down my suitcases and went in to calm you. And since nothing would calm you, I made you that promise so you would stop crying.[111]

Orphée has caused destiny to yield, but only temporarily and without changing the final result: only an illusion has been created that man can change destiny. It is important to remember that Orphée is of the heroic race, and that he has brought about this suspension of destiny by his refusal to accept the reality that destiny had tried to force upon him. Thus, the picture left us by Eurydice is that of a universe ruled over by an omnipotent destiny that can be influenced to a certain degree by heroic man. This yields to the hero his freedom, in the sense that the hero believes he can create himself, as opposed to the mediocre man who believes that "our beloved liberty, after all, consists of accepting ourselves as we are . . ."[112]

The Chorus in *Antigone* tells us: "There's nothing to be done. Her name is Antigone, and she's going to have to play her role to the end . . ."[113] And he underlines the absurdity of such inevitability: "It's a question of casting."[114] From this the power of destiny is clear, and Henri Perruchot is correct in assuming there is "nothing simpler, in its intense sobriety, than this tragedy hastening implacably to its end, carefully led on by Destiny."[115]

On the other hand, Antigone is free insofar as she realizes her potential self through her actions. She acts gratuitously, with no apparent motivations, only becoming herself as she meets the particular situation in which we see her. Her actions are intuitive rather than rational, and represent what Bergson might call the ensemble of her intimate feelings, thoughts, and aspirations.[116] She asserts her freedom to choose, and because she has never said yes to life she feels she remains free. As Perruchot states in the conclusion to his study of this play: "Antigone is her own fatality."[117]

In *Roméo et Jeannette* God is recognized for the first time as a part of Anouilh's world. It is principally through the words of Lucien that we learn of Him, and Gabriel Marcel has warned us that we should not take Lucien too seriously, for he is an obsessed maniac.[118] Be that as it may, Lucien seems worthy of a certain degree of trust, for he has at least pierced through the superficial comedy of life and seen the absurdity that lies beneath it all. If he has accepted life, he has done so with the knowledge, if not the dignity, of a Créon. He is represented as having the intuitive insight of those unencumbered by reason. It is Lucien who announces the arrival of Jeannette as destiny breaking upon the house, and it is he who explains to the others the nature of God: an indefinite God, either nearsighted or sleeping. One thing awakens Him: the odor of happiness, for He is a cruel God, and He wakens to destroy happiness: "everything that's good is forbidden. . . . the fellow up there. Whenever anyone is happy it makes him terribly angry. He doesn't like that."[119]

After the suicide of Frédéric and Jeannette, Lucien turns to his sadistic God and admits bitterly that this was after all how everything was bound to turn out.

In the face of this, Jeannette still asserts her responsibility. She has tried to stop eating meat, but cannot, for she likes it too well. "Then it's not your fault either," says Frédéric. "Yes," replies Jeannette somberly, shaking her head. She realizes how pleasant it must be to lay the responsibility elsewhere, and when she has grown old and made the compromise with life, she too will undoubtedly excuse herself.[120] But being young, spontaneous, and heroic, she cannot help but feel her own responsibility, for in spite of the deterministic outlook implied by the presence of a cruel God who sniffs out happiness wherever it may exist, the hero is free in the sense of being aware of his real self and aware of his choice.

In *Médée* Jason speaks of the indifference of the gods[121] who are apparently unmoved by human suffering. At the same time, he makes it clear when addressing Médée that he believes the gods are in control and man is not free:

> I can't prevent you from being yourself. I can't prevent you from doing the evil you carry within you. The die is cast, anyway. These insoluble conflicts come to an end, just like the others, and someone probably already knows how all this will finish. I can't prevent anything. All I can do is to play the role that has been assigned me from the beginning.[122]

If Jason is helpless, Médée is not, for she will wreak vengeance by acting. Thus she will be aiding destiny, for she knows that destiny must always be aided: "Count on Médée!" she cries after the departing Créon. "We have to help destiny a little!"[123]

Médée understands her role both as victim of the gods and as their unique instrument, when she takes her blade in hand to commit the multiple murder of her children and of the innocent young girl that she once was. Lesser humans escape the notice of the gods, but the heroic soul is too beautiful a prey to let slip past. The gods have their eyes fixed upon Médée: "They're waiting for this blood up there. They can scarcely stand it, they're so eager!"[124]

All four of these central plays present contradictions that suggest a confusion in Anouilh's mind regarding the functions of destiny and free will. God or destiny is present, sometimes indifferent, sometimes extremely interested; man has been assigned a role to play, and he has no choice but to play that role: all of this implies a deterministic attitude. But the assertion of free will and moral responsibility on the part of the heroes suggests that Anouilh believes, or wishes to believe, man may be free.

The most admirable characters in Anouilh's world are aware that there is a choice to be made. Without this awareness they could make no true decisions, nor could they have any feelings of responsibility. They might simply excuse themselves for their weaknesses by saying that they are unavoidable—this is what Jeannette refuses to admit when Frédéric tells her she is not to blame for her inability to abstain from eating meat. Rather, she feels she has a definite choice to make and that her weakness in following her decision is not dictated by exterior force, nor is it an inherent weakness in herself. It is owing simply to laziness which she has the power to correct, but instead she has followed the way of least resistance—has failed to break through the crust imposed by habit and has not acted with what Bergson would call her entire soul or personality:

> The free decision arises from the soul as a totality; . . . Here, in the very center of the fundamental self, a parasitic self takes shape and continually encroaches upon the other. Many people live this way, and die without having known true liberty.[125]

In this instance Jeannette has resigned her freedom through sluggishness or indolence, allowing the local process to run its course when instead, as Bergson says, her whole personality ought to be vibrating.

The members of the mediocre race follow the line of least resistance even though they may realize there is another possible choice. But even the recognition of a choice to be made is usually restricted to the members of the other race. And their freedom is represented not so much by the choice they do make as it is by the very awareness they have of their ability to choose. In other words, Anouilh's free will is an inner liberty intuited by the characters even when they feel themselves dominated by fate, and opposed to that exterior force represented by destiny, God, or human institutions. If the exterior forces assert their superiority ultimately, the hero is inwardly victorious and can continue to assert his liberty, for he is expressing, even in apparent defeat, his truest self. Free will is, in this instance as in the philosophy of Bergson, a corollary of consciousness: "We are free when our acts arise from our total personality, when they express it, when they resemble it in that indefinable way that a work of art resembles the artist."[126]

Consciousness thus distinguishes the hero who lives on an intellectual as well as on an intuitive plane from the mediocre man who, unconscious and unthinking, is sunk in being rather than constantly becoming. Submitting, without an effort to understand, to the coagulation of religious, moral, and social codes, the mediocre man lives the life of an animal—following instinct and the easy way. He is not committed in a positive way to anything, and therefore is not really living. The average man is dominated by his role, whereas the hero tries to dominate it by becoming himself through the anguish of decision.

In the plays of the third period, in which the mediocre people dominate, God remains for the most part indifferent to man, if He exists at all. Madame Desmermortes is not sure that God exists, but if He does, man is hardly worth his attention. When at the end of *L'invitation au château* a fireworks display is set off, Lady India is terrified, and cries, "The fire from heaven, already?" "No," replies Mme Desmermortes. "We don't deserve so much, my dear."[127]

Julien is more pathetically skeptical when he reminds Colombe of their marriage vows, "in the cold little chapel where there were no guests, perhaps not even God."[128]

When God's existence is taken for granted, characters tend to renounce any claims to freedom and make God responsible for their weaknesses. In *Ardèle* the General expresses the belief that God is too busy to pay any attention to him. Life has taught him that good intentions are of no avail, and so he has abdicated.[129] These people have followed the way of least resistance, consoling themselves with the thought that they are helpless. "That's the way the world is, my dear," says the Countess in *La Répétition,* "and we can do nothing about it."[130]

Ornifle continues the cruel picture of God we have seen in *Roméo et Jeannette.* "He gives nothing free," Ornifle tells his wife, who is about to go to a ball. "He'll make you pay dear for your enjoyable evening."[131] And later he explains to his natural son's fiancée that God was avaricious when it came to distributing love among men; he is only generous when it is a question of epidemics or railroad accidents.[132]

In *Pauvre Bitos* God has disappeared to make way for the Idea of Duty and the deification of the People. But the People is only an abstract, and Bitos, in his desire for perfection, cannot abide men. "I like no one,"[133] he cries, and maintains that he will kill all those who try to cheat: "I'll guillotine everyone!"[134] Here there remains an abstraction which corresponds to nothing in reality. The perverted "humanism" of Bitos is another facet of the perverted religion of the Grand Inquisitor of *L'alouette.*

In *Becket* God returns, but in name only, for his presence is never felt except as an adjunct of the absurd destiny that separates Henry from Becket. Like Antigone and Créon, they can only accept the roles that have been assigned them, and play them conscientiously. In a lonely and discouraged moment not long before he is murdered, Becket murmurs, "Another solu-

68

tion, O God, would have been to love mankind."[135] But in this world whipped by an absurd wind, man is abandoned by a God who has apparently chosen cruelty or indifference rather than love.

It is in *L'alouette* that we find the most thorough discussion of the problem of God and his relation to man yet to come from Anouilh's pen. The romantic revolt that so many critics have pointed out, particularly in the early plays, was perhaps partly responsible for his refusal to discuss God as such. God was another man-made concept that his hero rejected along with the others. By the time of the production of *Eurydice* he had, as we have seen, realized the necessity of dealing at least summarily with the problem of man's relation to a higher power. This does not indicate a turning toward religion, of course; on the contrary, the plays are still peopled with cynical men and women who doubt the goodness, or the very existence, of God. He is usually only vaguely there, if there at all, except for the more vigorous images in *Roméo et Jeannette* and *Médée*. In *L'alouette*, however, we get a radically different concept of deity.

In Jeanne's mind, God is the creator of man and it is He alone who has the power to save or to damn. It is He who has made Jeanne what she is by sending voices to her, and if she is proud, the responsibility is God's: "If only he had let me guard my sheep, and spin by my mother's side, I would never have become proud . . ."[136] If God is responsible for Jeanne's pride, it is difficult to see why He is not equally responsible for not having made Charles brave.

> *Charles.* All He had to do was give me courage. I was willing enough!
> *Jeanne* (*severely*). Do you think He's your nursemaid, and you're the only person He has to take care of? Couldn't you try to work things out with what you've got?[137]

The difference seems to be that Charles is seeking an

excuse for a negative attitude, whereas Jeanne seeks a justification for a positive one. Charles has been given the same intelligence as everyone else, but he has failed to put it to use. "You can put it to good or bad use, Charles. For that God leaves you free,"[138] Jeanne tells him. There is, then, a margin of will which allows men to bring to fruition the potentialities given them by God. Most men fail to tap these resources and lazily blame their weaknesses on God. "Real miracles," says Jeanne, "the ones that make God smile with happiness in his Heaven, must be those that men do all by themselves, with the courage and intelligence that He gave them."[139]

Cauchon strengthens the case for determinism: "We can only play our roles. Each one his own, good or bad, in his turn, just as it was written."[140] How, then, if Charles' role is already written, can he assert his free will and become strong? Either God has given us a role, complete in all its details, or else He has given us nothing more than a biological locus which we proceed to develop or to have developed more or less freely. The concept of the role is opposed to any such freedom.

On the other hand, we learn that God has confidence in man, and the obstacles we find in our way are evidences of that confidence. God is waiting for man to make the first step, then He will crown his efforts: Jeanne's soldiers must fight hard and courageously, and only then will God give them victory. Action is necessary; prayer is supplementary. God is as dependent upon man as man is upon God. In fact, we may go so far as to say that God can have no meaning except insofar as He is related to man, for man is God's greatest miracle.[141] To destroy man and leave nothing but the vacuum of God, as the Inquisitor desires, would be taking away from the glory of the divinity rather than adding to its prestige. In the universe that Anouilh has described, man's actions are a result of God's will, and unless man acts, that will cannot be disclosed on earth, which is the only place where it has any true meaning if man is the end of creation.

Whether God has assigned each man a role, or has borne witness to his confidence by leaving him free before certain obstacles, He is no longer man's overseer. For all practical purposes, God has disappeared and man is alone, and Jeanne's voices might have been nothing more than figments of her imagination. Cauchon expresses this sentiment:

> God had remained silent since Jeanne's arrest. Neither she, whatever she may have said, nor we certainly, could hear him any longer. *We* continued with our routine; we had to defend the old house first of all, that large and reasonable human construction which is actually all we have in this empty wilderness on the days that God is absent. . . . But it's in this solitude, in this silence of a God who has disappeared, in this animal nakedness and misery, that the man who continues to hold his head high is great. Great, all alone.[142]

The beauty and sincerity of expression in these last lines is unmistakable: it is not too much to say they are the summing-up of a desperate humanism which is the most mature attitude of Anouilh. It is in the spirit of these lines, imbued with that grandeur of man left to himself, that Jeanne, her eyes lifted to a silent heaven, realizes she must answer for herself the question of God's purpose with her life. It is with this knowledge that she chooses death, and becomes through death her truest self: the immortal lark singing in the sky of France.

Man, his role assigned, has been deserted by God and left to make his decisions for himself, or so he believes. And this belief in the freedom of his choice and in his ability to aid destiny, to take the first step, is one of the distinguishing characteristics of the hero. Even in the face of a destiny that dictates otherwise, the hero con-

tinues to have faith in his free will. Whether this freedom is real or only apparent is not the important point.
The inner freedom that lies in the hero's faith in his
choice is what makes him heroic, and he thus creates
himself.

If such a confrontation of what appears to be an
obvious determinism with an apparent inner freedom is
absurd, it is but one more indication of the absurdity
of man's condition, and of the chaos of a universe in
which death has no more meaning than life, and in
which man, in order to live and find a cheap happiness,
must build an illusory wall between himself and the
nothingness of life, as Jason has done.

The possibility of justice existing in such a universe
is obliterated by the chaos that is the world, and the
shallowness that is a society that blinds men to that
chaos. Justice, to the hero, is something more than the
equity mapped out by little men who are painfully
busy sweeping aside the shadows and building walls.
It is the victory of that truth that each is seeking within
himself, and which can never be on earth, for the truth
of the hero is opposed to the truth of society.[143]

But the optimism of Anouilh is an ever-present element, however obscured it may be beneath the black
of the capricious gods, a tyrannical environment, and
disappointments ending in death or escape. This is no
universe of *The Lower Depths* in which all are dominated by life, and in which there is no dissenting voice
to rise and affirm its liberty. On the contrary, Anouilh's
faith in heroic man indicates that there is an element of
greatness in an absurd universe, and man, lifting his
head amidst the silence and the chaos, is greater than
the fate that dominates him, for he is not only conscious
of his liberty—he asserts it by acting with his whole
being. In a review of Jaspers' *Perennial Scope of
Philosophy*, Sidney Hook, in reference to a philosophy
that also places heroic man at the center of the universe,
points out the optimism of such a concept:

72

Existentialism is certainly a cure for superficial optimism about the career of man on earth. But like every religious doctrine it is based on the most stupendous optimism concerning the order of the universe and man's privileged place in it. Utopianism is no less romantic when projected on a cosmic scale.[144]

Although both Anouilh and the existentialists are ultimately optimistic in their placing of man at the center of the universe and in their conception of man as a free being, their understanding of that freedom differs. For the existentialists, man is not a creature, for he has not been created; God is dead, and man is an existent who is constantly creating himself by his own free choice. His birth and death were willed by no one and governed by no law save that of absurdity. The heroic race of Anouilh is free to choose also, but only within the bounds of their parts, for they are creatures and owe their beings to a God or destiny, however vaguely that force may be conceived. In the chaos of the universe there is at least sufficient plan for us to realize that each man has his place, whether that place has any meaning or not. And ultimately it cannot have meaning unless the creature asserts his liberty by living to the very depths of his being. It is a kind of liberty through self-realization, akin to the liberty attained by realizing the will of God and resigning one's self to acting within that will. But Anouilh's heroic liberty is not a resignation. On the contrary, it is a revolt against human standards and a refusal to take a place in a solidified universe; a refusal to lose one's plasticity and become caught in the *viscosité*, to use Sartre's word, of the bourgeois ideals. Here again Anouilh and existentialists join hands.

The solitude consequent upon the absence, death, or indifference of God is likewise common to the existentialists and to Anouilh. Neither the characters of Sartre nor those of Anouilh have a God to help them in their choices. Lost irremediably in a solitude they cannot understand, they are akin to Kafka's protagonists who can never get through to God.

Anouilh's man who makes a choice is analogous to Sartre's "authentic" man who faces the absurdity of existence and possesses a sense of responsibility, whereas the others correspond to the placid bourgeois —the *salaud* who lives the life of a machine, believing in principles of existence, and looking at himself through eyes invented by the society in which he happens to live.

This fundamental distinction between those who make a choice and those who are unaware there is any choice to be made, seems to be of particular importance to contemporary dramatists. T. S. Eliot, for example, has made the distinction quite clearly in *The Cocktail Party*. Edward and Lavinia are of what Anouilh might call the mediocre race, for they are willing to go on compromising so that some sort of happiness may be found, whereas Celia is of the good race for whom there can be no question of a betrayal of the true self. She is aware of a choice to be made, and she takes the way of enlightenment, which is a way of pain. Eliot is also concerned with the solitude of the individual and the impossibility of men understanding each other, but he is more human in his acceptance of a compromise in order that life may go on, and more optimistic in his conclusion that "every moment is a fresh beginning and life is only keeping on."[145]

Despite the obvious parallels between Anouilh's outlook and that of the existentialists, we cannot conclude that Anouilh is a member of that group, or has even been influenced by them. All the ideas that the two outlooks have in common were expressed by Anouilh before Sartre had developed and popularized his brand of existentialism: man's solitude; the hero's refusal to accept any standards other than those he creates for himself; the hell created by the realization that we are

74

what others believe us to be as well as what we desire to be; and the "dreadful freedom" of heroic man who realizes that he must choose his own being or dominate his role.

We must resist the temptation to impose any particular philosophical frame upon Anouilh's concepts, remembering that he is a dramatist first of all, or even exclusively, and any philosophy expressed through his plays must be considered an indication of the dramatist's sensivity to and awareness of the tragic sense of life which is so much a part of our time. He has founded no system, and has established no school. But his ideas are significant because, although sometimes contradictory, they reveal Anouilh as a writer who is bound to the cause of man's freedom, and an author whose work is valid first of all for his contemporaries. He shows us the difficulties and the anguish in store for the man who will accept his responsibilities, and the dignity of man true to himself.

2

The Illusions of Love

FOR MANY OF Anouilh's characters life is a simple matter. Their major preoccupation is what they call "love," and their major necessity, money. We have heard M. Delachaume in *Le rendez-vous de Senlis* speak of the simple life in just those terms. Orphée's father describes it as a combination of wealth and respectability with passion. For the mediocre race, love is sometimes a mere convenience, often a purely animal passion, and always a consolation that serves as a mask to the solitude of life. Général Saintpé ends *La valse des toréadors* as he puts his arms about the new maid and leads her into the garden: "It's better this way. Not that it means much, but just the same, it helps to make you feel less lonely in the dark."[1]

For the members of the heroic race, love is all-important. When they feel they have found real love they are willing to sacrifice almost everything else to it. Only when they finally realize—as Anouilh believes all who see life in its true perspective must—that love is built upon a lie, do they renounce it. The hero will never sacrifice his integrity. For that reason, the picture of love, as society understands it, is to be found in the compromises of the mediocre. True love, as Anouilh envisages it, as Tristan and Iseult exemplify it, must always end in death or renunciation, for it is tainted with certain weaknesses that prohibit the realization of a perfect love in life.

Each play contains, then, two aspects of love: the renunciation of the heroic characters and the compromise of the mediocre. The first group of plays includes two kinds of solutions. In the more serious plays—*L'hermine, Jézabel,* and *La sauvage*—the hero renounces love because the obstacles between him and his beloved, usually expressed in terms of background, are too great. In the other plays of the period, some sort of happy solution is found through escape or compromise, and the difficulties confronting real love receive little attention. The four plays of Anouilh's second period deal with the more fundamental problems that separate the couple. The heroic renunciation that dominates these plays includes, of course, the renunciation of love. On the periphery, and contrasted to this renunciation, is the "love" of those who have accepted life. The third group of plays includes the most exhaustive discussion of the problem. With the author's camera focused upon the mediocre race we are able to see just what are the various forms of compromise in love.

Love's Obstacles

In *L'hermine* Frantz is seeking happiness with Monime, but he believes love touched by poverty soon becomes tainted and dies: "I want my love to be immaculate, I want us to be lovers without calculations, without fears, without shame."[2] Frantz has no illusions and no scruples: he knows that love is not as it is described in the storybooks and that even great love can die from petty wounds. To love is to fight constantly against the hidden forces that attack through others and through the lovers themselves. With poverty beside us, he maintains, we are not strong for the struggle.

Frantz's separation from Monime is imposed by his love for her. His despair at losing her dictates his confession at the end of the play. As the police bind him, Monime cries "I love you, Frantz" and falls at his feet. Without his confession and arrest Monime could never have uttered these words. He has purified himself in her eyes by his willingness to accept the responsibility for his action. And he has purified their love by making any further relations impossible. Only thus could it remain an idealized kind of love.

In Monime's mind, and in the audience's mind as well, there lurks the suspicion that Frantz is deceiving himself when he attributes such great importance to money. We wonder whether his insistence upon procuring the money of the Duchess, and his excuse that it is to preserve the purity of his love, are not rationalizations in the mind of a young man who has been burdened by poverty and whose burning ambition is to rise above his past by any means.

It is not so much any inherent weaknesses in love itself as it is the power of their varied backgrounds which pulls Monime and Frantz apart. It is impossible for them to understand each other. For Monime, money is unimportant, because she has always had all she needed. Like Lady India of *L'invitation au château,* she has a highly romantic conception of poverty. Because she has never tasted it, she believes it is palatable. Frantz, having known nothing but poverty and the condescension of the rich, sees life from a different angle. For the rich, it is easy to have hope; to think all will turn out for the best. For the poor, life is quite another thing: they are unable to rise above the hopelessness of the past; unable to have that faith in love which comes so easily to the rich. This is so precisely because the rich tend to see only the surface of things, Anouilh tells us, whereas the perspicacious poor are aware of the absurdity that underlies everything. Frantz lacks the faith of a Monime. "Oh, my God!" he cries. "Why did you give me this love without also giving me the necessary faith?"[3]

A similar difference in backgrounds is also the obstacle that lies between Marc and Jacqueline in *Jézabel*. For Jacqueline, all is possible, whereas for Marc, sunk in the moral filth of his family's past, life offers no hope.[4]

We see the same struggle between the poor and the rich in *La sauvage*. Florent, rich and happy, has never suffered a day in his life. But when he falls in love with Thérèse, he discovers a being from another world. He and Thérèse can never come to an understanding, for their pasts, their ways of thinking, are entirely different. Thérèse cannot forgive Florent his wealth or his sheltered life: he is a conqueror who has never had to fight —a being who is hardly human, for he does not know what suffering and struggle are. Florent does not even need Thérèse: she is for him but one joy among many, and she cannot swallow her pride and resign herself to becoming a mere accessory to his life.

In contrast to the heroes, who will not make the compromises required by marriage with a wealthy mate— renunciation of their past, which is as much a part of them as are their desires and hopes—there are a group of pathetic people who have lived out their comedy of marriage and love in various ways. In *L'hermine* we see Mr. and Mrs. Bentz who live together as though happily married, whereas in reality neither is satisfied with the other. The Duchess makes clear that her marriage was one of convenience and that she did not even conceive that marriage could be anything else; Florentine and Philippe continue cheating to satisfy their appetites. In *Jézabel* Marc's parents reveal another form of compromise that parades as marriage: his father amuses himself with the maid while his mother seeks the pleasure of what she terms "love" wherever she can find it. She explains to Marc that she felt herself dead with her husband, for he thought only of his money, whereas with other men she could become a living woman and feel a human contact. But her desperate

79

search has resulted in emptiness. When Marc asks her if she has ever really loved, she responds: "Never. I was looking for *my* man among all those men, but doubtless it wasn't among them that I was destined to find him. . . ."[5]

The case of Mme Tarde in *La sauvage* is similar. For years she has been living as mistress of Gosta, the orchestra's pianist, and now that she is growing old she is losing her attraction for him. In order to hold him she would make a further compromise: give him her daughter Thérèse, so that she may have him for herself at the same time. Her husband is too weak to prevent anything that goes on. He is aware of the affair between his wife and Gosta, but dares do nothing about it.

The *Pièces roses* of this period, as well as *L'invitation au château* and *Cécile ou L'école des pères* which are essentially *rose*, are unfinished tales, and only because of this do they end happily. For a time the protagonists are able to make their imagined world dominate their lives. This is particularly true in *Le rendez-vous de Senlis*. One day, however, Georges must waken to the realization that he and Isabelle cannot understand each other any more than he and Henriette his wife have been able to understand each other. Between Georges and Henriette there is, once again, the obstacle of money, in addition to the fact that Georges was forced unwillingly into the marriage by his parents. In *Le bal des voleurs* the compromise is already beginning as Juliette leads Gustave into the garden to convince him that he should accept the little comedy they are playing, in which he will pretend to be the long-lost son of Lord Edgard, thus becoming a suitor of sufficient wealth and position to be considered.

For Gaston in *Le voyageur sans bagage* there can be no question of renewing the dishonest liaison with Valentine, his brother's wife. Gaston renounces forever the person he used to be, in order to become someone else. His brother Georges and Valentine are in a situation similar to that of many couples, such as Robert and Barbara in *Le rendez-vous de Senlis,* the Tardes, and Marc's parents: the wife is faithless and the husband, although not entirely indifferent in this instance, accepts his position.

Ludovic in *Y avait un prisonnier* has also renounced the compromise of marriage, and refuses to renew his relationship with his wife for whom he no longer feels any affection. In contrast to this "leftist" ex-convict is Ludovic's daughter, a victim of society who is not only willing but eager to make the necessary compromises with her integrity in order to marry into a family with a name.

Love's Flaws

Throughout the plays of the first period, the obstacle of money is ever-present for the minor characters who have compromised, as well as for the heroic ones who refuse to do so. Money is the excuse for Valentine's marriage to Georges in *Le voyageur sans bagage;* for Georges' marriage to Henriette in *Le rendez-vous de Senlis;* and for Robert's acceptance of his wife's prostitution in the same play. In the later plays, money continues to be an obstacle in some instances, and the cause of much evil in others, but the problem of love is stated in more fundamental terms. Difference in background no longer rends the couple apart, but certain weaknesses inherent in love make it impossible for the hero to accept such a union. In these four central plays we witness the heroic renunciation of love.

For Eurydice, everything could be so simple, if only Orphée would stop thinking and accept things as they are; if he would but let his hands love her, and speak no more. This superficial love of hand for body and body for hand—nothing more than a contact of surfaces—is what the people of Anouilh's world call happiness. Orphée cannot accept such happiness, for he realizes what Eurydice and all those who lean toward the simple and easy cannot realize: that "life is not a matter of gestures." For the hero, life must be lived deeply, on levels other than the purely physical. To realize that each man is alone and can never understand another is a painful discovery. And herein lies one of the inherent weaknesses of love, as Anouilh pictures it: love's original sin, which condemns it irremediably to failure. Love for his characters is only a touching of surfaces. In spite of his desire to vanquish the sense of solitude which pervades the life of every thinking being, Orphée realizes that the couple is inevitably two: "Two skins, two envelopes about us, completely impermeable, each one for himself with his oxygen, with his own blood no matter what, completely walled-up, very much alone in his sack of skin."[6] The couple may establish a physical contact, but the pleasure it brings is only an illusion and one finds himself alone again with his only friends: "his liver, his spleen, his intestines."[7] Words are of no help either: "Two prisoners who will never see each other. Everyone is alone. Don't you think everyone is too terribly alone?"[8] For a moment Orphée will lose himself deep in Eurydice's eyes, believing they are two stems on a single root, but quickly they will separate and again become two: "Two mysteries, two lies. Two."[9]

This desire of the lover to lose himself in the beloved constitutes a second weakness in love as Anouilh depicts it, for it involves a loss of the authentic self. In his efforts to understand or please the other, the lover must make certain compromises with himself. We have already seen that one cannot be true to himself without hurting others; in love the inclination is to be more compromising than ever. Even Orphée, as we shall see, must give up a certain part of himself for Eurydice.

There is yet another weakness: love threatens to become a habit and the couple seek each other because they are accustomed to one another—caught within the net they have woven. The relationship loses its spontaneity and becomes nothing more than the gestures of love.

For the mediocre race such weaknesses offer no difficulty, since these people are unaware that anything else might be desirable. Eurydice's mother, a third-rate actress touring the provinces, and Vincent her lover, a member of the troupe, are the ridiculous examples of the aging couple who think they have really loved, whereas in truth their relationship has been a romanesque illusion fed by the verses they have played on third-rate stages:

> *The Mother.* What *I* don't understand is why everything seems so sad to these children! After all, my honey bun, we were passionate lovers too, but did it make *us* sad?
>
> *Vincent.* Not at all! Not at all! Besides, I've always said: a little love, a little money, a little success, and life is wonderful!
>
> *The Mother.* A little love? Lots of love! That child seems to think she has invented the whole thing with her little violinist. But we adored each other too, didn't we? We too wanted to kill ourselves for each other. Do you remember in Biarritz in 1913 when I wanted to throw myself from the top of the Virgin's Rock?
>
> *Vincent.* Fortunately, I held you back by your cape, my sweet.[10]

This scene, like the earlier one in which Vincent quotes Perdican's lines on love to Eurydice's mother, fills Eurydice and Orphée with disgust, and the young girl finally realizes they could not have been happy together: "You were right. By wanting to be happy, we should have become like them . . . How horrible!"[11]

The inherent weaknesses of love are not perceived immediately by Orphée and Eurydice, for the overpowering effect of love is such that Orphée feels completely at ease and happy for the first time. Love lends an aura of perfection to all about them. The railway café becomes "theirs," and the waiter himself takes on so noble an air that he appears to be a *sociétaire* of the Comédie Française. Orphée feels himself transformed and, although timid by nature, he becomes courageous, for love blinds the couple to reality. With their little, misunderstood happiness they feel stronger than the whole world. They begin to lose sight of man's absurdity and the solitude that, in Anouilh's view, is his basic condition.

They become blind to one another. Orphée describes Eurydice, and believes she is really as he sees her in his ideal of love. The terms he uses are typical of the hero. For him love is not a complicated game: it is a comradeship reminiscent of our childhood friendships in that it is based on a feeling of fellowship rather than sexual desire. In Orphée's ideal love we see the longing for the return to a paradise similar to that of childhood, where all is simple and spontaneous. His ideal Eurydice is a "little soldier"; a "silent little brother" who belongs to him alone; a man for others and a woman only for him:

> I had given up hope of ever finding a comrade who would go along with you, strong and alert, carrying her bag, and detesting the easy smile too. A quiet little buddy who'll take anything, and who in the evening is beautiful and warm against your body.[12]

Eurydice wishes to conform to what she mistakenly thinks is Orphée's conception of her: she will become a mysterious woman; she will try to be somber, and to smoke. She will play all the roles she thinks Orphée expects of her. She will have just a few moments now and then in which to be true to herself.

> *Orphée.* It's going to be a dog's life!
> *Eurydice.* That's what love is! . . .[13]

Now it is Orphée's turn to lose some of his freedom: Eurydice looks forward to sleeping upon his shoulder and holding his hand all day long. But Orphée is precisely the man who sleeps flat on his back across the bed; the man who loves long solitary walks. In order to become a member of the couple Orphée–Eurydice he must renounce a part of himself. Compromises begin on all sides. Eurydice becomes tangled in a skein of lies, and we discover that she has the same weakness as Général Saintpé: she lacks the courage to be cruel, and this is partly responsible for her compromises in life. Through pity, she gave herself to Mathias; through pity for the *petit régisseur* she gave herself to Dulac; and now through fear of hurting Orphée, she is lying to him about her past—piling up barriers between him and herself. She is not a *sauvage* who has the courage to appear as she really is. Love has given her a certain courage, but it is the courage of the happy who are cruelly oblivious to the feelings of others. Eurydice breaks with her past to go with Orphée, and he is able at last to leave his father. "There. We're alone in the world now,"[14] says Eurydice. And M. Henri sums up the situation of the new couple: "A handsome young man and a beautiful young girl! Ready to play the game without cheating, to the very end. Without those little concessions to comfort and ease which make aging and prosperous lovers."[15] But realizing that even Orphée and Eurydice must wake up some day as man and woman and engage in the war of "love," he adds: "Two courageous little animals, with supple limbs and long teeth, ready to fight till morning, as they should, and to fall wounded together."[16]

Eurydice soon realizes that the image in Orphée's mind is what he is in love with, and that she can never resemble it. She runs away, but death overtakes her, and Orphée pleads with M. Henri to give her back to him at any cost. He is willing to make a compromise: he will accept; he will say yes to life, "with its stains and scratches, its giving up and beginning all over again—with its shame."[17] But in the course of his conversation with Eurydice returned from Hades, Orphée learns that he cannot make such a compromise, for he sees Eurydice as she really is. He sees that they are forever alone, separated from each other by two walls of flesh and a past that is forever present and yet cannot be seized by any other than the person who has lived it. When Eurydice invites him to make the compromise, he refuses. He has understood the ugliness of life—the emptiness of the grotesque figures making theatrical gestures:

> Live! Live! Like your mother and her lover, perhaps, with displays of tenderness, smiles, weak moments of indulgence, and good meals too, and afterward you make love and everything is fine. Ah no! I love you too much to live.[18]

Life is love's irreconcilable enemy, with its piling-up of habit and compromise—its destruction of spontaneity. The longer we live, the further we go from that kingdom in which Antigone takes her stand. Even Eurydice finally agrees with Orphée when she sees the ridiculous display of their past made by her mother and Vincent.

When Eurydice has once more returned to the dead and Orphée is disconsolate, M. Henri paints for him a picture of what his life would have been had Eurydice lived. Orphée does not want to accept this picture because he, like every man in love, believes his case is different from all others. Monsieur Henri shows him that it is not, and that his love was doomed from the start as every love is. In five or ten years Orphée would have discovered that, without having stopped loving her, he no longer desired Eurydice, or that she no longer desired him. Orphée would have wished to deceive Eurydice; to follow other women. He would have walked beside her, "with the look of a man who is trying to lose his dog in the street."[19] Or they might have decided to become complaisant and to tolerate each other's deceptions. To Orphée's protestations of his and Eurydice's eternal fidelity, M. Henri replies that life would not have allowed their love to escape: it too would have disintegrated and disappeared as though they had never meant anything to each other.[20] Moreover, what M. Henri does not mention, but what Anouilh himself has indicated, is that Eurydice's love was already vitiated and sullied at its incipience by the lies to which she had to resort in order to hide her previous relations with men.

There is but one way for Orphée and Eurydice to become the eternal couple, and that is through death: "Death is beautiful," says M. Henri. "It alone gives love its true climate."[21] This is the ultimate lesson of *Eurydice:* life sullies everything it touches—even a love that appears to have every chance of enduring and is sanctioned by fate itself. Only death washes clean. It is the same sea of death we see in *Roméo et Jeannette* and which not only purifies their love but insures it against the ravages of life and time.

Anouilh seemingly believes that the story of Orphée and Eurydice is the only story of true love which can be told. All other tales, which end "happily ever after," are either unfinished or are tales of compromise and lies. We see this adequately illustrated throughout Anouilh's theater, as well as in the works of other contemporary dramatists.[22] For the hero, there are only two possibilities: death or separation. There is no other answer to the imperious demand for purity which the hero feels within himself.

In *Antigone* the refusal of love is only a small part of Antigone's refusal of life. She realizes that even her love for Hémon could not endure the ravages of life and time, and that one day they might become indifferent to one another. Créon, attempting to convince Antigone that she must live, reminds her of Hémon and asks her if she does not love him. She replies that she loves him as he is now—young, faithful, and exigent— but if life and happiness change him into "monsieur Hémon" and he learns to say yes, then she no longer will love him. Although her refusal of love is only incidental to her renunciation of life and of "filthy happiness," her death and that of Hémon make possible the eternal existence of their love.

We see the same conclusion in *Roméo et Jeannette*. Although Frédéric and Jeannette come from different backgrounds and cannot understand each other completely for that reason, the difference in background is not considered the major obstacle in the complete realization of their love, as it would have been in the earlier plays of Anouilh. Rather, it is life itself which prevents the perfection of love. Jeannette realizes this and offers to make their love eternal by dying with Frédéric. But Frédéric cannot understand, and it is only at the last moment that he is able to take the heroic step. As he and Jeannette are cleansed by the sea, Lucien watches from the window and describes to his father what has happened. Through Lucien's words the contrast between the true couple and those people who go on living is emphasized. As the curtain is about to fall, Lucien, looking out to the sea, says sadly:

> Love, sad love, are you satisfied? Dear heart, dear body, dear romance. Aren't there jobs to do, books to read, houses to build? Aren't there other good things in life too: sunshine on flesh, cool wine in the glass, spring water, shade at midday, a fire in winter, the snow and even the rain, and the wind, and the trees and the clouds and the animals—all the innocent animals—and children before they become too ugly? Tell me, sad love, isn't everything good?[23]

Life must go on with its little pleasures and illusions—the same pleasures vaunted by the Nurse and the Guard at the end of *Médée*—while love, sad love, requires of its true devotees the sacrifice of everything that might have made for a happy mediocre life.

Médée and Jason, in the last play of this period, are two essentially different people who have succeeded in establishing for a time a satisfactory relationship. Jason refers to his life with Médée in the same terms Orphée had used in speaking of his ideal Eurydice: little brother; soldier. If at first he and Médée were man and woman, or rather mother and son—"I lost myself in you like a little boy in the woman who gave him birth"[24] —their love soon ripened to something more nearly resembling comradeship. By day they were brothers, "and in the evenings, when they stopped to rest, the soldier and the captain undressed side by side, surprised to discover under their clothing that they were man and woman, and that they loved each other."[25]

The memory of those days can never be taken from them, for they were days lived fully by two people who had found the secret of love in comradeship and equality. But, doomed to failure as always in Anouilh's world, this love soon lost its fraternal quality. Médée became a woman and Jason a man, and they sought to hurt each other. Lies and deception took the place of their candor, and hate was born—a third person to walk between them. Then began the inevitable life of compromise and pretence. Médée, accustomed to Jason, could no longer free herself from him: "I had to stick again to your hatred, like a fly; I had to take up again my life with you; and the next evening lie against your bored body in order to sleep at last."[26]

This is the way of all marriages, Anouilh suggests. And even when Jason makes the compromise with society and goes off to marry Créon's daughter, Médée, although freed from him and become once again the authentic being she was before, still knows the force of habit and of long years together. Even more than that, she feels Jason belongs to her and that now he can never really escape her, even though she be dead: "For you the world is Médée, forever."[27]

The contrasting attitudes of Médée and Jason reveal one of the basic differences between man and woman; one of the principal causes of their misunderstanding. For Jason, Médée is no longer necessary; rather, he longs for liberty, to escape the woman who has become a weight upon him. For Médée, such a liberty does not exist. Since Jason once loved her, he has become exclusively hers; he cannot free himself from her or see the world in any other form. Jason himself admits later: "The world has become Médée."[28] Their life together has accustomed them to each other, so that for Médée no other man is satisfactory. When she felt Jason was slipping away from her, she tried to desert him first: "I tried, Jason, didn't you know? I've tried again with others since. I couldn't do it."[29]

Woman, we are told in *Médée*, is so constituted that she desires one man, becomes accustomed to him, and can see the world in no other form than his. Man, on the other hand, desires his liberty, and can belong to no one. It is only in the perfect form of comradeship that love can exist. When the man becomes a man, and the woman a woman, then the two begin to hurt each other, or else they accept the yoke they have imposed upon themselves, and become slaves to the habit they have formed. Life loses its spontaneity and goes on only on the surface. Compromise follows compromise and the authentic self is lost sight of.

Médée is made of heroic stuff: when Jason abandons her she is able to become again her authentic self. She might have followed the path of the General's wife in *La valse des toréadors*, but instead, destroying as best she can the vestiges of her compromise with Jason, she reacquires her lost purity. But still she cannot completely suppress the feeling that Jason belongs to her. As she stabs herself and disappears into the flames of her burning wagon, she shouts to Jason: "Look at them, your little brother and your wife, it's I. It's I! The horrible Médée! Now try to forget her!"[30]

Love's Compromises

Anouilh's third group of plays concerns chiefly those people who have accepted the contamination that the dramatist sees as a necessary adjunct of life. In *Colombe*

Madame Alexandra is an unmistakable representative of the group. So often has she compromised with love that when the newspapers ask for a statement of her opinion on love, she is advised by Poète-Chéri to answer that she *is* love. How true this is we discover at the end of the scene when she goes off with Poète-Chéri to discuss her investments, leaving her manager nonplussed as to what sort of statement to make:

> *La Surette.* So what should I tell them about Love, Madame-Chérie?
>
> *Madame Alexandra.* Stop plaguing us with your Love, stupid fool! Can't you see we're speaking of serious things?[31]

But she does not leave before playing a scene on the given theme, prompted by her official poet, Poète-Chéri. His first definition of love, as "an absolute giving of the self . . . But all that it gives is for itself,"[32] impresses her as profound but hard. She, who has run through more than half a dozen husbands and as many fortunes, would show her public a faith in the ideal, "in all that is noble and beautiful in love."[33]

> *Poète-Chéri.* "So that true love may flower, we must first pull the weeds of desire and passion from our hearts."
>
> *Madame Alexandra.* But, Poète-Chéri, great poet! What is this nonsense? Come now, love is nothing but passion! How can you say that? Why, when I was that child's age, I had already committed suicide four times over love![34]

For Madame Alexandra, and for all her cronies, life lies in the gestures one makes. She believes she has really loved because Salvatore-Dupont entered a lion's cage for her sake or ate a raw rat at Maxim's; because one of her husbands took the horse's place and pulled her home in her carriage; or because Boni Despinglettes set his mansion on fire and took her in his arms amidst the flames. But these are only melodramatic gestures— the surface that appears as passion and satisfies the whims of a spoiled and jaded actress. Anouilh, we feel, would agree with Poète-Chéri when he says that love is selfish at the same time that it is self-giving. Again Poète-Chéri expresses Anouilh's view when he speaks of weeding out desire and passion, for when they are present there cannot exist that comradeship of two brothers marching through life together, each with knapsack on his back, and surprised at night to discover that the other is of the opposite sex. This is the love that Julien would share with Colombe. It is different from the sexual desire of man for woman, which may change; it is built upon esteem. Julien sees certain qualities he admires in Colombe (whether they are real or imagined is another question), and it is for these that he loves her and calls her "my ally," "my little brother." Colombe, however, wants to be loved as a woman—for her beauty and her sexuality. An animal passion is what appeals to her. She is a student in the school of Madame Alexandra, whose false brilliance of paste jewels and studied attitudes she admires. Like every couple, in the last analysis, Colombe and Julien cannot find true happiness together. Indeed, no two people can find true love and understanding, this bitter play tells us. Armand would have suited Colombe better, but their passions could not have lasted forever either, and Colombe, we see, will become a less colorful Madame Alexandra. Of this play, Marsh says, "*Colombe* takes up the love-story where the *Pièces Roses* used to put it down. The young lovers have married happily, and this is the 'ever after.' "[35]

In *La répétition* Anouilh shows us what his characters find to be one of the most convenient compromises with love—the *ménage à quatre*. The Count and Countess, although fond of each other, have never been in love.[36] Each has taken a lover, readily accepted by the other as well as by their circle of acquaintances. Ironically enough, the Countess' lover, Villebosse, is more punctilious about the honor of the Countess than is Tigre. He goes to such lengths that the Countess claims, "My dear Villebosse, you have accomplished the rare feat of making sin more boring than virtue."[37] The Count's mistress, Hortensia, is a worldly-wise woman who has decided never to suffer; she prefers to live superficially. But when Tigre is about to become involved with Lucile—a person beneath him socially—wife and mistress join forces to end what they consider to be an infatuation, which threatens to become serious, for Tigre is really in love, and for the first time in his life. He experiences the same feelings that Orphée had experienced upon meeting Eurydice: "Imagine, Héro [he says], that one day everything around you falls into place. That everything becomes simple and peaceful; but at the same time, inaccessible."[38] Through love, Tigre has found again a glimpse of the purity of his youth, and he desires to "give all" for Lucile. But through the machinations of his wife, the liaison is broken off and Lucile flees.

Héro, the Countess' instrument, is a pathetic figure. Only by living in a constant state of drunkenness is he able to face the emptiness of life, for he had once known the purity of youth and the possibility of a real love with Evangéline. But Tigre had convinced him that such a marriage would be inadvisable, and Héro has lost forever the one woman he really loved. His seduction of Lucile is a bitter revenge against Tigre for having made him miss the one chance for happiness that life offered him. There is an ironic twist to the situation, however, when we see it in the perspective of Anouilh's entire theater: if Héro had married Evangéline, his love would have died and ended in some pitiful compromise. It is only because Tigre prevented him from marrying her that Evangéline can still symbolize ideal love for Héro.

Anouilh's attention is centered on the problems of the couple and love and its illusions even more in his later plays than in the early ones, although from the beginning of his career it has been one of his central themes. In *Ardèle ou La marguerite* and *La valse des toréadors* Anouilh has left such themes as man's predicament and the force of money on the periphery, in order to concentrate on "love." In *Ardèle* we see what one of the characters calls love on trial:

> *The Count.* Liliane, it's not your trial, nor mine, nor the general's, or Ardèle's or Villardieu's. We're putting love on trial. Aunt Ardèle has love hidden in her hump like a devil, naked blazing love hidden in her deformed body, under her aging skin. And we who have been cheating with love for I don't know how long, here we are face to face with it now. What an encounter![39]

The encounter is complete, for in contrast to the love of Ardèle for her hunchback stand the multiple kinds of compromises made by the other characters of the play. This multiplicity is typical of *Ardèle*, for in it we find a synthesis of elements contained in other separate plays. Although the surface is gay and the dialogue witty, the underlying feeling is one of bitter pessimism. The picture we see is what Anouilh depicts as the inevitable result of marriage; and if the love of Ardèle is pure, it is only because it remains in the realm of the ideal and is consummated in death.

The play opens upon a scene of gross compromise as the General leaves his flirtation with the maid to answer the demented cries of his wife who, it is said, has gone out of her mind because of her disappointed love for her husband. Every fifteen minutes she calls "Léon! Léon!" to assure herself of his whereabouts and of the innocence of his activities. The General, whose weakness was that he never broke with his wife when he no longer loved her, feels burdened by her love. Such a possessive love is "a piercing cry every fifteen minutes, to check my whereabouts."[40] On the other hand, the maid is a symbol of liberty for the General. He feels it is only natural to be fickle, for such is man as he was created by God himself:

> If God had wanted love to be eternal, I'm sure he would have arranged things so that the conditions of desire would remain eternal. When I do what I do, I have the obscure feeling that I'm following His design.[41]

The General is not in love with Ada, the maid, but she is necessary to him: "Without your odor, without the daily contact with your body, I'm like a little boy all alone in the world in this house."[42] It is the contact of two walls of flesh, "two prisoners tapping against the walls of their cells,"[43] which will make the General feel less alone. His desire is an animal passion, uncomplicated and superficial. He takes his pleasure where he can find it, along with the consolation that it affords. But there is no deep emotional involvement: with Ada, he is free. We will see the same situation in *La valse des toréadors* where, in the end of the play, he takes the new red-headed maid by the hand and leads her into the garden.

In the General's inability to understand that death is the only possible ending for true love, Anouilh sees a clear indication of his lack of heroic qualities. The General simply accepts the fact that love is not eternal and shifts the blame to God. When Ardèle says she wishes to die, the General is outraged: "Die! Die in despair over love! I've felt like dying of despair a good half-dozen times. Am I dead, for God's sake? No!"[44] And yet the General conserves something of his youthful self: a small remnant of the love he once felt for Amélie is still alive. As the Doctor in *La valse des toréadors* will tell us later, Léon has a soul, and this is the root of his unhappiness. He feels the world is full of happy people and that they have some secret which he could learn. The General's brother-in-law Gaston, who is also the voice of the author, explains that the happy people are those who have never loved. The General was once overcome with love for Amélie, and now he is paying the price of that love, and between him and Amélie the struggle is a real war, for "one must always destroy the other, that's all there is to it."

Liliane, his wife, accuses the Count of cynicism and asserts that everyone knows love is first of all "the giving of the self."[45] These are the very words of Poète-Chéri. But the Countess forgets the second part of this aphorism: all that love gives is for itself. However, the Count supplies the necessary clauses:

> You believe that too. I strip myself, I tear myself apart, I kill myself for the person I love? It's true. As long as the one I love is that ideal projection of myself, as long as he is my possession, my thing, as long as he's me. It's so good to come out of our foul solitude. To ourselves, sincerely, we wouldn't dare. But to give all to that other person who is your-self, what a refreshing summer rain on a shrivelled-up heart! Until, by caprice, or by chance, the other becomes another once again, nothing more. Then we stop paying, of course. What do you expect one person to give to another on this earth? That would be philanthropy, not love. . . . If we persuade Aunt Ardèle to forget about giving her all to her hunchbacked lover, that is to say, to herself, then there's a chance that we can all be cured.[46]

Love, then, is but the projection of an ideal self into another person, and when we say that we love another, it is really our idealized self that we mean. This is at the root of the comradeship that is the only acceptable form of "love," in which each loves himself in another. But the day when the other becomes himself—when the comrade becomes a member of the opposite sex—the claws and teeth are bared, and open war is declared. Then the only alternatives are to run away, as did Lucien's wife and as Jason tries to do; to cheat on the side, as the General does; or simply to accept the situation and set up the most convenient form of compromise, whether it be that of pretending that all is well and continuing as before, as Mr. and Mrs. Bentz do (*L'hermine*), or that of the *ménage à quatre*—the solution adopted by the Count and Countess.

The *ménage* that the Count and Countess have arranged along with Villardieu is somewhat discordant. Villardieu is insanely jealous of the Count, for he believes Liliane still loves her husband. As the General says, "Liliane is capable of anything." Villardieu's fortune makes it possible for him to spend his time observing Liliane and Gaston. At night he does not sleep, for he watches the Count's door, fearing a secret rendezvous between husband and wife. Since Liliane is equally jealous of her husband's attentions to his "petite amie," she never lets him out of her sight:

> *Villardieu.* And at night while I watch her door, she watches his. The Count is the only one of us who could sleep. I say "who *could*" because his mistress, whom he can never see, is always making scenes, and I'm convinced that he doesn't sleep either.[47]

The Count has brought his mistress with him, and has lodged her at an inn in the village adjacent to the chateau, so that he may have her near him during his sojourn in the country. Whenever he can escape Liliane he makes brief telephone calls to the child, who is desperately in love with him and constantly threatening to poison herself. It is a heavy burden for a man of his age: Gaston was looking for a flirtation, and love fell upon him.

The Count is the sanest of the characters in *Ardèle*, and the only one possessed of a true sense of humor and a perspective that permits him to see the ridiculousness of himself and the people about him: all struggling for a little happiness, looking for love where it cannot be found, and when they find it, trying to escape. As in *La répétition*, it is the lover who resents and is jealous of the husband, whereas the latter is cynical about the affair. The Count's witty comments are particularly annoying to his wife and to Villardieu, who take themselves very seriously and wish to pretend there has been no rupture. They believe it is only decent to exhibit the feelings society expects, even if they are not sincere. Gaston prefers not to confuse an already complicated situation.

Nathalie, the wife of the General's soldier son Maxime—a brute and a rake who is away in Tonquin—and Nicolas, younger son of the General, who has returned home for the conference, had been in love before Nathalie's marriage. Driven by poverty, the girl had agreed to the older brother's proposal in order to find security. Although she hated her husband, she had submitted and given herself to him, enjoying him in a purely animal way. Now she is no longer capable of the pure love she once felt for Nicolas. Nicolas is the only person we see who is untainted, but he is young. Nathalie leaves him with the admonition, "Never think of love again."[48]

Two minor characters caricature the love of the grown-ups they see about them. Marie-Christine, Liliane's child, and Toto, the General's youngest son, engage in a game called *se faire des scènes*, in which they pretend they are married. The scenes consist of bitter arguments, scratching, biting, and kicking. The play ends as the two children argue noisily over who loves whom the most, and as the curtain falls they are still struggling, savagely beating each other, and shouting imprecations. Anouilh comments significantly: "The curtain has fallen, hiding them, but they probably continue behind it . . ."[49]

In this melée of animal struggle, there is one touch of purity and idealism, represented by Ardèle—a mute character who never appears on the stage. Cloistered in her room, Ardèle suffers the solitude of the idealist.

The capital scene of the play is that in which the various members of the family step up to the door one by one and try to convince Ardèle that she must give up her impossible dream and face the reality that the others wish to force upon her. It is here that the sharp contrast between the two attitudes toward love—with all its irony, its tragedy, and its humor—becomes most apparent. Only Ardèle is really in love, yet she is the only one who is denied the freedom to realize her wishes. The others had selfishly asserted that love permitted anything, but this applies only to themselves. When it comes to the universal application of the rule, they object. It is the Count who defends Ardèle's rights. If Liliane and the General do as they please, then why should not Aunt Ardèle do likewise:

> *The Count.* Why won't you grant her the same rights you grant yourself? . . .
> *The Countess.* You know very well that it's simply a question of keeping up appearances. . . . In spite of her age we must consider Ardèle as an irresponsible child. What can she possibly know of love?
> *The Count (calmly).* Of love as you and I understand it, as the general and Villardieu and Nathalie understand it, nothing perhaps. But of love as Ardèle understands it, everything, I am sure . . . And who can say if that isn't precisely what love is?[50]

The Count realizes that what he and the rest of the family think of as love is nothing but a selfish passion, and that Ardèle, with her naïve affection for her hunchback, is probably nearer the truth than anyone. The family's answer to the Count's defense is that he is talking nonsense. Love as Ardèle envisages it could not possibly be real love: the family cannot rise above the concept of physical passion which they identify with love, and they are incapable of comprehending the possibility of two hunchbacks enamored of each other. The General says he will force Ardèle to take food, and soon enough she will forget her hunchback, eat normally, and take up her piano again. All will be as before. It is easy for the General to imagine this; he has never died for love, or even starved himself. The idea itself is beyond him now. The young lieutenant might have made such a gesture—might have understood Ardèle—but not the General of today. The compromises have grown too thick about him, and this is precisely why Ardèle criticizes him. "It's through an excess of scruples that we've come to this," comments Gaston. None of them has had the courage to be himself—the General to put away his wife; the Count and Countess to separate. By some misconception of their duty, they have acted wrongly. The petty, commonplace joys—which Gaston tries to make attractive to Ardèle, but without any personal conviction, for they are the joys he has known—have sufficed to satisfy these weak-willed people. As the Count says, "life is made of pennies, and you can make a fortune if you know how to hoard them." Ardèle responds that she has found a thousand-franc note. "When you've found a thousand-franc note," the Count reports her as saying, "you mustn't let it get away."[51] In the end, Ardèle keeps her thousand-franc note, but in the only possible way: through death.

When Gaston has finished speaking with Ardèle, Nicolas springs to the door, and with the spontaneity of youth cries out to Ardèle that she must love regardless of any scandal: "You must love against them, Aunt Ardèle! You must love against everything. You must love with all your strength in order not to become like them."[52] The force of love is such, then, that it can save us from the ugliness of life; it can keep us from becoming like the compromised adults we see about us. But, if we would believe Anouilh, there is only one way in which love can do this. Death is the only possible path to salvation, and it is the way not only of Orphée and Eurydice and Ardèle but of many great couples of literature—of Tristan and Iseult, Romeo and Juliet,

Antony and Cleopatra, Paolo and Francesca. The message of *Ardèle* is an old one.

The last scene of the play is a demonstration of the impurity of the General's family. It is played on and about the central staircase of the chateau, with a continuous coming and going of ruttish animals from one room to another. The Count returns from his mistress in the village and tries to steal a brief moment of conversation with his wife, but they are soon separated by Villardieu, and Gaston retires to spend the night on the couch in the library. Ada has rendezvous with the General in his study while Nathalie and Nicolas hold a hushed but impassioned conversation beneath the stairs. Toto goes to the vestibule to steal hats and canes so that he and Marie-Christine may play their game of "love scenes" in a more adult fashion. A dark, cloaked figure glides through the shadows and enters the room of Aunt Ardèle. The climax of the scene is reached when, suddenly, out of the hushed darkness comes Amélie's shrill cry: "Léon! Léon!" The door to her chamber bursts open and Amélie emerges in her nightgown, her hair wild, and clutching a robe about her shoulders. Morbidly sensitive, she feels the animal instincts alive in the house and abroad. She cries hysterically that she cannot sleep, for the animals and the insects are fornicating. Moreover, she smells amorous activity in the house itself, and demands that it be stopped. Scarcely have the others understood that Amélie is referring to Ardèle when two shots ring out, and, breaking down the door, they discover that Ardèle and her lover have shot themselves. "The imbeciles," says the General. Mediocre humanity, Anouilh suggests, can never learn that life cheapens everything, and that death, in the final analysis, is the only noble way. In spite of the general gaiety that prevails in this play, its true color is black.

In *La valse des toréadors* we become better acquainted with the General's wife. We discover what married life with the General has meant to her: a few years of love, suffering, blows, and reconciliations. But the General soon tired, and turned to the seduction of waitresses and maids, gained some weight, and lost some hair. "And under this carnival disguise the heart of an old youngster who is still waiting to give his all. But how be recognized under this mask? This is what they call a fine career."[53] The Doctor who listens to Léon's explanation could speak of his own life in almost the same terms, for marriage, according to this play, always gives the same results: a few years of happiness, followed by many of compromise.

The entire fourth act is a heated discussion between the General and his wife. The latter, having discovered her husband's love for Ghislaine, has attempted to kill herself by fleeing from the house and lying upon the nearby railroad tracks—after the daily train had passed. This is a surprising feat, because Amélie is supposedly paralyzed. The Doctor explains that her condition is a nervous one in which the unconscious mental process is: "I won't walk so he'll feel sorry for me and won't be able to leave me."[54] Amélie's position is, she feels, that of a martyr who has sacrificed all for her unappreciative husband. She alone suffers, she thinks. She refuses her meals, then orders snacks secretly—insisting continually that she has lost sixteen kilos. Amélie, who renounced a career at the Opéra to marry Léon, has not stopped performing for the past twenty years, and in Act IV we see her playing scene after scene; dramatizing her past; suffering a feigned heart-attack.

Although she maintains that she is dying because of Léon's cruelty and indifference, it soon becomes apparent that Amélie has hardly been any more faithful to Léon than he has been to her. She says that he has never satisfied her, and if he had been "good for something" he would have kept her love. The General, in turn, objects to "this same cold meal" served up day after day during the long years of marriage, and says

that his infidelity was a means of proving his manhood.
He cannot accept that Amélie should do likewise. She
must defend her honor. There is a tragic misunderstanding of the sexes at the bottom of this couple's incom-
patibility. Neither one can realize what drives are
working on the other. Each is selfishly excusing himself
while condemning the other. The first thrill over, none
of them have done anything but pretend:

> *Amélie.* Both of us closed our eyes in bed. But
> while you were doing your little business thinking
> of God knows whom—you don't imagine it's you I
> was thinking of?
> *The General.* How vulgar you are, Madame, and
> how immodest! But let's forget it. If we had both
> reached that point, why so many tears and re-
> proaches, why so many cries these many years?
> *Amélie (sits up, terrifying).* Because you're mine,
> Léon. You're mine, do you understand?—forever—
> no matter how pitiful you are. You're mine, like my
> house, like my jewels, and my furniture, and your
> name. And I'll never allow what's mine, never,
> whatever happens, to belong to anyone else!
> *The General.* And that's what you think love is,
> Madame?
> *Amélie (with a frightful cry, standing on her bed
> in her nightgown—nightmarish).* Yes!
> *The General.* Hell and damnation, Madame! I re-
> fuse. I don't belong to you.
> *Amélie.* Then to whom do you belong?
> *The General.* To no one. To myself perhaps.
> *Amélie.* No! You don't belong to yourself any more.
> I'm your wife. . . . You belong to me.[55]

This is the same basic difference between male and
female which was described in *Médée:* the woman feels
she owns her man, whereas the man desires nothing so
much as his liberty. The General has not abandoned his
wife completely, but he is estranged from her. Unlike
Médée, Amélie does not have the courage or the

strength to turn her back upon her husband and seek a more authentic self. She becomes bogged down in the habit from which Médée was finally able to free herself. For Amélie, love is a selfish and blind ownership which gives the "owner" a feeling of security. It is a feeling of belonging with someone, and having a place to occupy in the universe. We see Ghislaine express a similar idea when she has given herself to Gaston: "I'm no longer a dog without a collar, I have a little chain around my neck with the owner's name on it."[56] Opposed to this desire of belonging and ownership is the General's desire for freedom. He refuses the love offered him by his wife, just as Gaston will some day cease to accept the love offered him by Ghislaine. To a certain extent this refusal is, in the General's instance, a refusal to become a "thing." Amélie seeks to make an object of him: "you're mine, my object, my thing, my catch-all, my garbage can . . ."[57] And Léon tries to rebel by fleeing the attentions of his wife, and finding consolation with the maids he seduces. But he cannot really escape, for he is too cowardly to hurt his wife. Only when the Léon of the old days—the young lieutenant—comes to the fore, does he once attempt to rid himself of her.

Anouilh suggests that life itself was responsible for the brief duration of Léon's married love. Why then has Léon's love for Ghislaine endured for seventeen years? Simply because it was never consummated, and life did not have the opportunity to affect it. Even so, we cannot say that it endured in a pure state, for Léon was never really faithful to Ghislaine, and her love for him, although it has stayed the same, has not grown in the years between.

The Doctor is the wisest voice in *La valse des toréadors*. He would have the General follow the path of Thérèse and Ludovic—that of escape. He would infuse him with a feeling of his duty to Ghislaine, with a power to act and to make others suffer by his independence. Failing this, he advises that the General remember he is aging, evening is falling, and it is time to sound the *extinction des feux.* The General finds this difficult to accept. He still wishes to give his heart, but no one wants it. The Doctor sums up the moral of the General's life: "My poor friend, shall I tell you the moral of this tale? One must never understand his enemy—nor his wife . . . One must never understand anyone, or one dies of it."[58]

To appreciate the implications of such a moral, we must remember that the verb *comprendre* has a special connotation in this play, as, indeed, it often has in other plays of Anouilh. "To understand," as used here means not only to grasp intellectually but to renounce that purity that preceded the comprehension, and to accept what one has understood. To "understand" that life is ugly is to accept it as such, and this is why we hear Antigone objecting, "I don't want to understand."[59] To understand one's enemy is already to have compromised with him and agreed that he is right. To understand one's wife is to lose the individual self: a renunciation that love requires to a certain extent.

The Doctor succinctly describes the cause of the misunderstanding of the couple. Unfortunately, men and women differ in their concept of egoism which they develop in love. Men take everything as theirs and attract it toward themselves in a centripetal fashion; women, on the other hand, act centrifugally, projecting themselves into the world, and more particularly upon the man who is to become their means of expression. For this reason, man feels himself captured and longs for his native freedom, whereas woman bitterly resents man's promiscuity and what the General calls the ingenious system of balances, which allows a man a moment of ignominy inevitably followed by good resolutions. This is another tragic flaw in love: man and woman are different—they are not two halves of the same being. In order not to perceive this, if they remain together for even a brief time they must begin piling up compromises and looking the other way. They are inconvenienced by each other. Thus, Jason and Médée have dreamed of a world in which the other did not exist, and the General envisages a world in which medical science would have found a means to make women sleep forever, except for a few moments at night.[60]

This basic difference between men and women is illustrated in *Ornifle*. The aging libertine is surrounded by adoring women, each more eager than the others to devote herself to him. Among them is his wife Ariane, who for many years has tried to close her eyes to her husband's infidelities. Together they are living one of the convenient arrangements of "love"—more convenient, it may be noted, for the husband than for the wife.

The love depicted in *Ornifle* is, like that which we have seen in the other plays, more a purely physical pleasure than what we are willing to call real love. Ornifle realizes this himself, and points out to his agent Machetu, in one of those metaphors so typical of Anouilh—prosy and banal, yet so apt that it is painful—that love is the only thing that can quiet our hunger, and yet most of us can never find it. Instead we spend our lives eating the candy and bonbons of amorous adventure, always insisting that this one will be the last, until we suddenly discover that the box is empty and we have a stomach-ache.

Speaking to his wife, Ornifle maintains that, "No one loves, my dear, except in those cheap novels they sell in railway stations . . . We simply play the little ballet of desire like the doggies."[61] We are like so many dogs on leashes held by we know not whom. We encounter a dog we think we like, sniff about a bit, and soon someone pulls on the leash and we are off to a new encounter. *Ornifle* leaves us with the feeling that men in "love" are little better than animals.

In Anouilh's world, love is conceived of as a form of self-deception in which the lover gives himself to the beloved because he sees himself in her. This love is completely selfish, for it is the giving of the self to the self, and it is a deception because ultimately the love-object is not the self, and when this is discovered, love cannot continue. Perfect love is conceived of as a comradeship in which man and woman are equal, but even this love is threatened with inevitable ruin, for it is based upon a fiction: the belief that man and woman are alike. In reality, each is distinct from the other and incapable of understanding the emotional approach of the other. For woman, love becomes a feeling of ownership, whereas for man it results in the desire for escape and freedom.

Anouilh's view is that perfect love cannot be maintained in life. He sees in it certain weaknesses that make its failure inevitable. It is always superficial, for the human being is so constituted that he can never break through the wall of flesh which is himself in order to understand and truly become one with another. Even the desire to give oneself completely is a delusion, for not only is it impossible but the person to whom one wishes to give oneself does not exist except in the mind of the lover.

Love, moreover, tends to hide the real self. Even the hero, Anouilh believes, loses a part of his true self when he loves. He longs to become what the mate believes him to be, and he tends to live a part rather than to be his real self.

Not the least of the weaknesses of love, as Anouilh's plays reveal it, is that it results in a loss of spontaneity. The relationship becomes a habit within which the lovers are caught, helpless to release themselves. There exists no longer the daily re-creation of a love that is felt deeply and involves the entire personality. The relationship is merely accepted as such, and life goes on in the same meaningless rut.

For love to be true and eternal it must end before the stage of habit is reached, and the only way that it may end is in death. Separation is no answer. The love of Thérèse for Florent may remain pure because it was never consummated, but we cannot say that it is an eternal love, for the years may bring many changes in feeling. The only eternal love is that of Orphée and Eurydice, of Antigone and Hémon, of Frédéric and Jeannette, of Ardèle and her hunchback. Only in death can love find eternity.

Those who go on living must necessarily resort to some sort of compromise, for love cannot last forever. When two people realize they are no longer in love, whatever may happen their purity is already tarnished, for the relationship has gone too far—has lost its spontaneity and ideality. There are several arrangements that a husband and wife may make. They may remain together, accepting the fact that they are bound to each other, pretending that all is well, while each one realizes that he no longer loves the other. To the stranger, and sometimes even to each other, they give the impression that they are content. This is the arrangement of Mr. and Mrs. Bentz; it is the adjustment that Frédéric and Julia would have made one day; and the one that Adeline would try to effect with Ludovic upon his return from prison. It is the story of M. and Mme Delachaume, and of Orphée's father.

A second form of adjustment is that represented by the *ménage à quatre*. The couple remain together and keep up the social pretense of a marriage, but they are not faithful to each other. They accept the fact that they are not in love with each other, and each tolerates the other's lover. This arrangement, it would appear, is sanctioned by society as long as the third and fourth persons are within the same social stratum as the husband and wife. This is the arrangement that Gaston and Liliane have made in *Ardèle*, as it is that of Tigre and his wife in *La répétition*. The characters of the middle class are not so particular as are those of the nobility in observing the proprieties in this relationship. In *Jézabel*, for example, the mother is enamoured of the chauffeur of her son's wealthy fiancée, while the father is busy seducing the maid and buying gifts for her to ensure her coöperation.

The third form of accommodation, and the one which, it would appear, is by far the best in Anouilh's opinion, is that of separation. To leave the person we no longer love is to regain to a certain extent our lost integrity. But the separation must be a clean one, and the one who remains behind bemoaning his fate is as lost as he who never effects a separation. Général Saintpé could have become a more heroic person had he had the courage to break off with Amélie when he ceased to love her. It is the path followed by Ludovic when he realizes what a farce his marriage would be, for Adeline is not at all what he had imagined her to be. Médée regains her lost purity by reëstablishing her freedom when Jason leaves her. On the contrary, Lucien is nothing but a miserable cuckold, embittered by life and unable to free himself from the past which haunts him.

Such arrangements exist wherever there are two people who desire one another, unless they realize that their love, because of its inherent weaknesses, cannot— indeed, must not—endure.

That it is impossible for the couple to meet on a common ground and to find genuine happiness is a natural consequence of the solitude of the individual. And it is a sad commentary, for if there is any hope of finding a comfort in the solitude that is part of the human predicament, it is in the company of the beloved. It is possible for a moment to feel less alone by finding a comrade in one's mate, but the comfort is illusory, for the comrade we believe we have found is nothing more than a projection of ourselves.

3

Money and Social Classes

THE IMPORTANCE of money and social caste is one of the
main themes in Anouilh's plays, for these factors often
color the attitudes of the characters, and are presented
as having a great deal of influence on love. The *question d'argent* has been a frequent theme in the French
theater. Since the days of Dumas the younger and
Augier the essence of the question has been seen to lie
as much in the problem of the *nouveau riche* as it does
in the attitudes toward money assumed by the characters in the plays, and in the relationship of poverty to
wealth. In the theater of the Second Empire the golden
calf has many faithful devotees; the acquisition of
money is the goal of the poor, and its preservation one
of the major preoccupations of the rich. To the poor
it represents prestige, and affords the opportunity of
mingling with the rich bourgeois and aristocratic soci-
eties they so admire, or of entering the higher strata.
Money is a power which brings together the most
disparate castes: newly rich valets, not without in-
solence, shake hands with impoverished nobles. To a
certain extent, it is a leveling agent, although class
distinctions are still strongly felt. But the distinctions
are of a descending order, and felt by those at the
top of the social ladder, rather than by those at the
bottom whose unique concern is usually to rise as close
to the top as possible. The poor man can forgive the

rich anything if he has a chance to enrich himself also. In the mad rush of activity which typified the era of Napoleon III there was ample opportunity for large numbers among those possessed of ingenuity and ambition to make a small fortune for themselves.

In the theater of Anouilh, however, the situation changes radically. The rich in many of the plays belong also to the idle nobility,[1] and this makes them feel they are a distinctly different species from the others. There is no longer any common ground upon which the poor and the rich may meet. With few exceptions, the poor are not imbued with the desire to become rich. On the contrary, they do not wish to become like the moneyed people who are insensitive to life and its suffering. The rich, on the other hand, have little prejudice against the poor. Instead, they have a feeling that is worse than prejudice: a feeling of such utter superiority that they cannot even consider the people of the poorer classes as belonging to the same human race. They do not consider themselves superior because they are rich. Rather, they consider that they possess wealth and social position because they are superior, and that the poverty of the poor is a sign and a result of their inferiority. With patronizing hauteur, when not with outright contempt, they look upon the inferior creatures as beasts; as a convenience to aid them in their enjoyment of life. Each wealthy duchess has her "pauvres," for whom she knits sweaters and upon whom she occasionally makes charitable calls. But these poor are on the same level as the horses, the pets, and the other possessions of the wealthy—a part of their *train de maison*, to help maintain their prestige and flatter their vanity.

The Duchesse de Granat in *L'hermine* is the first, and perhaps the most heartless, of the line of wealthy dowagers to appear in Anouilh's plays. For her, it is inconceivable that Frantz or Marie-Anne could place themselves on a level with herself and Monime, or that Frantz could dare to aspire to the hand, or even to the affection, of Monime. For the Duchess, there are two distinct worlds, and each person must live according to his own. She makes this perfectly clear to Frantz when she speaks to him of his failure in his projected business:

> If you were my son, I would forgive you for having neither business sense nor a taste for study. But you possess neither the fortune that would allow you, nor the name that would oblige you to live an idle life. . . . You must work, my boy; for the people of your world, that's all there is.[2]

The Duchess rules the poor about her with an iron hand. They are the slaves she has bought to satisfy her whims, and if they cease to satisfy they are no longer her employees. She comes between Monime and Frantz, just as she had been the obstacle between Marie-Anne and her lover, and now stands between one of her scullery maids and her lover: "The hussy claims she's in love! It's magnificent! What's the matter with all of them? Let them think of work and decency first of all, and leave the rest to the cocottes."[3]

If the wealthy ladies of later plays are content to see their spoiled children marrying poverty-stricken lovers, it is not because they no longer entertain the same feelings as the Duchess de Granat, but because they feel able to buy in order to satisfy their sons and daughters. Lady Hurf and Lord Edgard wish to force a compromise upon Gustave to insure the happiness of Juliette; the fantastic Duchess of *Léocadia* has pounced upon poor Amanda without a thought for the girl's feelings or for her economic condition, so that she might serve her ends in wakening the Prince to the present; and Isabelle in *L'invitation au château* is hired by Horace to satisfy his selfish wishes, without the least consideration for her personal feelings. These paupers are merely so many pawns for the wealthy and idle nobility to move about in their diverting game of life.

The resentment felt in Anouilh's plays rises from the lower rungs of the ladder. A human being could not very well resent his dogs and horses: he tolerates them, he plays with them, or uses them for his own ends. It is the poor who cannot forgive the rich their immunity to suffering and their feeling of superiority and complete lack of sympathy for the poor. For the latter, poverty is a stark reality—something they have lived with for years. "You speak of it like a rich girl . . ." Frantz cries to Monime:

> You don't know its daily drudgery, its ingenuity, its patience. For twenty years I've had it at my heels like a vicious dog. I know that nothing can withstand it, not even youthfulness, which is as alive and as strong as love . . . I'm afraid of it . . .[4]

Nothing in life can withstand the slow corroding effects of poverty, Frantz believes. Love is weak, and youth itself gives way. Anouilh's rich fail to understand this, for their money has made them blind to life as it is lived outside their own group. Thus, wealth and their caste divide them from other men. The wall of flesh which divides man from man, no matter what his condition, may be a more fundamental barrier, but that imposed by poverty or wealth is no less insuperable. In order to understand how this can be true we must remember the emphasis Anouilh places upon the role of the environment as a determining factor in the make-up of the individual. Just as the hero must be true to his most real self, whatever that self may be, he must also be true to his environment. Thérèse cannot deny her past any more than can Eurydice, and both of them must leave the men who cannot understand what their pasts have been. For Eurydice it is not so much a matter of difference in background as it is the impossibility of two people ever understanding each other, and her resignation is to one of the inherent weaknesses of love which dictates that the beloved renounce her real self in favor of the self imagined by the lover. Eurydice is weak, and can only flee. Thérèse is stronger, but in addition to those forces tearing Eurydice and Orphée from each other, there is in her instance the force of a background different from that of Florent— the power of poverty and wealth. For a moment, during an effective scene in which Florent, strong as only the rich are strong, throws away his money, Thérèse strives to rise above her past, but she cannot live a lie and finally throws herself sobbing at Florent's feet to gather up the precious coins.[5] This scene highlights the easy strength of Florent contrasted to the painful pride and shame of Thérèse, and the vulgar avidity of M. and Mme Tarde, who show the ecstatic eagerness of the poor about to receive an inheritance. Unctuous and abased, like many of Anouilh's poor, they bow and scrape for the favors of the rich. They are devoid of pride, and eager for the consolation that only money can give them. Although this is their nature, they will pretend that it is not, and in the second act we see M. Tarde's ludicrous attempts to play the role of the gentleman and his insistence that this is his real milieu. Thérèse knows it is not, and in order that Florent may realize she belongs to another world and hates the quiet immunity represented by his world, she pulls his books from their places, for they are a part of his past from which she is forever barred. She spits upon his mother's portrait, and tries to make Florent believe things about her past which are not true, but which are typical of her milieu and incomprehensible to Florent. Thérèse feels alone in his home, for the world of the rich is not her world. It is characterized by tranquillity and dignity. The rich alone can smile, can be strong as conquerors, although they have won without fighting. The fundamental criticism that Thérèse makes of them is that they are inhuman. Because they have never suffered, never hated, or been ashamed, the rich cannot understand these emotions in others. To make it worse, they are strong and sure of themselves, completely walled up within their insensibility to the problems of the poor. Thérèse not only resents the rich—she hates them. And in spite of her love for Florent, she hates him for what he represents—for his past that separates them. When Florent, weary of her accusations, asks her what she would have him do with his money, she cries:

> Oh nothing, Florent! You could throw it all out of the window, laughing, as you did the other day, and my pain wouldn't fly away with it . . . You're rich not only because of your money, don't you see? You're rich because of the house you lived in as a little boy, rich because of long years of calm and happiness, yours and your grandparents' . . . You're rich because of your joy in life which has never had to attack or defend, and because of your talent too. You see, there's really too much to throw out of the window . . . And above all, don't think you're a monster. Hartman misled you when he used that word. You've tortured me, and you're good, you know, and it's not your fault, because you just don't know anything.[6]

We see Florent's lack of comprehension of the feelings of the poor when he states, in the faces of the miserable creatures trembling in anticipation of picking up the money he had thrown away so lightheartedly: "It's perfectly easy to live without money!" At the beginning of Act III, in a scene of striking contrasts, we see more clearly how the rich misunderstand the poor. Florent's aunt—Mme Bazin—and his sister Marie are watching Thérèse being fitted for her wedding dress. The scene is painfully ironic, for Mme Bazin and Marie make remarks about labor and the laboring classes which ring hollow in the presence of Thérèse, and she leans now and then toward the poor child apprentice to ask her if she does not agree with the shallow judgments of the rich.

Madame Bazin is a delightful old lady who plays

at being busy, knowing that she will not have to account for a speedy and careless job. As she chats, she is knitting sweaters for the poor:

> I take a long time to knit these sweaters; and I drop stitches now and then—I've never been a good worker. But the poor are so grateful when they know that you have made them yourself![7]

. . . .

> I'm not one of those idle people who can sit around with empty hands. I have two gardeners, but I sometimes cut my rose bushes myself.[8]

Marie, a "revolutionary," believes all women should work; it is sporting and amusing:

> Actually, the shopgirls and secretaries envy us; they don't know how lucky they are. The liberty you gain from money you've earned, money that is your very own. If they knew how stingy parents are with girls of the best French families, under the pretext of a good upbringing . . .[9]

As an example of the joy of working and the liberty afforded by earning one's own income, Marie tells of a friend who has worked for almost a year in a bank, and is now going to buy an automobile. Her father will pay for part of it, of course. With her car, this young "working girl" will make a tour of Greece and Italy. "But her bank?" asks Thérèse. "Will she have a long enough vacation?" "Of course: it's her uncle's bank. He'll give her all the vacation she wants."[10]

It is all Thérèse can do to refrain from explaining to these innocent rich what life is all about. She is trying to understand (that is, compromise with) them, but cannot see why they are "so charming, so bright and hard without realizing it."[11] Already, however, Thérèse is learning to seek the easy way out. She is becoming less exigent, and her sorrows will soon be only "bird sorrows," like those of the rich. She has begun to understand the happiness of the rich, which, like all happiness in Anouilh's world, consists in living on the surface where everything is easy and there is no struggle. But at the last Thérèse will realize she is not one of them. She cannot forget her past and close her eyes to the misery she has known. She is irremediably a Tarde, a pauper, and she can never understand the rich as they can never truly understand the poor.

In *La sauvage* we can see the change in perspective which Anouilh gives to the money question in the French theater. No longer are the different classes able to meet on the common ground of finances, and level their differences with cash. Rather, that money now forms a barrier between them, which prevents forever the possibility of any understanding.

More important perhaps than this function of money is the attitude of the poor toward the rich. It is no longer one of admiration or of a desire to climb socially. There is not even the desire to ape the rich or to mock them which we find in the lackeys of the seventeenth and eighteenth centuries. The pauper is aware of his own personal dignity as a human being and he hates the rich for not being able to recognize that dignity, for being invulnerable to life itself and immune to the sufferings that are the common lot of man. The insistence of this theme in Anouilh's theater, particularly in the early years, leads one to wonder whether it is a reflection of personal attitudes engendered by the conditions of his own life. The gradual decline in his emphasis of this theme would suggest that this is a reasonable assumption, for as Anouilh has become more successful he has tended to mute the bitterness of his early poverty-stricken heroes. However, he has not relented: the criticism of avarice, of the domination of money, and of the shallow "good-breeding" of the rich has become more subtle, but no less acid. In *Ardèle* we have seen how poverty forced Nathalie into a compromise she would otherwise probably not have made. In *La répétition* the rich are painted as indolent ne'er-do-wells who spend their days giving parties, drinking, and making love to women they are not in love with. Lucile, the poor girl of the play, believes in the dignity of labor. In *Colombe* La Surette, secretary of the grand tragedienne Madame Alexandra, cowers before "Madame-Chérie," but behind her back he gives vent to his hatred for her—the hatred of the underdog for the person who makes it possible to live and at the same time denies him any human dignity. If La Surette has not asserted himself—has not become a human being instead of an animal—it is because, as he himself explains: "I have a peculiarity, monsieur Julian: like all asses, I graze. Twice a day. And since it's she who allows me to graze, I swallow the rest with the oats."[12] La Surette is aware of the ignobility of his position, but he puts it on Madame Alexandra's account. He is not of the heroic race. Because he has a soul, he can realize his indignity, but unlike the hero, he cannot revolt.

In *L'alouette* Anouilh makes the poor assert themselves again as they did in the early plays. Jeanne, who is of the people, is the only one in the play to realize the true dignity of her being by remaining true to herself. The other characters, particularly the rich— Charles, Agnès Sorel, the queens—are content to live on the surface, to find life's greatest thrills in the acquisition of a new hennin; and the Duke of Warwick, pleased that Jeanne has recanted, tells her how inelegant it would have been to die under such conditions:

> *Warwick*. That would have been, as I told you before, a bit vulgar, a bit common, a bit stupid, to insist upon dying no matter what, in order to defy everyone and shout insults at the stake.
>
> *Jeanne (gently, as though to herself)*. But I am common, I am stupid . . . Besides, my life isn't so embellished as yours, Monseigneur—all smooth and straight, between the war and the hunt, pleasure and your beautiful fiancée . . . What will *I* have left when I am no longer Jeanne?[13]

The true heroes of Anouilh's world are almost always poor, *du peuple*. In *L'alouette* Anouilh has shown more than ever his faith in the people. If the milieux of the later plays display signs of wealth, it is because there are no heroes there, or if there are, they are invaders from another world with which the rich are unfamiliar.

In *Ornifle* and *Pauvre Bitos* we see this world of the wealthy where the poor feel ill at ease. Machetu, Ornifle's materialistic agent, cannot forget the differences that exist between him and his patron. When Machetu calls Ornifle, "bougre d'animal," it has no effect, for Ornifle knows his superiority; when the latter uses the familiar term "vieille canaille" in addressing Machetu, his agent becomes indignant, for he fears there may be a germ of truth in it. Because polite behavior was not bred into his bones, he must always be on the *qui vive,* and he is never far from resentment in his attitudes toward his wealthy client.

The same is true of Bitos. The enmity that exists between Bitos and his rich acquaintances among whom he passes the evening dressed as Robespierre, is based ultimately upon social differences. Bitos was taken as a charity student into the school where his mother worked as a cleaning woman, and because he was the best student he was always disliked by his wealthy classmates. Their hatred in turn strengthened his determination to outstrip them and to develop those unbending moral qualities that make him the unsympathetic character he is. Throughout the play we feel a tension between the two worlds represented, and as the curtain falls this tension is stressed by the words of Victoire, the wealthy young woman Bitos would have liked to marry. She reminds him that his poverty is the most precious thing he has, and that on his family crest there will always be the two red arms of his mother.

Becket is also, in a sense, a poor man among the rich, for he belongs to a conquered race, and must assert himself by his strength and intelligence among the weak-willed conquerors. The vanquished Saxons can never forgive the wealthy Normans who use them as animals or objects, killing their sons and ravishing their daughters. The overbearing inhumanity of the rich and the rankling resentment of the poor are effectively presented in the scene in Act I where King Henry attempts to appropriate the house and daughter of a Saxon peasant for his private pleasure.

Among the plays of the third group one stands out for the light it sheds upon the question of poverty and wealth: *L'invitation au château*. For the rich, as usual, life is a game to be played at the expense of the poor. This attitude prevails throughout *La répétition, Colombe, Ardèle, La valse des toréadors, Ornifle*, and *Pauvre Bitos*. We see the same bitterly ironic attitude toward the rich who, with insulting condescension, believe they may purchase the poor to serve as flesh to satisfy their whims.

Horace, in *L'invitation au château*, has no room for feelings, and since he has paid Isabelle, any emotional entanglements are incomprehensible. Isabelle, another Thérèse, spurns his money, while her mother, another Tarde, vilifies her for not accepting the hand of Romainville, a mundane gentleman who would have assured her security for life.

Madame Desmermortes, mistress of the chateau, is a later Madame Bazin, but she differs from the rich women of *L'hermine* and *La sauvage* in that she is aware of her attitude, and is direct and cynical in expressing the nature of her feelings for the poor, whereas the others were sanctimoniously rationalizing about it. With the incontestable logic of the rich she tells Capulat, her reader, "I've always given you my old dresses. You owe me everything."[14] Like Florent's aunt, she too has "her" poor: "I had my poor, of course, just as I had my horses and my lorgnettes. We must live with our own class, whether we like it or not."[15]

The rich guests of Mme Desmermortes have a picturesque conception of poverty. It appeals particularly to the romantic Lady India, who, like Florent's sister, has no idea of what the stark reality of poverty means. In her description of poverty Anouilh parodies Marie Antoinette's bucolic holidays in her Petit Hameau:

> I would adore being poor! Only I would want to be really poor. Everything excessive enchants me. Besides, misery must certainly have its own great poetry, . . . How amusing it would be! I would wash your dishes. I would cook, my dear, for you. I would ask Roeséda Sisters to make me some cute little aprons. (They're the only ones who could do that well.) Oh, nothing fancy, a scrap of cloth, a little pleat, but with their *chic!* We would have little pots and pans and little brooms. You would work in a factory. (With my connections in the Ironworks Board, I could get you a job in the foundry right away.) You would come home in the evening harassed with fatigue and smelling very bad. It would be marvelous! I would wash you, darling, with a little washcloth. Ah! How beautiful it is to be poor![16]

At the end of the play we see that Lady India is serious, although fantastically mistaken, and when she believes Messerschmann has lost all his money she cries out that she will follow him barefooted to his native Warsaw, in the depths of Siberia, where she will be his squaw and cook for him in his log hut.

Messerschmann—once a poor tailor of Warsaw, and now so fabulously wealthy that he controls the fortunes of hundreds of people, including all those invited to the chateau—is a particularly significant and exceptional character in Anouilh's plays. He is the rich man who cannot forget that he was once poor, and the desire to humiliate those people who once humiliated him is behind his will to wealth. To the masses, Messerschmann is a happy man, but those who know him realize he is far from blissful: his mistress is unfaithful, he suffers from insomnia, and his stomach forces him to live on a diet of boiled noodles without butter or salt. His daughter is no happier, for she feels scorned not only by Horace, whom she desires, but by everyone in the chateau except Frédéric, who follows her like a dog and whom she has accepted as her fiancé, since she knows she cannot have Horace. Her father is quite upset to think there is something his money cannot buy, but Diane tells him in no uncertain terms that this is, nonetheless, the bitter truth:

> Money is useless! You can hoard together ten times as much as you have, but you'll never have enough to keep from being humiliated, and to keep your daughter from suffering. They're stronger than we, papa, with their dusty family portraits and their crumbling mansions. They're willing to accept our money to pay for repairs, but that's all. Ah! I hate you, I hate you because I'm your daughter! I would have liked so much to be like them![17]

Diane makes clear something we might not have realized before: money is not the greatest evil. It is the background that money gives, and which has gradually built up the wall between the poor-born and the well-born to such a point that now it forms an insuperable barrier. Anouilh makes clear that no matter how much money Messerschmann accumulates, at heart he will always be a pauper, for he grew up with paupers and his thought processes are theirs. His way of thinking cannot be understood by the rich, and, until his fortune has passed down through generations, its origin lost, and his descendants immunized by many decades of wealth from sympathy or understanding for the poor, Messerschmann's family will not be accepted as a rich family.

Not only is money powerless to make Diane happy but it has, to a certain extent, imprisoned her, for a whole world of experiences is now inaccessible to her. As she tells Isabelle, she can never again have the exciting experience of being "invitée au château." She cannot be thrilled by her beautiful clothes or jewelry because they are common things to her. Diane maintains earnestly, quite unaware of the irony, that money means nothing to her, and if it has established such a reputation for itself, that is only because all books and plays are written by paupers, to whom money seems particularly useful. Florent, or a Lady India, can see only the colorful aspects of poverty, whereas the poor are forced to live the sordid reality. But in Diane's mouth the words have more meaning than they would if spoken by Florent or Mme Bazin, for Diane has passed through poverty and knows what it means. And now she has learned what wealth means, and discovered that one can buy everything save those things that matter most. When she tells Isabelle that it is not easy to become poor, we are inclined to be skeptical, but her father proves her point when, to restore his faith in the power of money and in his own power as a mighty financier, he tries to ruin himself and all the capitalists depending on him. The foreign markets believe he is engaging in a sly maneuver, the speculators buy instead of selling as he had intended, and he finds himself twice as rich as before.

Messerschmann's great disillusionment, one which prompts the gigantic attempt to ruin himself and hundreds of others, comes when he meets Isabelle. She is a pauper: "little paupers don't know how to play. They're too badly brought up."[18] Messerschmann cannot buy his daughter's happiness from Isabelle. When he offers to pay her so that she will leave immediately, she refuses his money, saying that she was about to leave in any event. Messerschmann cannot endure this, for it is an indication that there is someone who is not only beyond his power but beyond the reach of money, and "that's not in the order of things."[19] For Isabelle to leave for nothing is too expensive a price for Messerschmann. He offers to write her a check: he will place the number one at the left and will continue writing zeros until she stops him.

Now it is no longer a question of Diane's happiness, for that seems assured. It is for his own peace of mind that Messerschmann is bargaining. His whole life has been built on the belief that everyone has something to sell, and he could no longer believe in himself if Isabelle proved to be an exception. All he asks is that she accept some money from him. He is bound because he has agreed long ago to play the game, whereas Isabelle is free to refuse his money and Messerschmann can do nothing about it. Like Antigone, Isabelle's greatest pleasure is the freedom to say no to all the realizations of her dreams which Messerschmann offers her. The old financier finally admits that he has no faith in money either, for it has only made him miserable.

There follows a scene reminiscent of *La sauvage*. Desperately, Messerschmann takes all his franc notes from his pockets and starts tearing them to bits. Isabelle, unlike Thérèse, joins him and destroys the equivalent of a country house with a beautiful garden, a hat firm, dresses, furs, and jewelry. Being practical, she also tears up a bill for a valise in which to put all the clothing. Surrounded by the scattered bits, they sit upon the floor, miserable and alone. Money is no guarantee for happiness. It serves as an instrument of humiliation to the poor, and as a prison to the rich. That money should bring man happiness, or be a means of preventing it, does not concern Anouilh particularly, for "filthy happiness" is not something to be desired. Its great evil is that it hides the authentic man by making the rich insensitive to the real life led by the poor, and, by the same token, it widens the breach that separates man from man, and loses us more irremediably in the solitude that is our condition. In many plays the satire of the rich is a social satire. But—and this is Anouilh's contribution—the accent is upon the moral questions involved. Money, whether it be a social necessity and a benefit, or not, is, morally speaking, an evil that separates, hardens, makes complacent and self-satisfied on the one hand, and rouses bitterness, hatred, and vindictiveness on the other.

Anouilh's originality does not lie in his examination of the money question, but in the stress he has placed upon the attitudes of the classes toward one another, since the attitudes he describes are indicative of an important change in the outlook of the present generation.

Reflected also in the treatment of the money problem, and to some extent in the treatment given to the theme of love, is an implied criticism of contemporary society. Even without the barrier of money, men are so selfish that they seldom take their fellows into consideration. The primary social unit—the family—has broken down, and acts not as a group but as a heterogeneous mixture of individuals. With little regard for conventional morality, each goes his own way. The husband and wife are usually unhappy, and either separated or living under one of the convenient arrangements possible in society. The children do not love their parents, nor do the parents exhibit any particular affection for their children, except as tools to their own personal happiness, as in the instances of the Tardes, who would marry off Thérèse to a wealthy man, and the Delachaumes, who succeeded in marrying their son to a wealthy shrew. Eurydice's mother is too busy with her lover Vincent, and with her career, to do much else than admonish her daughter to sit up straight; and Orphée's father is only eager to have his son help to earn a meager living, and listen day after day to his pointless prattle of restaurants and menus.

Général Saintpé neither understands his wife, nor does he care for his daughters (in *La valse des toré-adors*). His sister, the Countess (in *Ardèle*), is selfishly concerned only with her own happiness. Even the parents of Jeanne d'Arc cannot understand their daughter. In *Becket* several scenes depict the unpleasant home life of Henry with his nagging wife and unloved son who cordially returns his father's hatred. The family is nowhere presented as a real unit, but only as so many selfish individuals, each bent on satisfying his own whims and impulses. We may see in this another result of man's solitude. But it is also a criticism of man's selfishness, and of his inability to feel true compassion for his fellow-sufferers. Only the heroic soul at times rises to such a sentiment. Thérèse, at the end of *La sauvage*, expresses her love for all mankind, and points the way to the optimism of *L'alouette*.

Part Two: Dramatic Values

4

Modes of Realism

IN *La répétition* Anouilh offers us something like an *ars dramatica*. In the words he puts into the mouth of the Count, Tigre, he comes closest to a direct expression of what he believes the theater should be:

> Naturalness and truth in the theater, my dear, are the most unnatural thing in the world. Don't think that it suffices to find the precise tone of real life. First of all, in life the text is always so bad! We live in a world that has completely forgotten the semicolon, we all speak in unfinished sentences with three little dots at the end, because we never find the exact word. And then the natural tone of conversation which actors claim to have found: those stammerings, those hiccups, hesitations, and mistakes—it's scarcely worthwhile gathering five or six hundred people together in a theater and asking their money, just to show them that. They love it, I know. They recognize themselves. Nonetheless, we must write and perform plays better than they. Life is very pretty, but it has no form. The object of art is precisely to give it one, and through all possible artifices to create something that is truer than truth.[1]

These words make it clear that Anouilh's theater does not belong in that tradition of modern realism which advocates a slavishly photographic imitation of life, and which usually leads to the "desert of exact likeness to the reality which is perceived by the most commonplace mind,"[2] as T. S. Eliot has said. In fact, such a desert is precisely what Anouilh is trying to avoid by giving an artistic form to life, which for all artistic purposes is in itself amorphous. The stumbling and mumbling, the hesitations and back-turning, and the complete ignoring of the presence of an audience in the theater which characterized much of the realistic and naturalistic drama of the turn of the century, and was typified by the theatrical techniques of the Théâtre Libre, is left behind by Anouilh as he pursues something more elusive. "To create something truer than truth" is indeed a high ideal for the artist. In fact, the phrase in itself implies that there is something beyond the realistic scene: some synthesis of reality which may give insight into a more general truth beyond the scope of Realism. What this truth is need not be completely clear to the intellect. The intuitive processes may realize this truth as completely as the rational. The truth may be one- or many-faceted, lying below the rationalized level that must be the central one in our theater today because the appeal is not to the ritual instinct or the desire to worship, but to the desire to understand or enjoy.[3] Because our theater is not based upon any one tradition, either in the broad sense of the cosmos accepted by the Greeks and the Elizabethans, or the more restricted bourgeois parlor that formed the background of action for the lives of Ibsen's audience, and the enlightened drawing room that served the same purpose in the plays of Wilde and Shaw, the individual author must establish a tradition of some sort against which to build his play. Most contemporary authors continue to accept the bourgeois parlor of Ibsen, or something equally restricted, and present their plot within its confines. The miracle of Ibsen was that while using so confining a tradition he was able to go beyond it and present through the ultimately insignificant struggles of his characters, couched in the trite terms of the times, the more significant picture of man brooding over his condition. Ibsen created through that very parlor the feeling of something beyond it. Most dramatists have remained content to present the narrow reality within its confines with no suggestion of any transcendental values; and, indeed, the point has been reached where the parlor and the drawing room have achieved a feeling of stability which is comforting to the audiences who live within their confines.

One of the purposes of the dramatists in France since the First World War has been to undermine that stability. Like Gide, they would make man *disponible,* ready for each new experience, capable of growing in ever-changing and new directions. Such a purpose, which is evident in the theater of Anouilh, as it is in that of Sartre, brings us round full-circle to the "plus vrai que le vrai." The only truth that is entirely true, and which Anouilh would therefore present, is that which we each discover for ourselves in the intimacy of our deepest being. It is to free us for the discovery of this truth perhaps that Anouilh would break down the barriers that limit us to certain concepts.

Thus, we may interpret the quotation from *La répé-tition* to mean two things: the dramatist will present a composed version of life as it is lived which will give the illusion of reality, and at the same time will present, if not a deeper reality, at least a suggestion of how we may find that deeper reality. At the center of his theater there will be found the same convention of the parlor which we find in most modern drama, but behind we will feel something of deeper significance—not the ordered cosmos of the Greeks, but a chaos that underlies all life, including the ordered bourgeois life, if those who lived it would but consent to look. Anouilh presents not a story told for the simple pleasure of telling; he strives to express the universal behind what

Francis Fergusson calls the "diminished scene of rationalism" by which the dramatist is so often bound today.

This rational-realistic tradition within which Anouilh writes, and beyond which he strives to go, offers no strictly defined instrument with which to work. The Greek and the Elizabethan dramatist had the poetry both of language and of the rhythm that is an inherent part of ritual drama. In a more limited way, the authors of the French Classical theater could rely upon a poetry that is clear and balanced—even sensuous at times—but lacks the richness of Elizabethan language, which, suggestive and many-faceted, reflects not only the rational but all aspects of life. Anouilh—and the modern theater generally—lacks any such universal poetic instrument. His drama is distinguished instead by the same convention that one finds in Pirandello—the stage as a stage, and life itself as a theater in which all men are actors.

The Realistic Core

Before studying the acceptance of the stage as a stage, which will require a discussion of appearance and reality, let us look at the realistic core of Anouilh's theater. The earliest plays, in which the author is not so aware of the theater as a theater, resemble more closely the realistic drama of the last half-century than do Anouilh's later plays. The first scene of *La sauvage* is a good example of what might appear to be photographic realism. The setting is described in detail:

> A café in a resort town. Mediocre and pretentious decor. The stage is occupied almost entirely by the orchestra platform. On one side the door to the kitchen, which the waiters, their arms holding their tray, push with their foot.
>
> Three tables on stage. The first, near the platform, is used by the musicians; it is covered with music, instrument cases, the two others are empty.

132

> One of them has its chairs tipped to indicate that it is reserved.
>
> The rest of the room is invisible. On the wall a system of mirrors multiplies the orchestra and reflects the depths of the café.
>
> The orchestra is composed of the pianist: Gosta; the double-bass player: M. Tarde; the cellist: Mme Tarde; the first and second violinists: Thérèse and Jeannette.
>
> When the curtain rises, the orchestra is finishing a lively number. The waiter is listening near the platform; at the end of the piece someone calls the waiter from the other end of the room. He rushes off, wiping the table as he goes by.[4]

There is nothing exotic, romantic, or unusual about this setting. It is one of a thousand such cafés which anyone might enter. It corresponds to our everyday experience. The characters are for the most part commonplace, and they do exactly what we would expect such people to do. The same can be said for the people and settings of *L'hermine* and *Jézabel.* Even the luxurious settings are treated in the same manner, and the wealthy people act in that blind way which Anouilh, from the beginning, has accustomed us to expect them to act. They are mediocre people and everything they do is plausible. The settings are clear and look as we would expect such places to look in real life.

The dialogue is realistic also. There is no use of grandiloquence, rhetoric, or lyricism. This is true not only of the early plays but of later ones as well. In such a play as *Antigone,* in which, because of its roots in classical tragedy, we might expect some degree of lyricism, we are surprised by the tone of Antigone's sudden change to the declamatory style when she apostrophizes her tomb: "O tomb! O nuptial bed! O dwelling under ground . . ."[5]

The poetry of Anouilh's language lies not in any such

expressions but in a use of imagery which is integrated so closely with the thought of the characters that it is an essential part of it. Antigone is doing more than making a clever metaphor when she tells Créon that his preoccupation with happiness is disgusting: "You're like dogs who lick everything they find."[6] She is intimately identifying the masses who want nothing but an easy happiness with an animal that uses no judgment but instinctively heads for whatever appeals to it at the moment. The image is extended by Médée when she accuses her love for Jason because it has enslaved her to him and made of her "that bitch who comes back to sleep in her hole."[7] Général Saintpé's description of life as a long and boring family dinner reveals the hypocrisy that is an essential part of his life, and suggests the breakdown of any real meaning in the family, which has become a hollow mockery of what it was intended to be. Such metaphors are taken from everyday experience and are, in that respect, realistic rather than fanciful or exotic.

In *Eurydice* there is an imperfect mingling of the real and the supernatural, and this is reflected in the language, which, although mostly realistic, at times takes on that same aura of fancy that we find in Giraudoux. Thus, Orphée explains to Eurydice his feelings upon meeting her: "You possess just the weight that needed to be added to mine in order to hold me down to earth. Until just a while ago I was too light; I floated; I hit against the furniture and against people."[8]

However, the realism of Anouilh's dialogue is usually far removed from so Giralducien a tone and may even extend to such ungrammatical conversational usage as: "Tu n'as pas peur qu'il ne revienne pas, quelquefois?"[9] ("Aren't you afraid he might not come back, sometimes?") "Well!" exclaims Marcel Berger in his stylistic study of the first few pages of *La sauvage*, "a first-rate writer who in no wise rejects the 'photographic style,' who likes his characters to 'speak true'!"[10] The dialogue is skillfully handled, of course, so that in a few words we are told many essential things. In this way, by making his characters use an everyday vocabulary, but reserving the author's right of condensing their speech and composing it in a logical order and not in a haphazard sequence, Anouilh achieves his effect of "truer than truth," and gives an artistic form to what might otherwise have been pointless conversation, or tedious repetition.

Fantasy and Fact

While he was writing his early plays of unrelieved realism—*L'hermine, Jézabel,* and *La sauvage*—Anouilh was composing a parallel series of works of an entirely different nature. The contrast between *Jézabel* and *Le bal des voleurs,* both written in the same year, is striking. The former, with its somber pessimism of characters caught in the hopeless web of a lurid past, reminds one of the unhappy dramas of the naturalists. *Le bal des voleurs* stands at the opposite pole: it is a gay and frivolous vaudeville in which the serious thoughts occasionally expressed by Lady Hurf are quickly forgotten in the ludicrous happenings, and the dominant tone is optimistic. This play, with its fantastic plot and improbable characters, is a far cry from the realistic early *Pièces noires.* In later plays we see a gradual enlarging of the serious note in the "rose" plays and of the fantasy in the "black" plays. This combination of fanciful and realistic elements is already noticeable in the seriousness of Lady Hurf in *Le bal des voleurs,* and in the sharp-edged satire of the Duchesse de Granat in *L'hermine* and of Florent's aunt and sister in *La sauvage,* but it becomes more insistent as Anouilh matures. The skillful blending of the comic and the tragic has come to be one of Anouilh's most characteristic features. In *Le voyageur sans bagage,* the lightness of tone of the first part of the play seems to indicate a *pièce rose*, but soon the complications of Gaston's identity take on a seriousness that dominates the play, and the tone becomes at least edged with black. *Le rendez-vous de Senlis*, although classified as a *pièce rose*, follows the same pattern: the first act is amusing, but the second act becomes more serious, and this tone dominates to the end, although the outcome is a happy one, since the protagonist is able to escape his past and the sad world of reality.

Most critics have distinguished the *pièces roses* from the *pièces noires* by the fact that in the former the world of dreams is allowed to dominate reality, and the protagonists are permitted to make the compromises without losing their dignity. They can live because they give themselves entirely to their illusions, and play the game with all the enthusiasm of youth. The *Pièces roses*, according to Hubert Gignoux: "bring a bit of hope. Some, in effect, tend to show that some lies are allowed; and others, even more optimistic, that sincerity itself not only does not exclude happiness, but may build it— that loving and living are not incompatible with one another."[11]

This distinction between the two kinds of plays fails to strike the root of the problem. A key statement of one of Anouilh's characters—a most trustworthy one—gives us the basis on which to make a distinction. In *Là valse des toréadors* the General asks his friend the Doctor how all the complications will be resolved. The Doctor responds: "As in life, or as in the theater, in the days when it was still good. A trumped-up denouement, not too sad on the surface and which fools no one—and a little while later: curtain."[12] This suggests that Anouilh's critics may have been duped by the happy outcome of the *Pièces roses* into believing Anouilh considers such an arrangement as a final answer to the problems that exist in life. True, it may be possible for a time, but it is only an "arrangement," and does not really solve any problems. They still remain, and will return some time in the future. "And a little while later: curtain," has an ominous ring to it. It is the curtain not only of the play but of the "arrangement" and of the happiness that depends upon it. In other words, where the *Pièces noires* show us life with a finality, with its problems carried to their conclusion, the *Pièces roses* give us only a temporary view. They can end happily only because the author stops before the end. Gustave and Juliette, Georges and Isabelle, the Prince and Amanda—all of them must wake up one day and discover that the illusions in which they have been living are not reality. It will be a sad awakening, but under the right conditions it can also be a heroic one.

Because *Le voyageur sans bagage* shows the domination of the dream in its melodramatic ending, it too may appear to be "rose." But it is quite logically classified as "noir" when we reflect that every man does not have the freedom to choose himself which Gaston has. *Le rendez-vous de Senlis* is basically "noir" also, because we cannot all create a childhood like the one Georges deludes himself into believing he has created for himself. Indeed, all the *Pièces roses* are essentially "black"; only "rose" on the surface, through the lightness of tone and the frequently vaudevillesque humor and exaggeration.

The combination of *noir* and *rose* elements, the well-known romantic *mélange des genres*, which we see to some degree in every play except *Jézabel* and *Médée*, appears to appeal to Anouilh for two reasons. It permits him to present to us his sad picture of reality in a not-too-dreary light by covering it over, or touching it here and there, with a farcical note. Moreover, since life is neither all sorrow nor all laughter, neither all dreams nor all tedious reality, Anouilh, by welding sorrow and laughter together, can, like Pirandello, show us a more complete picture of life—a truer picture than can the realist, who tends to reveal only the seamy aspects of everyday life.

"This clowning, this absurd melodrama, are life,"[13] says M. Henri. Both buffoonery and melodrama have a place in life. Consequently, many of Anouilh's characters are condemned to a lucid understanding of the ridiculousness of their seriousness. Georges in *Le rendez-vous de Senlis* is one of them. Addressing the two players whom he has hired to impersonate his ideal mother and father, he says:

> You who are accustomed to a theater in which the comic and the tragic are never mixed, must look with astonishment upon this young man who, with a drawn look and trembling hands, is dragging you toward a light comedy of intrigue . . . Others have tragedy quite naturally at their beck and call; upon the least provocation, the smallest pain, they can wave their handkerchief or shed a tear surrounded by unanimous sympathy. It so happens that I, however, must play my life in the style of light comedy.[14]

Later in the same play, Isabelle converses with the actors:

> *Isabelle.* Do you play drama or light comedy?
>
> *Philemon.* I play everything, Mademoiselle. Classic or modern, tragic or comic.
>
> *Isabelle.* And you never mix the genres?
>
> *Philemon.* In my day that wasn't done, Mademoiselle! But with the plays they put out now, evidently . . .[15]

Ardèle ou La marguerite is the consummate example of this *mélange des genres,* for in it the two aspects of the comic and the serious are blended so skillfully that there is no dividing line between the two. The grotesque element represented by the hunchbacked lovers accentuates the fusion. It is neither a serious play with

Jean Anouilh

Dupont-Dufort father and Dupont-Dufort son, disguised as thieves, clumsily hold up two real thieves parading as visiting Spanish grandees, in the wartime revival of *Le bal des voleurs* at the Atelier.

Madame Renaud and the Duchesse Dupont-Dufort vainly attempt to evoke Gaston's childhood, in the Théâtre Montparnasse revival of *Le voyageur sans bagage*, directed and designed by André Barsacq.

Lady Hurf "discovers" her visiting grandee is only a talented pickpocket, in the Atelier revival of *Le bal des voleurs*.

Isabelle (Dany Robin) proudly refuses the bribe offered her by Messerschmann (Robert Vattier) in the 1947 production of *L'invitation au château* at the Atelier, directed and designed by André Barsacq.

(*Courtesy Lipnitzki; French Cultural Services, N.Y.*)

Jeanne d'Arc (Suzanne Flon) at the stake, a moment before her reprieve: the penultimate scene of the 1953 production of *L'alouette* at the Théâtre Montparnasse.

(*Courtesy Bernand; French Cultural Services, N.Y.*)

The aging Don Juan (Pierre Brasseur) comes face to face with death and his own irresponsible past, in the 1955 production of *Ornifle ou Le courant d'air* at the Comédie des Champs-Elysées, designed and directed by Jean-Denis Malclès.

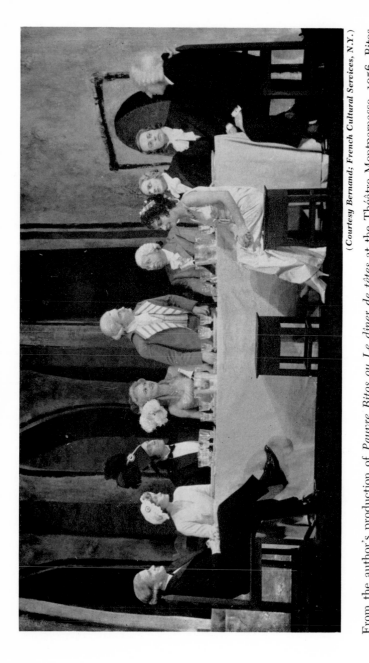

(Courtesy Bernand; French Cultural Services, N.Y.)

From the author's production of *Pauvre Bitos ou Le dîner de têtes* at the Théâtre Montparnasse, 1956. Bitos (Michel Bouquet), impersonating Robespierre, defends the intransigent dictator to his not-so-intransigent friends.

farcical elements, nor a comedy with serious elements. It is both, and the fusion of tragic and comic effect underlies the entire play. The laughter is always tinged with bitterness, and reflects the tragedy beneath it: "Fortunately we are ridiculous," observes the Count, "otherwise this story would really be too sad."[16] *Ardèle* possesses all the grotesque humor of the *Pièces roses,* but its essence is "black."

This mingling of the grotesque with the serious has been criticized in *Ardèle,*[17] but such an objection is no longer valid if we remember that for Anouilh life is a paradox. It is absurd and not worth living, and yet it is all that we have, and death is equally absurd. To take such a life seriously is an error, and yet it is often difficult to laugh in the face of our shattered illusions. The presentation of life in terms of the tragic that is ridiculous makes more patent this feeling of paradox, and hence plays like *Ardèle* seem to be the full flowering of Anouilh's manner, rather than the last abortive attempts of an author who has nothing more to say.

"The comic element is," as Lester Crocker says in regard to *Don Quijote,* "superficially predominant, although it serves ultimately to enhance the tragic."[18] "He [Don Quijote] embraces the inseparably comic and tragic sides of man's striving, elevating them into the unity of myth."[19] Without going so far as to maintain that Anouilh has elevated his characters to a mythical universality, we may at least assert that he attempts to reveal the inseparably comic and tragic sides of man's striving. In *Ardèle* the characters are tragic in their inability to rise above the evil and compromise which is part of their condition, and comic in their inability to see themselves as they really are. It is only the heroic creature of Anouilh's world who sees himself as he is and thereby becomes tragic rather than comic. "The distance between wanting to be and believing that one already is, is the distance that separates the tragic from the comic,"[20] says Ortega y Gasset. Don Quijote is a world in himself. The heroes and the nonheroes of Anouilh represent various aspects of this world but do not achieve the completeness of Cervantes' prodigious creation.

By the time he wrote *Ardèle* (1948), Anouilh was no longer striving to present on the stage the same kind of realism we see in *Jézabel* and *La sauvage*. His method is more an impressionistic one, and we see life through the eyes of the dramatist rather than presented in what the realist likes to call an objective way. Anouilh's plays present what the author himself has called "a poetic and imaginative interpretation of reality."[21] With the railway café in *Eurydice* we bid farewell to the detailed low-class settings. It is no longer the everyday reality of the realists which we see, but the halls of chateaux, strange old country houses falling to ruin, backstage life in the theater, and, in *L'alouette*, a courtroom that is really a stage upon which the life of Jeanne d'Arc is reënacted. Here we are far away from the apparently photographic realism of *La sauvage*. The world is a theater; our imagination is called into play to create for ourselves the scenes that Jeanne is reënacting, and the world of actual reality, represented by the crowded courtroom with its judges and executioner and by the stage itself, is brought more closely than ever before into conjunction with the inner world of the heroine.

The realism that lies at the core of Anouilh's plays varies in inverse ratio to the emphasis placed upon the theatrical aspects of life in each play. In the first plays there is no question of the characters presenting themselves to us as characters, or even of presenting a play of some kind within a play. They are there before us as though we had suddenly intruded upon life as it is being lived, although it is life that has been composed to a certain degree by some artistic process that gives it form. In the *Pièces roses*, on the other hand, the characters are highly theatrical; they are puppet types in many instances, and we can see either the strings that the author pulls or those that one of the characters, who has planned a play within the play, and who really represents the author, is pulling. There is no attempt at a realistic presentation. The world of illusion that the characters are able to create for themselves is unreal to us and often illogical.

Appearance and Reality

The theme of the play within the play, or that of the play frankly accepted as such, is closely related to the theme of appearance and reality. This theatricality is, in fact, but another way of putting the problem of appearance and reality. The stage, accepted as such, corresponds to objective reality, and the play that is being played, to the inner subjective reality. Our problem is to discover which of these Anouilh feels to be the reality and which the illusion as it is revealed through his dramas.

For Don Quijote at the beginning of his knightly adventures, as for Hamlet before the death of his father and the young prince's subsequent disillusionment, the highest reality corresponded to that inner vision of a better possible world, whereas objective reality was branded as appearance or illusion. But for the disillusioned old Don at the end of Cervantes' novel, who is no longer the *caballero andante* Don Quijote but the country squire Alonso Quijano, and for Hamlet at the opening of Shakespeare's play, it has become clear that the inner vision is truly an illusion, unrealizable on earth, and that what had previously been called appearance is the only reality that has importance for society as a whole. Segismundo in *La vida es sueño* almost comes to the same conclusion, but he avoids it by accepting the Catholic interpretation of the problem: that this life and its objective reality may be illusion, but beyond that there is an ultimate reality, which is neither dream nor illusion. Thus, he is able to act,

141

whereas Hamlet, lacking any sound basis for a system of values, was lost through indecision.[22] The Prince of Denmark was troubled by the same doubts and anguish of which Miguel de Unamuno speaks to Don Quijote:

> Life is a dream certainly, but tell us, unhappy Don Quijote, you who woke from the dream of your madness to die abominating it, tell us: is not death also a dream? Ah! And if it were an eternal dream and a sleep [sueño] without dreaming [ensueños] nor waking, then, beloved Knight, how was the sanity of your death more worthy than the madness of your life? If death is a dream, your desire for immortality was only profound madness.
>
> And if your madness was a dream and a vanity, what but dream and madness is all human heroism, all effort in behalf of others, all help to the needy and all war on oppression? . . . If it were thus, it would be better for us never to have seen the light of the sun, or breathed the air of life.[23]

This is a similar accent to that which we find in *Roméo et Jeannette*, for example, where we are told that life and death are equally absurd. Is there no hope for a happy solution? The problem is one that has preoccupied Anouilh since the beginning of his career. Even in the plays where there is no element of theatricality as such, the problem of appearance and reality is suggested.

In *L'hermine* Frantz is already a disillusioned young man. He has no faith in the power of love, and realizes that his love is doomed from the start: "Oh my God, I'm a monster! Other lovers believe in eternity, in love in a cottage. Why did you give me this love without giving me also the necessary credulity?"[24] Yet, in spite of this lack of faith, Frantz desperately tries to create a vision of happiness buttressed by money, and then to realize his vision by murdering the duchess. It is almost as though the vision had for a moment dominated his despair and made him play a role that was not really his. As in Pirandello's *Enrico IV*, the dream world he has created becomes suddenly more real than the actual world, and without even stopping to consider the money offered him by Bentz, which might have afforded him some measure of solace, Frantz, like Pirandello's character, commits a crime that makes the dream as true and base as the reality. Unlike Pirandello, Anouilh does not make any clear contrast between the actual and the visionary reality. The contrast lies implicit in Frantz's situation rather than being explicit in Anouilh's treatment of it. Frantz follows through his murder, defending his innocence as though still caught in his dream. It is only when Monime wakes him abruptly at the end of the play that Frantz realizes the ugliness of what he has done. The vision has vanished. He is once again the disillusioned youth, and he gives himself up willingly to the police.

Marc in *Jézabel*, like Frantz, would escape his past and find a refuge in a vision of happiness in the future, but his dream is still-born and never becomes anything positive; it remains only an abortive attempt to deny the past that is his only reality.

Thérèse, *La sauvage*, discovers the many facets of reality also. At the beginning of the play she is optimistic and hopeful; her love for Florent is a beautiful thing in her own mind. Then she discovers that her family and friends have other conceptions of what this love is, and Thérèse feels that these attitudes toward her love, although they may not be true for her, are the only reality for her family and friends. For them her marriage to Florent is based upon the desire for money and comfort. Her love is not only what it is, but what it appears to be. Because she is honest, Thérèse must make Florent aware of this aspect of her love, just as she must try to make him understand all that she is and stands for by revealing her environment and her past. The social lies, the hypocrisy, and the deceptions upon which society is based are even more obnoxious to her than the vicious background from which she has come, and Thérèse would reveal to Florent her real self—both the heroic savage that she is and the unpleasant light in which she is framed by her background and the attitudes of her acquaintances.

Ludovic of *Y avait un prisonnier* is also a bitter opponent of the social lie—"Vice is nothing," he says. "It's the comedy it plays that makes life frightful."[25] Because he refuses to accept this game, Ludovic must flee from society, and he and La Brebis leave the ship to swim ashore where they will seek an ideal life of happiness away from the pretense and hypocrisy that society demands. Ludovic does not attempt to reform society. He is no Don Quijote. On the other hand, neither is he an Alonso Quijano who accepts society as it is. He refuses society for himself and turns to the ideal that is his truest self, for only away from society can he be true to himself, and the reality that seems to be an illusion may become a reality.

In other plays we learn that this vision is unrealizable in life, and as far as life is concerned is an illusion. The appearance–reality equation is more complex than it at first appears. We may say that there are two sets of values. The first is objective reality, which is ugly and corrupt, with its corollary, the social lie, which is not in itself real, but because of its general acceptance and its necessity in the world, acts together with objective reality as though the two were one reality. In the *Pièces noires* this two-faceted reality is taken as objective reality in itself. The hero or heroine opposes it, sometimes for its basic ugliness and always for its hypocrisy, by bringing against it his concept of reality, which is the second set of values. According to this concept, the real man is the inner man of whom the hero is aware within himself, and to whom he must remain true. This reality is a subjective one, and is termed most often by society as illusion or mere appearance. Such a subjective reality, which according to

144

Anouilh cannot exist in society, and which cannot even be long-lived because of the compromises that will ultimately corrupt and hide it, is the reality that the hero is seeking to affirm. Paradoxically, the affirmation of this truth sometimes carries with it the affirmation of the truth of the ugliness of reality which the ideal self would like to reject, but realizes that in all honesty it must accept as an inescapable reality of life. Thus, there is often a struggle of the inner self envisioned as the basic reality and cognizant of the ugliness of objective life which is recognized as actual reality, against the social lie or any kind of mask that serves as a convenience rather than as an ideal.

In the *Pièces roses*, where there are no truly heroic characters, and where illusion dominates, the second set of values does not come into play, and the two parts of objective reality—the ugliness of life and the rose masquerade—are opposed to each other, with the latter winning the upper hand. Speaking of the *Pièces roses*, Perruchot reverses the title of Calderón's well-known play, and says Anouilh tells us that "dream is a life."[26] He might well have added, along with Hubert Gignoux and the majority of Anouilh's critics, that in these plays dream is the only life. "To lie or to die,"[27] is the alternative as Gignoux states it. In the *Pièces roses*, then, we will see the dominion of the illusion, and learn that a lie of some kind is necessary for life to go on. Man cannot bear to look reality in the face and go on living.

In *Le bal des voleurs* all is masquerade. The one honest note is sounded by Gustave who tries not to cheat, but as the curtain falls we know he will accept the lie that has been prepared for him and will enter into the dream that his life with Juliette can be for a time. If we learn from *Le bal des voleurs* that illusion can make life possible, we also learn that illusion cannot be trusted too far, for even within the realm of dreams there are tricks and lies. The thieves are so well disguised that they pick each other's pockets; Peterbono who starts off to dupe Lady Hurf is for a time duped by her. Masquerade follows upon masquerade until everyone in the play is confused except Lady Hurf who is pulling the strings. Even she is a puppet and behind her we can feel Anouilh controlling the situations playfully and willfully, like some mischievous destiny. "Here are our marionnettes,"[28] cries Lady Hurf, and we know she is speaking of all the characters, including herself. The play is light and happy precisely because it is a play and a game, not life itself. At the end, when Lord Edgard says "The play is over"[29] and the clarinetist takes his instrument from his pocket to play while the company performs a ballet, exchanging beards among themselves, we feel that the marionnettes will be laid away, "like corks,"[30] to use Lady Hurf's image. The dance and the exchanging of beards make clear, if nothing else had, that this is nothing but a masquerade—not to be taken too seriously—and that what we have seen is a *guignol,* not life.

Life comes later when we wake from the dreams of youth and love. If Juliette is happy it is because she is unaware that what she was playing was a comedy —an illusion, not reality. The disillusioned who lack faith in love and youth because they have passed through and beyond them, continue to play their roles, but without experiencing the joy of a Juliette. There is a hollow ring in it for them.

In *Le bal des voleurs* the "rose" illusion dominates almost to the exclusion of the "black," and in *Léocadia,* as we shall see, the Prince is finally awakened from his "rose" dream only to be lulled into another that is masquerading as reality—the reality of love and youth, which is also an illusion.

Le rendez-vous de Senlis is a *pièce rose,* but there are elements of the "black" in it. All the ugly reality represented by the family grouped about Henriette is typical of the *pièces noires.* When they arrive in the rococo salon of Georges' rented house and meet Isabelle, who personifies happiness, the "rose" and the "black" encounter each other, and the latter threatens for a time to destroy the former. Its ultimate destruction is certain, in any event, for Georges is not a puppet; he belongs to the "black" world, and he realizes his dream is false. All that part of the play which centers on Georges' dream is "rose," whereas all that which centers on his past, his true parents, and supposed friend, is "black." It is significant that the evening that Georges had planned to be the one ideal evening—totally "rose," spent with Isabelle and the ideal parents—does not materialize at all. The entire lie is a fiasco: the actor and actress hired to impersonate the mother and father make no attempt to play their parts. Georges cannot realize his dream. Reality is too strong. The ideal parents can remain ideal only so long as they are not materialized. That is why Georges does not hire an actor to impersonate his best friend: "That way he will have every chance of remaining a perfect friend."[31] But ugly reality imposes itself even upon this im-materialized ideal, and the picture of the perfect friend painted by Georges for Isabelle is destroyed by the appearance of Robert. Not only is Robert more real in his selfish attachment and hatred for Georges than is the ideal friend, but he is more real than Isabelle, who is happiness itself. Though he leaves and Isabelle is free to accompany Georges as he goes to dine with his "family" of third-rate actors, we feel Robert is more real and will continue to exist after Isabelle has vanished.

Besides a real pessimism, Gignoux[32] has pointed out, we find in Anouilh an optimism of the theater. The un-real characters are the ones who contribute to a belief in the possibility of happiness and the dominion of illusion, but they are not substantial enough for us to have faith in their solution. We see this again in *Léocadia,* where the characters are devoid of any real existence.

When Amanda affirms her reality in the face of the dream world of Prince Albert, we feel that this real Amanda is almost as ephemeral as the world of the Prince or the happiness of Isabelle in *Le rendez-vous de Senlis*. The reality she affirms is not the ugly reality of everyday life, but the illusion of the possibility of love in life, and an acceptance of the small change that life offers, which is a compromise in itself and part of the social lie that makes life possible. Such a reality is nonetheless as much an illusion as the dream of the Prince, and destined to vanish just as the vision of Léocadia vanishes. But Amanda is still more real than Léocadia, for she is not so fantastic, and while she plays her role she often stops to remind us that it is only a role and that she, Amanda, does not munch orchids or put her gloves on her plate.

The Prince tries to cling to the memory of Léocadia as his greatest reality—as a comfort for the boredom of everyday life—for she had taught him the value of a lie: "That madwoman had time to make me understand the worth of appearances."[33] But the illusion is not strong enough to conquer reality, and the Prince feels himself slowly falling back into the dullness of his pre-Léocadia existence. This is why he is almost hysterical in his efforts to hold on to the memory and so cruel to anyone who would change anything that he identifies with Léocadia. But slowly he is weaned away from one illusion and won over by another, the illusion of everyday actuality, which is nearer to what is real only insofar as a response to its claims is a necessary condition for survival. The struggle in *Léocadia*, then, is not so much between reality and dream as it is between two different dreams.

Like Prince Albert, Gaston in *Le voyageur sans bagage* becomes most disturbed and angry when his past, which is becoming only too real, is brought before him. Because he has forgotten it through his amnesia, it remains only a shadow, but it is a shadow of that unpleasant reality that Gaston would deny. He prefers his dream of a man without a past, to the acceptance of a past that does not conform to his dream. "If I am your son," he tells Mme Renaud, "I'll have to accustom myself to a truth so far from my dream . . ."[34] The words Gaston chooses indicate clearly enough that he realizes which is the truth and which the fiction in his life. Even if Jacques Renaud is only a phantom to Gaston, he is more real to everyone else than Gaston can be. In spite of this, Gaston must kill the real person he once was in order to live his dream, and in a symbolic gesture he breaks the mirror in which he perceives his reflection.

This mirror scene recalls Pirandello's *teatro dello specchio,* which depicts man suddenly confronted with the image of himself:

> Either he is astonished at his own appearance, or else he turns away his eyes so as not to see himself, or else in disgust he spits at his image, or, again, he clenches his fist to break it. In a word, there arises a crisis, and that crisis is my theatre.[35]

This crisis often lies at the center of Anouilh's plays. The protagonists of the *Pièces roses* drape the mirror so that the ugly reflection is no longer visible. The protagonists of the *Pièces noires* usually refuse to turn their backs upon the image, and, because they realize it cannot be changed, they must die in order to be honest. Gaston, however, breaks the mirror. The symbolic gesture, effective for the moment, will not be effective always, for if life is what Anouilh has led us to believe it is, Gaston will some day come before another mirror, and this time he will not be able to break it.

In *Eurydice* the mother and her lover Vincent cannot see themselves as they are. Their life is built upon appearances and has no real marrow to it. Their every action is a scene to play, and the events of their past are so empty and meaningless that they can be evoked only in terms of certain styles of clothing or archi tecture:

> *Vincent.* I was still wearing sideburns then. . .
> *The Mother.* The waxed moustaches of the gyp sies, the great mauve irises and the pale green renunculi decorating the walls. . . . It was the era of eyelet embroidery . . . I had a white dress.[36]

Life itself tends to be nothing more than superficial appearance in most peoples' eyes, and M. Henri suggests this in his metaphor: "Your life is there waiting for you like an old jacket you have to put on in the morning."[37]

In the *Nouvelles pièces noires,* with the exception of *Jézabel,* which belongs to Anouilh's first period, the author is not preoccupied with the problems of appearance and reality as such, although they are, as always, implicit in the relationship of the heroine to ugly reality. Antigone, Jeannette, and Médée refuse to accept what they know is the only reality possible in life. With equal determination they refuse to cheat by covering the truth with pretty illusion: "I don't play,"[38] says Antigone; "I don't want to learn to say yes. Everything is too ugly,"[39] cries Jeannette; and Médée shouts mockingly at Jason, "Play the game, make the gesture, say yes! You're preparing a beautiful old age for yourself!"[40] That intimate reality which resides in being true to themselves is opposed to the reality of life, and so these heroines go down in death.

In the *Pièces brillantes* we are once more in the world of appearance and the theater. Like the *Pièces roses,* each of these plays has within it a masquerade or a play of some kind.

L'invitation au château is a lively and sometimes fantastic farce with an air of fairy tale about it. Perhaps it is dangerous to take too seriously the ideas expressed in this play, but there are certain elements worth noting. The roles of Horace and Frédéric are played by the same actor. They are thus physically identical. The only distinction lies in their personalities, and, as Frédéric points out, "If I resembled Horace morally too, I would be Horace."[41] In other words, the apparent reality would so dominate the truth that the two brothers would seem one. Actually, this may be so, for the theatrical aspect of the play is stressed, and Anouilh winks at his audience as everyone breathlessly expects the two brothers to appear on stage at the same time. But the butler appears instead of Horace, and Frédéric exclaims, "I was sure he wouldn't come."[42] Horace sends a note: "For reasons which you will all understand, I cannot join you in the midst of general rejoicing."[43] This playing with the audience and letting them in, so to speak, on the backstage secrets, emphasizes the artificiality of the play and makes us realize that the happy ending of the charming diversion is a contrived one, and that the whole picture is to amuse us, and not to present any true image of life. *L'invitation au château* is essentially a *pièce rose* and possesses the characteristics of the earlier *Pièces roses*. The action is fantastic in its complications, and the characters are unreal. Again there is a *meneur de jeu,* who is really none other than the author himself. This permits the play to assume that lightness of tone which life does not really have.

In *Colombe* we are in the theater itself, backstage, and we see the ugly reality that lies beneath the enchanting surface of the stage. Madame Alexandra is revealed on the one hand as actually a *monstre sacré:* selfish, cruel, sensuous, and faithless—a Jézabel who has been successful in life. To her public, however, she is presented as a devoted mother; as love personified. Colombe is the central figure of the play, and in her we see the appeal that the glamour and artificiality of the theater can have for a person who is not really evil but is only weak. It is so pleasant to forget the hardness of life as Julien had revealed it to her, and to lose herself in the theatrical illusion and in the belief that all is permitted to the artist (the delusion of father Tarde, and of Orphée's father). She sees life as the gestures that one makes rather than the hard reality and fidelity to an ideal self.

The particular charm of *La répétition* lies in the ingenious manner in which Anouilh has blended his dialogue with that of Marivaux's play which the characters are preparing, so that it is sometimes difficult to distinguish whether the people are speaking their own words or are quoting from the play they are rehearsing. The entire play is performed in Louis XV costumes, although it is clear almost from the beginning that the period is modern. This fact is undoubtedly partly responsible for the artificiality of the play, which, as Marsh says, "makes it far less disturbing than usual— it is somehow too remote to be the direct attack on the audience, the prosecution of our basic values, that we have discovered in Anouilh hitherto."[44] The use of the eighteenth century costumes with the modern speech accentuates the theatrical aspect of *La répétition,* and of life itself as a comedy. The Count stresses this when he tells Héro that women do not understand the theater: "When they have to depict someone other than themselves, they don't enjoy it."[45] Héro also draws the parallel between life and the theater: "I have to be a bit disgusting," he tells Lucile. "It's part of my role. Not the one in Marivaux's play, but in the other—the one I really play."[46] Life is a play. Like Pirandello, Anouilh here sees human life itself as theatrical, and man condemned to play a certain role. The parallel is carried throughout the play, not only in the analogies between the situation in *La double inconstance* of Marivaux and the lives of the people who are rehearsing it, but by references to the role, the game, and the play—all of which are parts of life. The Countess suggests that Héro may aid in ridding them of Lucile by seducing her:

Héro (*declaiming*). "And what do you command

at present, my lord? That I please that woman and become her lover?"

The Countess. You can do it, Héro, if you want to. The child is a romantic little fool, a little shop-girl, if not worse. All Paris knows you're irresistible. Seduce her. So much the worse if we play *Ruy Blas!*[47]

Lucile is the only one who is not playing a role.[48] Simple and honest, she is always herself and unblinded by any rose-colored illusions of life. She realizes there are two lives. One is pleasant and brief; the other dull and long. Of her love for the Count, she wants, "Nothing but to feel good for a minute in his arms. . . . Afterward, if I have to live the other life, the real one, the one you have to earn. . . . it doesn't matter."[49] Like Sylvia in Marivaux's play, Lucile knows that the milieu into which she has stepped is a false one:

Sylvia. This country is something frightful! I have never seen such obliging women, such virtuous men. Such gentle manners, so many bows, so many compliments, so many signs of friendship. You would say they are the finest people in the world—kind and conscientious. What a mistake![50]

Reality is not the polished surface—the few delightful moments in which we succeed in deceiving others and ourselves. It is the tedious everyday life which all of us would like to escape in our dreams, but which we must face if we are to be honest. Héro and Lucile are the two poles: one refuses to be deluded and the other forgets his sad reality in drink.

Cécile ou L'école des pères (1949), also one of the *Pièces brillantes,* is a one-act masquerade in the style of Molière. Once again the characters are conscious that they are part of a play, although they may pretend not to be. When Araminthe tells M. Orlas that the Chevalier is going to abduct his daughter that very night, he replies: "Ah! Ah! That's a fine joke! Do you take me for a fool? For a comedy father? Do you

153

imagine I'm going to wrap myself in a dark cloak and catch cold in the garden just to see if I can't find a ladder?"[51] And this is precisely what he does. He is, in fact, a *père de comédie*. The play continues on this self-consciously theatrical note as Araminthe tells the audience she knows M. Orlas will show up in the garden. "He may catch cold there, he may find love there . . . Or perhaps both. We'll see. The author doesn't know himself."[52] Anouilh is winking at us again. As in *L'invitation au château*, we see that this diversion is only a diversion and not life. As the play draws to a happy ending, Araminthe, using the same words as Mme Desmermortes in *L'invitation au château*, complains, "This little comedy is becoming a bit long."[53] But she has not been worried; she is the *meneur de jeu* and as such can explain to M. Orlas, "I was in on the secret of the play, monsieur, and in the theater all ends well always."[54] The inference here, presumably, is that in life all does not end well. This is the lesson of the four *Pièces brillantes*. The two that are frankly false and theatrical through and through are gay and have happy endings. The other two in which the theater plays a part, but in which ugly reality is also present to a large degree, end unhappily, with the dream withered and reality dominant. *L'invitation au château* and *Cécile* appear optimistic, as do the *Pièces roses*, but when studied in the light of the author's key phrases as well as in the context of his entire theater, they are seen to represent the superficial world of dream and illusion which we would like to enter into wholeheartedly, but which is inevitably destroyed in life by reality itself.

The characters in *Ardèle* and its sequel, *La valse des toréadors*, have fought a losing struggle against life and have no illusions left. There is little attempt in these plays to combat reality with dreams, or to impose the image of an ideal self upon ugly reality. The Antigones and Thérèses have vanished. The Juliettes and Georges are on the periphery only, and in *Ardèle* we see their last struggles as they drown, surrounded by the morass of reality—Ardèle and her lover together, Nicolas alone —playing their losing game with life.

What we see in these plays is not reality alone but a fusion of reality and theatricality. There is still a consciousness of the play as a play, especially in *La valse des toréadors,* where the Doctor answers the General that all will end well as in the good old days of the theater,[55] and where the General, growing impatient with the intrigue, demands, "Will this comedy never end?"[56] He is referring both to the play in the theater and to his own situation within the play. The theatrical consciousness is introduced toward the end of the play and in such a way that a certain contrast is established between the reality of the ugly part of the play and the unreality of the happy ending.

L'alouette is built on two levels. The first is that of the courtroom and the burning. The second, played within this framework, which represents a stage, is made up of the most important scenes from Jeanne's life; and they are clearly scenes in a play, contrasted to the more striking reality of the trial, which, for Warwick the skeptical materialist, is the only reality:

> *Warwick.* Are we all here? Good. Then let's have the trial, right away. The quicker she's judged and burned, the better it will be for everyone.
> *Cauchon.* But, Monseigneur, there's the whole story to play out. Domrémy, the Voices, Vaucouleurs, Chinon, the Coronation . . .
> *Warwick.* Masquerades! That's the story for children. The beautiful white armor, the standard, the tender and hard warrior virgin. That's how they'll make her statues later to conform to the needs of another regime. . . . You aren't going to reënact all the battles at any rate, are you? Orléans, Patay, Beaugency . . . That would be extremely disageeable for me.
> *Cauchon* (*smiles*). Rest assured, Monseigneur,

155

there are not enough of us to reënact the bat-
tles . . .[57]

The scenes from the life of Jeanne are frankly theatrical—played before the tribunal (the audience) by
a set of characters. There is no attempt to evoke the
scenes by a series of flashbacks. In fact, there is some
doubt in Warwick's mind as to the authenticity of these
presentations.[58] Jeanne, as she relives the decisive moments of her life, remains the Jeanne of the trial. She
wears no "white armor," rides only an imaginary horse
with La Hire, and weaves back and forth from the
present reality to the past scenes, which are presented
as not being quite so real. All this has a dizzying effect
upon Jeanne, so that when the Inquisitor asks her if she
believes herself to be in a state of grace at this moment,
she replies:

At what moment, Sire? It's hard to know just where
we are. Everything is mixed up. At the beginning
when I hear my Voices or at the end of the trial
when I've understood that my king and my friends
have also abandoned me, when I have doubted,
when I have abjured and then taken it back?[59]

It should be noted that this speech occurs near the
beginning of the trial long before Jeanne is abandoned
or abjures her Voices. Jeanne's foreknowledge of the
trial's outcome tends to establish the courtroom scene
as a part of a play also, and to destroy the reality–
fantasy distinction that Warwick would uphold.

The play reminds one of a rehearsal in which, at
times, the play characters have become confused with
the real characters, and the two levels are so inter-
mingled that it sometimes becomes difficult to distinguish between them. *L'alouette* is reminiscent of Pirandello's *Six Characters in Search of an Author*. The
theater accepted as a theater is parallel to the courtroom
in which the members of the court form an audience
while viewing the play of Jeanne's life. The difference
is that Pirandello's six characters, although more real in

their suffering than the flesh-and-blood actors, are creatures of fiction and exist chiefly, if not exclusively, in their roles as characters; whereas Jeanne lives on both levels, in the "present" of the courtroom, and in the "pasts" and "futures" of the scenes she reënacts. Jeanne is placed in the timeless light of the stage, and, like Antigone, in a neutral setting. The Pirandellian method is evident, but Anouilh's treatment is not the same. Jeanne's scenes represent what the Inquisitor calls man's "unconquered image of himself,"[60] and to which he would oppose the Idea—abstract, impersonal, inhuman, and for Anouilh we may safely say, nonexistent. *L'Idée* can be equated to the nothingness of life to which man gives meaning by constructing an ideal image of himself. For most men—we have seen it in the previous plays—the image serves only as a screen, and hence has no value. When it is an ideal image representing the hero's truest inner self, it cannot withstand the corrupting forces of life, and can be victorious only through death. Even then it may be an illusory victory, for there is no one but the hero to appreciate it, and he has perished. In *L'alouette*, however, Jeanne's death, or rather her decision to die in order to remain herself, results in her becoming her ideal unconquered self forever, not only in her own eyes, but in the eyes of the world, and as the play-scene of Charles' coronation at Reims is reënacted, the curtain falls upon "this lovely prize-book illustration . . ."[61] We have no reason here to believe that the ending is a contrived one to give a rose-colored glow to what would otherwise have been "black." The implication is not that Jeanne was not burned, but that the reality of her achievements is greater than the reality of her death. This is what Charles expresses:

> The true ending of the story of Jeanne d'Arc, the true ending that will never end, the one that will be told and retold forever when all the other names have been forgotten or confused, is not in

her misery of a hunted animal in Rouen—it's the
lark high in the open sky, it's Jeanne at Reims in
all her glory . . . The true ending of the story of
Jeanne is happy. Jeanne d'Arc is a story with a
happy ending!⁶²

And Beaudricourt, joyously clearing away the fagots
from about Jeanne, cries: "Fortunately I arrived in
time . . . The idiots, they were going to burn Jeanne
d'Arc! Do you understand?"⁶³

In *L'alouette* Anouilh presents us with a view of the
theater accepted as such, and thus continues the trend
we noted particularly in the *Pièces roses* and the
Pièces brillantes. But in this play we see the stage even
more clearly as a stage. It also continues the trends of
the *Pièces roses* and the *Pièces brillantes* in that the
image dominates reality, but in *L'alouette* we feel for
once that this inner image is the ultimate reality, and
the world of objective reality, represented by the courtroom, is less real ultimately, although it may appear
more real at the moment. The "rose" and the "black"
come together. The seriousness of tone, and the theme
of heroic man refusing to accept ugly reality as final,
blends with the conscious theatricality and the domination of the vision. But this optimism is short-lived.

With *Ornifle, Pauvre Bitos,* and *L'hurluberlu* we
have returned to the disillusioned world of the earlier
Pièces grinçantes. There is no longer the victorious
vision of a Jeanne d'Arc, and the unpleasant everyday
world resumes its place in the foreground. Reality and
theatricality blend once again. Ornifle is living the Don
Juan role that he forces upon himself, "par rigueur."⁶⁴
He even plays the later part of the play in seventeenth-
century costume, for he has been invited to a costume
ball. His doctors, likewise guests at the ball, play their
scenes not only dressed as doctors out of a Molière play
but actually using the words of some of Molière's characters. We are clearly in the world of the theater.

In *Pauvre Bitos* the world of make-believe is suggested from the beginning by the *dîner de têtes* at which each guest will impersonate a character from the French Revolution. When Bitos arrives dressed as Robespierre, his host and the guests torment him by treating him as though he really were the tyrant, since his role of petty official in real life corresponds in a small way to Robespierre's tyranny. As if this were not sufficient, in the second act Anouilh shows us a Bitos who has actually become Robespierre. Along with the other guests, now become the personages they were originally only impersonating, he, like Jeanne, plays over the scenes of his life. There is an interplay of realities as Robespierre watches his own life played before his eyes, and at the same time remains Bitos who, over his powdered wig, wears his modern derby hat. The guest playing the part of Mirabeau reminds Bitos, "We are in the theatre."[65] And, indeed, we are quite obviously in the theater, and life is a masquerade.

In *L'hurluberlu* the characters are once again preparing a play, and in the last act most of them are in pseudo-Spanish costumes. Before climbing onto the stage for a dress rehearsal, the General turns to his young son with a word of advice: "We must play the play gaily. Man is a disconsolate and cheerful animal . . . You'll see, as you grow up, Toto, that in life, even when it appears to be serious, it's really nothing but a Punch and Judy show. And we always perform the same play."[66]

The Multiplicity of Personality

Intimately related to the theme of appearance and reality is that of the multiplicity of personality. We have already seen evidence of the problem in *Léocadia* where the Prince attempts to build up an imaginary woman and convince himself that he loved her. His case is not so tragic, however, for Amanda is there to take the place of his vanished illusion.

Marc in *Jézabel* is not so fortunate. He clings desperately to the memory of his mother as she was when he was a child. As we see her in the play, Marc's mother is a ruined creature who has given herself to drink and sensual pleasure in a vain search for happiness. For Marc, she is a hated being and no longer his mother. His true mother is the woman whose photograph he keeps hidden with his papers. She is the young, innocent, and kind creature that "Jézabel" once was. In a dramatic scene the two mothers confront each other; while rummaging through a drawer the mother comes across the old photograph:

> (*She caresses it with her finger, arranges her hair, pulls back the wrinkles around her eyes, smiles at the photograph.*) Marc, you kept it? You kept this photograph! And yet I've looked for it, but you didn't want to tell me you had it here, with your young man's letters, like the photograph of a mistress . . . (*A pause.*) A mistress in leg-of-mutton sleeves. Then you do love me a little? (*A pause.*) That one perhaps, but *me*? (*She goes to the mirror, looks at herself without moving, her face expressionless. Suddenly she tears up the photograph without looking at it.*)[67]

When Marc discovers what she has done and asks her why, she responds:

> *The Mother.* It was my right. It was a photograph of me, wasn't it?
> *Marc* (*shouts*). No!
> (*A silence, they look at each other.*)
> *The Mother* (*slowly*). That's why I tore it up.[68]

The mother realizes, as does Marc, that there are two women, not simply two facets of one woman. The debased old mother of today in no way resembles the mother of the photograph. She destroys the picture not because it is a reminder of what she once was, but because it is a form of competition for the affections of her son and she is jealous of the mother in the photograph. That is the mother Marc loves. "But I?" she asks. This personality split in temporal as well as spatial dimensions recalls the dualism of the real and the apparent: the Jézabel we see on the stage is the actual mother, whereas the photograph represents a now-dead "idealized" mother who lives only in the mind of Marc. In truth, the idealized mother was the real mother, for she not only corresponds to Marc's need, but she was the young and vibrant creature who lived deeply. The old woman who has prostituted herself is less real; she is a puppet who is playing the game of life—a masquerade in which she neither feels the love she pretends for her men, nor experiences any deep emotion. She is a victim of habit, and her life is a lie. But, objectively speaking, this vulgar existence is all that remains to her. All Marc's efforts are in vain: no matter how real the mother of his inner vision may have been, he is forced to realize that for all practical purposes she is non-existent; that the ugly brute reality is the depraved woman he sees before him.

A similar problem exists for Gaston in *Le voyageur sans bagage.* He must decide which is the true Gaston —the unidentified amnesiac or the spoiled child of the Renaud family. "Me. Me. I exist in spite of all your stories,"[69] Gaston exclaims. What is this "me" he is asserting but a neutral personality that has no past and as yet no future, and no really perceptible present? This "me" is no person at all, whereas the memories of Jacques Renaud, his past, are very real for a whole group of people. If Gaston were a character of Unamuno, we might establish as his true personality the one that he was desiring to become, but Anouilh has not infused him with any creative will; his wish is a negative one. He desires to destroy the ugly reality of his past. His dream is another version of the social lie. In fleeing from his objectively real self Gaston clings to an illusion that will make life acceptable for him.

This quality of illusion which life requires is reflected in *Eurydice* by the fact that Orphée's Eurydice is a figment of his imagination and cannot live if he sees her as she really is: "Don't look at me. Let me live,"[70] she pleads with him. But Orphée must see reality as it is, so he looks at her and his dream vanishes. For Orphée to refuse to see Eurydice as she is—not to see her past which is forever a part of her—would be to escape into the world of illusion as Gaston does. Even if he had done this, M. Henri makes it clear that the illusion was destined to vanish and Orphée would have become "the gentleman who deceives Eurydice."[71]

Eurydice, for her part, realizes that her reality could never have corresponded to the ideal image of Orphée: "You saw me as beautiful, my love. . . . You saw me as strong, as pure. . . . I could never have lived up to it."[72] She is satisfied to return to death and there, idealized, to await her Orphée.

Even Julien, the intransigent hero of *Colombe*, seeks a certain consolation in the vision of the Colombe he knew when they first met: a Colombe who was an illusion doomed inevitably to disappear. Julien could no more possess a materialization of his ideal Colombe than Orphée could of his Eurydice. All he can do is to keep her in his memory; he attempts to do so and forbids the real Colombe to destroy that vision:

> *Julien.* Don't say anything against the Colombe of two years ago. I'm keeping that one! She's mine!
> *Colombe.* Yours, poor man? Because you knew that one too! An angel, wasn't she? At least you thought so? . . . Keep her if you want, your sugary sweet Colombe, but that sweet little hypocrite, I can tell you right now, was nothing but one of your day dreams, like all the rest, my poor darling.
> *Julien (has taken her by the arms and is shaking her insanely).* I forbid you, do you hear, I forbid you to tarnish her!
> *Colombe.* It's certainly my right. After all, it's me we're talking about, isn't it?
> *Julien.* No![73]

Like Gaston and like Prince Albert, Julien reacts almost hysterically to any attempt to destroy his dream. But

162

unlike the others, he is not able to maintain the dream. The real Colombe dominates the Colombe of his mind whom he had believed to be the real one. The world is even uglier than before: "everything has become too ugly. . . . I'm so lonely tonight."[74] He is alone, with not even an image left to cling to. The retrospective vision with which the play ends does not constitute a happy ending with the protagonist losing himself in illusion. On the contrary, Julien has already been rudely awakened. The end of the play serves to heighten the feeling of loneliness by showing us what hopes have been destroyed. This ending also, of course, points up Anouilh's belief that even the couples who seem destined from the start to be happy cannot win.

Colombe, as well as *Jézabel* and *Eurydice* (and *Le voyageur sans bagage,* indirectly), is a play whose progress is largely directed toward the recognition of the real personality as it unfolds inescapably in spite of the desperate efforts of the persons involved to create a desirable imaginary one.

In *La valse des toréadors* we see the old Général Saintpé who thinks he is still young beneath his disguise of old age, but both the young Lieutenant Saintpé and the youthful Mlle Sainte-Euverte are dead, and only a tender memory of them remains. Mademoiselle de Sainte-Euverte was in love with the young lieutenant. She does not recognize the touch of the old General, who has lost the purity of his youth. He cannot become what he is not, for he is irrevocably what he is. Man is trapped within his role, struggling vainly to become something he cannot become. The ideal man, the inner vision, the creature of childhood, is gone forever. The only reality it possesses is an evanescent one within man's vision. In the world of objective reality in which man lives and to which he is committed as a member of society, only the abject creature who has said yes to life has any meaning.

Ornifle and *Pauvre Bitos* suggest the same bitter conclusion. Ornifle, in the final analysis, is not a heroic Don Juan, but a cruel and facile man who has been defeated by life. Bitos at the end of his story proves to be a petty, vindictive tyrant and an unbearable prig. A synthesis of vision with reality is ultimately impossible, Anouilh tells us.

Becket, with its more positive vision, seems to suggest that perhaps the former Chancellor and playboy has at last, upon becoming Archbishop, found his real role. And yet, even as cleric, Becket remains to a certain extent "absent," for his role still seems too simple to him. Like Camus' Stranger, he is standing outside and watching himself live. And in the final analysis the positive value that he represents, and which serves as subtitle to the play, may simply be another of man's illusions in his constant struggle to impose meaning upon nothingness. The final note of the play is that of compromise sounded by the hypocritical penance of Henry in the interests of political expediency.

Unlike the Pirandello of *Right You Are*, Anouilh does not take a relative position in regard to personality. Instead of retaining their veils as does the mysterious daughter-wife who appears at the end of the Italian work, leaving everyone as bewildered as before, Anouilh's characters are unmasked in the cruel light of the stage, and shown to be only what they objectively are.

5

The Characters:
Psychology and Symbols

SERIOUS DRAMATISTS of France today, like Sartre, Camus, and Anouilh, seem no longer to regard character as the kernel of the drama. They present not so much a psychological study as they do a picture of man's predicament, in which the personages are representative of various aspects of man and of life itself. This is not to say that these authors are writing allegories in which men are stripped of lifelike qualities and presented only as symbols. But psychology is too abstract, says Sartre. "For us a man is a whole enterprise in himself. And passion is a part of that enterprise."[1] According to Sartre, the contemporary French playwrights present more specifically a conflict of rights, embodied in characters who are dominated by a passion at the core of which is an invincible will. In addition to being an individual, each character is a symbol as well, and this latter aspect of the characters is undoubtedly more important than a realistic psychology; yet without the presentation of the characters as living individuals, their symbolic meaning would fail to reach us effectively.

In the theater of Anouilh we find characters who are often convincingly alive, and at the same time possess a symbolic meaning, for Anouilh presents what René-Marill Albérès calls a "philosophical drama":

Like other modern writers, however, Anouilh has given up painting human passions in order to paint the human condition. One might thus find in all his work that philosophical drama which he constantly avoided before writing *Antigone*.[2]

Anouilh's characters are a mixture of the realistic and the exaggerated. Some are extremely lifelike, some entirely artificial; whereas others contain both characteristics in varying degrees.

Modes of Characterization

In the serious plays of the first period, the realistic note dominates. The protagonist who is unwilling to accept life as he sees it, profoundly aware of life's absurdity, is often a complex personage who is lifelike because of his very complexity. The other characters—those of the mediocre race who have accepted life without trying to understand it, without realizing the baseness of their action—live on a much more superficial plane than the heroic individuals, but they are also real on the stage. In their mediocrity, pushed to the point of caricature, they are pathetically real. In fact, one of them, Jézabel, is pathologically complex. All the characters have been formed by their backgrounds and environments to which they are hopelessly bound; tied forever to their old selves and to the filth of their past.

The complexity of the characters is apparent from the first play in the person of Frantz, the illogical young man who adopts an antisocial means to attain a position in that very society he hates. He is so dominated by his desire that even when the opportunity arises to better his condition by fair means, he blindly goes on with his original plans to murder the Duchess. Frantz's motives are never made clear to us, and his passionate reiterations that he desires purity above all else suggest he may be trying to convince himself of the purity of his motivations. Frantz creates himself before our very eyes. We are never aware of any intentions of the author in his characterization; those very doubts that we feel in regard to his words and acts make Frantz a richer creation, a more real person. As Ortega y Gasset has pointed out, in real life no person is presented to us neatly characterized. Instead, we get one impression today, a different one tomorrow, and finally form a concept of the person, sometimes one fraught with doubts and contradictions. We get such an impression from Frantz, of whom a reviewer said, "One feels the flow of human truth: a truth that springs from the intrepid flow of youth."[3]

This same "intrepid flow" is seen in *La sauvage,* of which Marcel Berger says, "The dramatist plays with us like a cat with a mouse."[4] We alternate between one opinion and another as we seek to understand the heroine. Thérèse has all the complexity of a living person with her pathetic hesitation between a shallow happiness with Florent and fidelity to herself in the wretched environment in which she grew up. She is different from Frantz, and more sympathetic than he, for she is more normally irresolute—not so blinded by one idea that she cannot see the advantages of the other side. Her tragedy is that her character, which demands utter purity, will not allow her to make the compromise that would have made life so simple and pleasant. Anouilh's portrait of Thérèse is thoroughly convincing and one of the most touching of his entire theater. Indeed, Jean Didier goes so far as to say: "Never, we believe, has a dramatist gone so deep into the unfathomable mysteries of the heart as in *La Sauvage.* Rarely has a man of the theater touched the depths of anguish with such rigor and lucidity."[5]

In *Jézabel* the characters are again presented in a realistic way, and even in the melodramatic situation in which Anouilh places them we are easily convinced of their reality. The mother is a pathological character, but she is consistent insofar as human beings are ever con-

167

sistent. She succeeds in awakening our sympathy to some extent, because we are shown the causes of her condition: her past, her unhappy marriage, and the natural weakness of her flesh. For her, life is suffering because she cannot see it in any terms except those of the sensual urges, which have acquired the mechanical nature of habit. She is caught, and yet she realizes the emptiness of seeking satisfaction in that habit.

Georges (*Le rendez-vous de Senlis*) and Gaston (*Le voyageur sans bagage*) both come alive through the visions of a happier life and of themselves which they have created. They reveal themselves not so much through their actions as through their dreams. Gaston is characterized by a contrast with the past his family is trying to force upon him, and Georges by the past he has invented for himself and for his ideal parents and friend. Both he and Gaston like to imagine their pasts in similar ways. Each of them has an imaginary friend. Gaston has invented a memory of such a friend:

> But among thousands of possible memories, it was precisely the memory of a friend which I was summoning up with most fondness. I've built everything upon the memory of that imaginary friend. Our impassioned walks, the books we discovered together, a girl that he had loved at the same time as I did, and that I had given up for him, and even —you're going to laugh—that I had saved his life one day in a little boat.[6]

Georges has transformed a commonplace and dubious friendship into an ideal relationship of boyhood in which it was his friend who made sacrifices. This is how he had presented that relationship to Isabelle, who now questions the "old friend":

> *Isabelle.* Is it true that you saved his life in a boat one day?
> *Robert.* In a boat? No, Mademoiselle, I'm sorry, but I don't know how to swim.

168

Isabelle (*after a pause*). Ah! And the girl that you gave up for him?
Robert. A girl I gave up? No, I don't remember. Forgive me, Mademoiselle, but I've never heard anything about such a girl.[7]

Of these characters of the first period, Thérèse, Frantz, and Jézabel attain a certain realism by the complexity of their natures. Gaston and Georges are much less complex characters and lack the lifelike quality of a Thérèse. Most of the secondary characters are even more simplified: people with one single drive, whether it be money, sexual passion, or drink. Frequently they are caricatures—simple types often broadly contrasting with each other, or with the major figures of the drama.

In the other *Pièces roses* of the same period we find a decided contrast to the realism of the *Pièces noires*. Although there are characters of the "black" world treated in a realistic way in *Le rendez-vous de Senlis*, in *Le bal des voleurs* and *Léocadia* we see people who have escaped into the play, who make of life a game. These people are clearly puppet-like: the pickpockets, the Dupont-Duforts, Lord Edgard in *Le bal des voleurs*, the Duchess, and the Baron and the valets of *Léocadia*. Characters like Lady Hurf, Juliette, the Prince, and Amanda are barely on the edge of realistic treatment; their suffering and their realization that there is some decision to be made gives them more reality than those unthinking creatures who merely exist.

The similarity to the realist dramatists which we find in this first group of Anouilh's plays might be misleading. Anouilh presents his characters and their realistic milieux not as ends in themselves but as representatives of man's estate. Rather than trying to prove, in the manner of Zola, that given certain conditions a person will grow in a certain way, Anouilh is presenting characters of symbolic significance.

In the second period realism occupies a less important

169

place than in the early plays. With Eurydice, fantasy has invaded the serious play. Although Orphée and Eurydice are both creatures of their environment, they are not complex characters. Through their suffering they come alive, and through their desire for purity they take on a new realism, for the seekers after purity are the favored children of Anouilh. As he has said elsewhere: "These characters exist. They are already half alive. Someone believes in them."[8] But already we see them more clearly as symbols. The air of fantasy which invades the play; the presence of M. Henri; and the title of the play itself; all prepare us for a more universal application of the characters and their predicament. In *Eurydice,* where the fundamental problems are treated as such for the first time, we also find for the first time that tendency toward abstractness which becomes patent in *Antigone.* In the four plays of the second group (*Eurydice, Antigone, Roméo et Jeannette, Médée*) we see the characters more clearly as representatives of man's condition. With the exception of Orphée and Frédéric, there is very little character development in the traditional sense, for the characters become only more like themselves, rather than changing in any way. They may pass through new experiences, but they are not altered essentially; rather, they are confirmed in their original strength or weakness.

Although the characters are less realistic in the conventional sense of the word, perhaps they are more so in their strength of will and their desire to find that inner purity without which life is impossible for them. As Marsh has said, "They present the essence of their predicament."[9] And the predicament of each one is similar to that of the others and to that of all mankind caught within the trap of life of which Médée speaks. They represent, therefore, the essence of the *human* predicament, as well as the private one in which they are enmeshed. They resemble each other, and yet they are different. Jeannette is not Antigone, nor could she ever be. Nor is Médée like Antigone or Jeannette. They resemble each other only insofar as each must remain faithful to what she believes to be her truest self. They are beings who act for no one but themselves. Proud or arrogant, they cannot abide the pity of others.

The puppet-like creatures of the *Pièces roses* whose bare strings are clearly visible have no part in the plays of the second period. The mediocre people who live fed by illusion possess a pathetic reality. Even if they are puppets, they are real insofar as they are accurate representations of types that are common in life. The method of emphasis through caricature and exaggeration is still employed.

In the plays of the third period the puppet characters dominate the scene. For the most part the spectator is aware of them as characters in a play rather than as living people. At times the realistic presentation typical of the first period is seen, as in the major characters of *Colombe,* and in the persons of Général Saintpé and Ornifle, who attain a complexity not usually found in this period. The others painted in light strokes are once again of an exaggerated simplicity: sometimes laughable, sometimes pitiable, often grotesque. Except for Julien in *Colombe,* the hero is no longer presented so convincingly; his inner fire is but a faint gleam compared with that bright flame burning within Antigone or Thérèse. In the last of the *Pièces grinçantes,* Bitos, the hero, has become an antihero; the characteristics of Thérèse and Antigone are perverted in such a way as to make Bitos appear despicable.

The most intense reality is possessed by the central figures of each of the serious plays, whereas the mediocre characters appear in a more superficially realistic light—real only as representative of a certain type. The hero is highlighted as a man of flesh and blood placed within a sort of vacuum of misunderstanding, within which the superficially alive people cannot penetrate. The hero's solitude is thus emphasized, and Anouilh's treatment of his characters is seen to be closely bound up with his major themes. Those characters who have accepted life and believe with Armand of *Colombe* that life is in the gestures one makes and the words one speaks, possess for the most part only the superficial reality of caricatures. The members of the heroic race burn with an inner fire, and by this fire create an intense life of their own.

Characteristic of Anouilh's theater is the narrow range of types who often recur from play to play. Since all his plays deal with the same problems, and Anouilh's view of man is essentially the same from his earliest plays to his latest, a kinship of characters is to be expected. A change in focus, emphasis, aspect, or detail gives sufficient variety to make each play an exciting exploration of man's problems.

The Personal Types

The most important of the recurrent characters is the hero, of course. The hero, from whatever period he may be, is primarily motivated by his desire for purity. This is his constant theme, but it is one that is capable of many variations. For Frantz, purity means the winning of wealth and a socially recognized union with Monime; for Marc, it lies in accepting the weight of the past of his family background while keeping himself free from easy habit; Thérèse sees it not only in fidelity to the past but in a renunciation of the shallow life she could have led with her rich fiancé; for Ludovic, it means flight from family and society to a life where he can preserve his spontaneity and his sympathy for his fellow human beings; for Gaston, it is also a flight from the past, but an easy and convenient refusal to accept his old self, as well; for Antigone, for Orphée, for Frédéric, and for Jeannette, purity can be found only in death; for Médée, the same is true, with the distinction that she must find death through a return to her real self. With varying degrees of fixity, they all have the same passion, but in some it is noble, in others it is an ironic distortion of nobility, and yet in others a desperate but convenient effort to reject the ignoble self. And again, in some it seems quite normal, whereas in others we feel it is pathological.

The hero, moreover, is aware that life is not all *rose*, and that one cannot ultimately escape into a happy illusion. When people like Gaston refuse to face their old selves, they are not being true to the heroic role. It is such differences in the solution of their problems which give variety to the heroes of this theater, and make some stand out as stronger characters than others. The keenest awareness is that of an Antigone, who realizes that the very act of living is impossible if one is to conserve one's purity. For this reason the heroines of the second period—those who are most heroic in their absolute refusal of life—invariably seek death as the only solution.

It is noteworthy that the most heroic characters in Anouilh's theater are young girls. Thérèse, Antigone, and Jeannette are heroines of the first importance, and such heroes as Frantz, Marc, and Orphée seem weak beside them. Related to them are the paler heroines of the rose or brilliant world; the poor girls who, in a wealthy milieu, attempt to remain true to themselves: Amanda, Isabelle, and Lucile.

The Relational Types

The lineage of Madame Alexandra in her role as mother may be traced back to Jézabel, through Mme Tarde, Mme Renaud, Mme Delachaume, Eurydice's mother, and Isabelle's mother (*L'invitation au château*). All Anouilh's mothers are cut from the same material, although there are individual variations. Selfishness is the dominant characteristic: instead of desiring the happiness of their children, they seek their own comfort and contentment. They prefer to satisfy their own physical needs, whatever they may be, and their own

173

petty vanity, rather than allow their children to have the happiness that they might have if freed from maternal ties. They are possessive women and, not infrequently, stingy. Jézabel cannot give up her dissolute life, even though her actions make it impossible for her son to find happiness. At the same time she maintains that she loves him and cannot live without him. She wants everything for herself—both her son and her weaknesses.

Madame Tarde, like Mme Delachaume, would push her child into a rich marriage so that she might enjoy the benefits of a wealthy son-in-law. She has no consideration for the real happiness of Thérèse. Or perhaps it would be fairer to say that she is incapable of visualizing happiness in any terms other than those of money, because her view has been warped by poverty. When she almost compels Thérèse to marry Florent, it is her belief that this is the way to happiness. Thérèse's renunciation is, of course, beyond the understanding of such people.

In *Le rendez-vous de Senlis* Georges describes his ideal mother to Mme de Montalembreuse, who is to portray her:

> *Georges.* The role of the mother . . . It's the most difficult. What a range of emotions—from the gray-wigged enemy who defends her heritage dearly, to the disturbing mother who trembles and loses the thread of the conversation, like a young girl in love, when her son enters or leaves the room!
>
> *Mme de Montalembreuse.* It's very simple: a good mother's role should include all mothers!
>
> *Georges.* No, I would like this one to be very simple. Obvious. A mother like those they describe in children's books. Like the ones little boys dream about in the kitchen near the maid while they're waiting for their real mother to come home— wearing too much perfume—from her endless afternoon errands. A mother who would have no

shopping to do, no friends to see. An admirable mother, in other words.

Mme de Montalembreuse. All mothers are admirable, my dear young man. Instinct speaks!

Georges. The slightest oversight is enough to spoil everything. A smile at a strange man which you fail to conceal. A single hard word on a day when you're exasperated and have in front of you only a disarmed, but intractable little enemy. A single kiss forgotten. And a child is there every day spying on you, requiring your all as tyrannically and minutely as a sergeant. Oh, I know the mother's role isn't easy. It's a role that won't allow stand-ins and which shouldn't be accepted lightly.[10]

The ideal mother aids, of course, in the search for purity; in the return to the prelapsarian world which all the heroes of Anouilh are seeking. But there exists no ideal mother, and the hero must seek alone, doomed to failure.

When Georges tests Mme de Montalembreuse by telling her he wants to marry a poverty-stricken young girl instead of the wealthy woman his mother had chosen for him, the actress, in the role of the ideal mother, falls right into the spirit of her role, and answers him: "if your happiness is somewhere else, don't hesitate; leave, and be happy. At your age, love is worth everything."[11] So convincing is her acting that Georges assumes she has actually experienced such an incident. As it turns out, she is a mother and her son had wanted to marry a poor girl. But the real mother's reaction was entirely different from that of the ideal mother: "Can you imagine! She was a little violinist . . . an insignificant little strumpet . . . Believe me, I smacked him down!"[12]

Madame Renaud had done much the same thing when her son Jacques, at the age of eighteen, had gone off to the war. There had been a fight between mother and son because she had refused to consent to his marriage with a poor seamstress. The son had shouted to his mother, "I hate you," and Mme Renaud, with wounded dignity and unbending pride, had locked herself in her room, refusing to make the first step of reconciliation. Thus, she had let him leave for the war and possible death without a farewell and without her blessing.

Eurydice's mother is too selfishly concerned with her own ridiculous affair with Vincent, and with her career as an actress, to pay much attention to her daughter. Her only constant admonition is, "Sit up straight." She is somewhat outside the stream of mothers; she is rather, as she calls herself, "an animal of the theater."

Isabelle's mother in *L'invitation au château* is foolish, sentimental, and selfish. She would have Isabelle make a marriage of convenience with Romainville so that their livelihood will be assured forever. She combines the romantic imagination of Eurydice's mother with the selfishness and moral weakness of the earlier mothers in Anouilh's theater.

In *Colombe* we are once again in the world of make-believe which is the stage. Madame Alexandra is revealed to her audience as a devoted mother, but Julien exposes the ugly underside of this picture when he describes his unhappy childhood—wasting away in a third-class pension, neglected by a mother too busy with her career and her lovers. Selfish and morally weak, Mme Alexandra possesses all the vices of the mothers in Anouilh's plays. Like many of them, she has not restrained herself sexually. Jézabel was hardly more than a prostitute, and Mme Tarde and Eurydice's mother were both living with men who were not their husbands. Isabelle's mother is unmarried. Jeannette's mother, we are told in *Roméo et Jeannette,* has run off with another man. And Mme Alexandra has gone through a good number of husbands and lovers, and she is probably not finished yet.

The fathers are shown in no better light than are the

mothers. Indeed, the parental couple is an abject pair. Real fathers, as Anouilh sees them, can hardly conform to the picture of the ideal father which Georges paints for us in *Le rendez-vous de Senlis:*

> *Georges.* You're a charming old gentleman, still quite young, with a youthfulness that time can't touch. You're the ideal father who gave up the "biblical" look along with his beard; the kind who was able to become a big brother in time. A big brother who wouldn't play at being a big brother, but a comrade; you're my comrade, papa. Besides, you dress just as I do, and even—it's so natural at your age—a bit younger.
>
> *Philemon.* But . . . a father just the same?
>
> *Georges (smiles).* Of course, papa . . . on the days when most big brothers would have the right to think of themselves first; the days when you have to be dedicated, to pardon, to give money too . . . On those days you become a real father, strong and reassuring, with whom your son can become a little boy for a while.[13]

The ideal father is conceived of, then, as being affectionate and capable of giving advice and help when needed; and when not needed in this capacity, he is a friend, not a commander. How far this is from the foolish, pompous father that is Georges' in reality; a man whom Georges supports, or rather, whom Georges' wife supports.

Marc's father in *Jézabel,* M. Tarde in *La sauvage,* Orphée's father, and Jeannette's father—are all weak, ineffectual, and lazy men who inflate their own egos and try to impress others with their importance. They are only deceiving themselves. They are frequently cuckolds, and too weak or insouciant to do anything about it. Marc's father gave up long ago, and has turned his attention upon his money and the maid. Orphée's father lives a dull day-to-day existence compounded of menu prices and a study of the best way to get the most for least. He is third-rate in every way, but he tries to make Orphée believe otherwise. At last he is reduced to admitting that he is not a good musician, despite his *second prix* at the Conservatoire d'Arcachon. He lacks what all these mediocre characters lack—the very quality that he lauds to Orphée and which he deludes himself into believing he possesses—a will of iron. Monsieur Tarde looks upon himself as an "old man to whom life refused everything,"[14] and is ever ready to place the responsibility for his weaknesses upon others, and to excuse himself on the grounds that he is an artist. "We are artists who are allowed all kinds of eccentricities,"[15] he claims. "I'm an old artist," says Jeannette's father, "I need a certain laxity around me."[16] All these fathers are men without character; lazy, good-for-nothing people without any real ambition, relying upon others and insisting at the same time that they are independent. They are optimistic because they are too shallow to see how pathetic they really are.

The friend occupies no better place than the parents in Anouilh's world. The ideal friend does not exist. As we have seen, he is twice described in somewhat similar terms as a person who is willing to make sacrifices; who will give up the woman he loves for his best friend; who will risk his life to save him. In reality, Anouilh suggests, friends are somewhat different. Georges in *Le rendez-vous de Senlis* had wisely decided not to have anyone impersonate the friend, so that he might remain a perfect friend. But Robert arrives at the house at Senlis, and it turns out that the real friend—stingy, selfish, jealous, petty, and vicious—in no way resembles the ideal one.

In *Le voyageur sans bagage* Gaston thinks he must have had a beautiful friendship as a young man. He imagines it in the terms described above. But when he discovers the real situation his dream fades. Rather than give up the woman he loved, or thought he loved, for his "friend," the young Jacques Renaud had quarreled

178

with his friend and pushed him down the stairs, causing a spinal injury that made him bed-ridden for life.

The other "friends" in Anouilh's world fare little better. Philippe (*L'hermine*) and Hartmann (*La sauvage*) are incapable of understanding the people whose friends they profess to be. Hartmann is from a different kind of background from Florent's, and his love for him is a mixture of envy and admiration. Héro in *La Répétition* is the Count's old friend, and it is he who, nursing an old grudge, gets back at Tigre by seducing the innocent girl who might have saved the Count from mediocrity. Perhaps the Doctor in *La valse des toréadors* comes closest to being the ideal friend, for he is sympathetic and devoted to the old General and helps him in every way he can to understand himself and his role in life. But even he fails to be effective, for the Doctor and the General, like everyone else, are shut off from each other by walls of flesh, and any true understanding is impossible.

Similarly, Becket and Henry, who at first seem close friends, are quickly revealed as fundamentally incompatible. Becket, proud and reserved, is incapable of giving himself to anything less than the absolute. Henry, pathetically weak and selfish, cannot forget the distance between king and vassal. "If you were my true prince," says Becket, "if you were of my race, how simple things would be."[17] Becket and Henry are separated by the abyss that lies between heroism and mediocrity: they belong to different races and must remain forever incomprehensible to each other. And yet despite their differences, in the face of overwhelming odds, a feeling of friendship subsists between the two, and it is with reluctance, one feels, that they separate for the last time, each incapable of expressing his real feelings for the other.

Even *L'alouette*, which in so many ways seemed promising of a new optimism, has nothing good to say for friendship, for in the end Jeanne is deserted by all

179

those who were her friends, including La Trémouille, her bosom companion. In fact, he is not even mentioned as present at her apotheosis with which the play ends.

The Social Types

Society, as Anouilh sees it, is divided into two groups: the rich, who are charming and blind, and the poor, who are bitter and humiliated. But within each social class, there are several distinctive types.

The rich are most often represented by the wealthy old dowager. We first meet her in Anouilh's first performed play, *L'hermine*. The Duchesse de Granat is a "sort of fabulous character."[18] Selfish, spoiled, and insensitive to the feelings of others, she is a symbol of the superficiality of the rich and of all those who live life in a shallow way, following the easy course. She has never had a real feeling, was never in love, and refuses to think of death. Ironically enough, in spite of her failure to live deeply, she dominates the lives of those about her, simply because she has money, and money is the measure of man's influence. The full meaning of her tyranny is seen in the person of her servant-companion Marie-Anne, whom she treats like an animal. The maid cowers before her, hesitates lest any action displease her, has warped her entire life to conform to the wishes of the egoistic Duchess, and is frustrated in her most meaningful emotional attachment.

Madame Bazin (*La sauvage*), Florent's aunt, a "charming old lady, full of lace, little jewels and ribbons,"[19] is ostensibly kind and thoughtful, but in fact she is every bit as insensitive to the feelings of others as is the Duchess de Granat. Because her experiences have been limited in scope, and she has never ventured beyond her own social class, she has no understanding of others.

Lady Hurf (*Le bal des voleurs*), we feel, has a broader experience of life, for she is aware that she is alone, and confesses that she is as bored "as an old carpet."[20] But she is willing to play the game. In fact, she is one of the chief organizers of this play where she (and Anouilh through her) pulls the strings of the other puppets. Like the Duchesse de Granat, she dominates the lives of those about her, and arranges them according to her will. But her rule is benevolent rather than malicious, and she wishes the happiness of others while it is still possible. She is clever, witty, amusing, and somewhat giddy.

This is true of all the other wealthy old ladies. The Duchess in *Léocadia* is, in fact, almost insane. Although extremely clever, she is so wildly extravagant that her actions are improbable. Again, she is incapable of understanding the poor. She has had Amanda dismissed from her job without a thought for the girl's wishes or her future. Like Lady Hurf, she is largely in control of the intrigue. Like her predecessors and the later dowagers, she is romanesque, absent-minded, dictatorial, wildly optimistic, and extremely theatrical. There is something of the nonsensical atmosphere of *Alice in Wonderland* in the scenes with the Duchess, as she chats with her deceased husband or goes hunting for birds in the hope that she will not catch any.

The Duchess Dupont-Dufort (*Le voyageur sans bagage*) is another charmingly deranged lady. She has romantically wild dreams about Gaston. She is certain that he is of a good family, and feels it would be nothing short of a national tragedy if he turned out to be from the lower classes. To a certain extent she dominates the characters of this play, but only for a time. She has undertaken to discover Gaston's identity and she almost pushes him into the arms of the waiting Renaud family. But when Gaston discovers the unpleasant truth about his past he frees himself from her influence.

In *L'invitation au château* we meet Mme Desmermortes, the last of these creatures who are often as puppet-like as the characters whose lives they seek to control. Just as Lady Hurf had done seventeen years

181

earlier, Mme Desmermortes exclaims, "I'm as bored as an old carpet,"[21] and like her earlier counterpart she creates an intrigue to amuse herself. Like the others, she is domineering and blind to the feelings of others, particularly in her attitude to her reader Capulat. She can be brutally insensitive at the same time that she is witty. Speaking to Capulat, she says:

> *Mme Desmermortes.* You are ugly. When one is ugly, one is never twenty years old.
> *Capulat.* Nonetheless, one has a heart!
> *Mme Desmermortes.* Ah, my dear girl! That instrument, without the others, is good for nothing. But stop making me talk foolishness . . . You've been happy all the same, Capulat, worthy and respected. For a woman like you that's the best thing that can happen. . . . You still have God. A life of boredom is an investment.[22]

She is extravagant and imaginative, but not so wildly romantic as her predecessors. Indeed, she is unusually clear-sighted and stable, and must often check the romantic cravings of Capulat.

All these characters show us the rich man's blindness, his insensitivity to the sufferings of others, and his selfishness. It is interesting to note that many of them are sick. Madame Desmermortes is confined to a wheelchair; the Duchesse de Granat suffers insomnia and must take her powders; and the Duchess in *Léocadia* is ready for a mental institution. Their maladies are but exteriorizations of the condition of their souls—warped by money and the sense of over-confidence, exaggerated self-importance, and self-righteousness which it brings. They are charming and cruel at the same time without suspecting the hurt that they inflict.

Two of the old ladies have as their friend and confidant an ineffectual old nobleman: Lady Hurf turns to Lord Edgard for advice which is not forthcoming; and the Duchess of *Léocadia*, to the Baron Hector. Both are simple-minded men who may now and then have an unexpectedly clever thought. They are treated lightly, but we may look upon them as another type found in the circles of the wealthy, ridiculous, and inept, with no purpose in life.

Villardieu and Villebosse, the jealous lovers found in *Ardèle* and *La Répétition,* are treated comically also. They are conventional and puritanical people, not only critical of the looseness of the husbands, but even jealous of them as if the roles of husband and lover were reversed. They are ridiculous and tedious with their constant attentions and complete lack of humor. They are hangers-on—neither one doing anything more than living in the home of another man with the latter's wife. Such is the pass to which wealthy society, as Anouilh sees it, permeated by immorality, has brought us.

The poor are represented by several types of characters. We have already seen the downtrodden maidservants of the dowagers: Marie-Anne in *L'hermine* and Capulat in *L'invitation au château.* Related to them is the poor kitchen wench who appears for a moment in *La sauvage* as she spies admiringly upon the beauty and happiness of Thérèse.

Although not pictured as poverty-stricken, the many valets who appear throughout the plays may well be included here, for they are all icily perfect, frozen impersonalities; people who have lost their identities in their service to the rich—for whom they are but another possession.

The poor working girls include four heroines, not the least of whom is Thérèse. She, Amanda (*Léocadia*), Isabelle (*L'invitation au château*), and Lucile (*La répétition*), poor girls in the homes of the rich, emphasize by contrast the unwitting narrowness of the rich who have purchased them as tools for their pleasure. The girls, true to their desire for purity, refuse to be corrupted by the wealthy milieu, in spite of its glitter.

Unlike the heroines, there are some poor girls who have made the compromise, and these are represented

in *Ardèle* and Valentine in *Le voyageur*
~ge. Both of them poverty-stricken girls de-
~nt upon wealthy aunts, they became tired of the
~umiliation that comes out of penury and servitude, and
sold themselves to the elder sons of wealthy families, although they were in love with the younger but in-
eligible son.

Perhaps the most impressive and pathetic representation of the poor occurs in *La sauvage*, in the characterizations of M. and Mme Tarde. The tyranny that
poverty has exercised over them is evident in their exaggerated reverence and desire for money, in their willingness to grovel before the wealthy to win favors, and
in M. Tarde's attempt to convince himself that he was
made for such a life as the one he leads at Florent's
home.

The social significance of Anouilh's plays is apparent
both in the satire of the rich and the poor, and in the
depiction of the kinds of lives the people lead. The poor
are depicted as more aware than are the rich (the hero
or heroine usually comes from the poor classes), for
they have suffered deeply, and learned through their
suffering that life is made up not only of joys and pleasures, which for the poor are few, but of disappointments and pains. Poverty, however, also warps a person's view, as we have seen. Rich and poor alike are
prisoners of their social spheres: incapable of understanding anyone who is not of their own world.

Both groups in Anouilh's view are completely amoral,
and accept free love and adultery almost as a matter of
course. The pursuits of the poor are love and money,
and with this in mind life seems extremely simple to
them. The wealthy already have their money, and consequently can devote themselves more single-mindedly
to the pursuit of "love."

Anouilh condemns society, we feel, for its lack of
real sincerity, and for its preoccupation with inessen-
tials which offer a temporary consolation, but which

ultimately bury man deep in habits that prevent him from seeing life as it really is.

The Professional Types

Two professional types are frequently depicted by Anouilh: the actor and the musician. The author's mother, it will be recalled, was a member of the orchestra of the Casino at Arcachon, and it was there that Anouilh first came into contact with the world of the theater. It is thus not surprising that the first artists we find in his plays are musicians. And M. Tarde speaks for them all, musicians and actors alike, when he insists that any extravagance is permitted to an artist.

The artists we meet in this world are almost invariably of third-rate calibre, but they have deluded themselves into believing they are fine artists whom the world has not yet recognized. They attempt desperately to convince themselves of their superiority, but in reality, with the exception of Mme Alexandra, they are all failures in their chosen profession.

In *Le rendez-vous de Senlis* we have our first taste of the actor's character, in the persons of M. Philémon and Mme de Montalembreuse. Imaginative, romanesque, and bulwarked by much self-esteem, this couple insist upon playing every scene for all it is worth, dramatizing the tiniest incident. But all their playing is hollow; we feel their emotions are as untrue as are their characterizations of Georges' ideal parents upon the arrival of Isabelle. When they play a scene it is to no purpose other than that of making themselves the center of the stage and giving themselves, for a brief moment, the feeling that they are all-important. It also brings out the ease with which they are prone to delude themselves into exaggerating their successes in the past. This is seen when Philémon and Mme de Montalembreuse describe at length their coincidental meeting at the station after years of separation; and it is revealed in their conversation as they go to the house

Georges has rented. Passing the Place Clemenceau, the actress is suddenly convinced that formerly the two of them had played in that very city:

Philémon. She pinches my arm: "Ferdinand, we've played before in this city!"

Mme de Montalembreuse. Something told me!

Philémon. Then, skeptical, I say: "There are Clemenceau Squares everywhere, my dear." "I tell you that something tells me we've played here!" And suddenly she shrieks: "Look at the statue!"

Mme de Montalembreuse (with a gesture). Ah! That statue.

Philémon. I look at the statue; I stop, glued to the spot . . .

Georges (cutting him short). And had you really played here before?

Philémon (simply). No, it was a mistake.[23]

This is much ado about nothing, but it gives the actors an opportunity to create a little scene for themselves. We see a similar situation when they suddenly recall a former colleague, laugh uproariously over his customary saying of "We're all ears," become quickly sad when they remember he is dead, and as quickly forget him when they turn back to Georges to hear the remainder of their instructions. They are constantly striking attitudes and making grandiose gestures. They conceive of themselves as people apart—the spoiled children of Mother Nature, gifted with their own special genius, eternally young and glamorous. Mme de Montalembreuse cannot play a very old mother—she must be a young one—and Philémon claims he has the profile of a *jeune premier*. To portray the roles of father and mother, each of them has a bundle of tricks up his sleeve, for as far as they are concerned there is only one type of father and one type of mother. It is only hesitantly that they finally agree to enact the characters Georges has in mind.

186

The mother in *Eurydice* and Vincent, her "gros chat," are no better. As vain as Philémon and Mme de Montalembreuse, they also believe themselves younger than they actually are, and artists of a much higher calibre than their success would seem to indicate. But the mother explains that "Paris no longer goes crazy over anyone but stupid little fools who have no bosoms and are incapable of pronouncing three words without stumbling . . ."[24] She is related to the overbearing duchesses, and whenever she enters a room, it is in a triumphant manner: *"Eurydice's mother makes a triumphant entrance. Boa, hat with a feather. She has not stopped growing younger since 1920."*[25] Vincent is no less theatrical: *"silver hair, handsome and soft under a very energetic exterior. Sweeping gestures, bitter smile, a wandering glance. He kisses the Mother's hand."*[26] All their life is contained in the wild melodramatic events or colorful scenes evoked through description of picturesque detail: attempts at suicide, petty jealousy, Mexican tangos, skating rinks, Monte Carlo. And all this is described in the most superficial way, until we cannot help but realize that for these two *cabotins* life lies in the gestures one makes and not in any deeply felt emotions or convictions.

So much is life a theater for Vincent that he cannot distinguish the point where the play begins and life ends. He declaims Perdican's lines on love from *On ne badine pas avec l'amour,* and believes he is expressing his own thoughts in original words.

In Mme Alexandra of *Colombe* we find another true "animal of the theater," as Eurydice's mother had called herself.[27] She is a *monstre sacré* in the old tradition, following in the footsteps of the more malicious duchesses. Selfish, stubborn, blind, and insensitive, she lives only for herself and her petty whims. For her, as for the other artists of Anouilh's world, life is simply the motions one goes through. Her "love" affairs have been one whirlwind after another, their sincerity sufficiently proved by the fact that they were melodramatic and colorful. Her interest in others is as false as her love. She never gives herself; nor even lends herself except for a moment. Her interest in Poète-Chéri, in Armand, or in anyone else, is based upon the benefit she may derive from those people, and not from any deep-felt love or concern for them, or even any awareness of them. Perhaps Mme Alexandra is one of the most isolated characters in the theater of Anouilh. But she does not realize her solitude, because for her the gestures are enough. The motion of a kiss is as good as a kiss, and so much the better if it is made midst the flames of a burning mansion.

The shallowness of the other backstage characters is evident. Their lack of true individuality, and their puppet-like natures are amusingly accentuated by their approach to Colombe. Each one, in the very same words, indicative of a stereotyped approach, invites her to meet him after the performance for "a drop of port, and two cookies."

Since Anouilh so often presents life as a game, and the world as a kind of theater in which man is assigned a role, his depiction of the theater takes on a deeper meaning. What he tells us of theater people and of the theater in general is true of all life, and the shallow people—gesticulating melodramatically, puppet-like, finding life on the surface rather than in any real feelings—are representative not only of players but of all human beings.

The Mouthpiece and the Meneur de Jeu

Certain of the plays contain a character who might be looked upon as the author's mouthpiece. They are characters who are either completely outside the action of the play because of the nature of their roles, or who are unaffected by what happens in the play because they can look upon it with a more objective eye than the other characters. Their attitudes range from a gently disillusioned kindliness to a bitter cynicism; from a M. Henri of *Eurydice,* or the Doctor in *La valse des toréadors,* to Lucien in *Roméo et Jeannette.* Between the two extremes is the Count in *Ardèle.* Off to one side, completely detached, is the Chorus of *Antigone,* who has no role in the intrigue of the play. These characters present nothing in common, except that their view of life is perhaps a little more coherent and presented at greater length than that of the other characters in the plays in which they appear. One feels that M. Henri and the Chorus are freer than the others, since they are not affected by what is going on. Lucien has lost a personal interest in life because of his bitter resentment, but he can hardly be called objective. The Count and the Doctor are characters within the frame of the plays. They are acting and acted upon, but by their intelligent attitudes we feel they obtain a certain immunity from events which is not possessed by the other characters.

Monsieur Henri is not only outside the game; he is, to some extent, directing it. It is he who brings back Eurydice for a brief moment, and who suggests to Orphée that death is the only answer. To a large extent, he is pulling the strings of the drama. There are characters of this type in many of Anouilh's plays, but the others do not possess M. Henri's omnipotence. They are characters within the plays, and yet they manage to manipulate the other characters like so many dolls. It is the wealthy dowagers above all who engage in this activity. Lady Hurf, the Duchess in *Léocadia,* and Mme Desmermortes are the most obvious ones. Actually Mme Desmermortes is but one of the two *meneurs de jeu* in *L'invitation au château.* Horace starts to manipulate certain events, but his plans are upset when Mme Desmermortes enters the game and starts pulling the strings behind his back, including those attached to Horace himself. The wealthy old ladies are old enough to understand life, and also old enough to be no longer in the game; hence they are the logical *meneurs de jeu.*

All these characters (with the obvious exception of such persons as M. Henri and the Chorus of *Antigone,* who belong to neither group) have a certain similarity, precisely because they are members of what Anouilh calls the mediocre race. Their similarities are ones typical of that race: selfishness, pettiness, blindness, vanity, weakness of character, a false pride in things they have not accomplished, and a picture of themselves which does not coincide with reality. Since Anouilh's characters are representative of his major themes, and those themes are few and oft-repeated, it is not surprising that these people resemble one another.

A further indication of the resemblance lies in their speech. It is typical of these plays that certain phrases are repeated from work to work. We have already noted that Lady Hurf and Mme Desmermortes were as bored "as an old carpet," and both Mme Desmermortes[28] and the old General of *La valse des toréadors*[29] note, in somewhat similar terms, that their plays are dragging on.

Another frequently repeated phrase—"Children are no longer children"—expresses disillusionment and despair. It is used by the father in *Jézabel,*[30] by Lucien in *Roméo et Jeannette,*[31] and by the General in *La valse des toréadors.*[32] The Duchess of *Le voyageur sans bagage* also uses the phrase, but in her instance it is used as an excuse for not understanding Gaston's attitude toward himself. But still, taken in the framework of Anouilh's entire theater, this repetition reminds us that beneath the brilliant surface is an ugly and meaningless reality.

Such repetitions as that of the "Second Prize of the Conservatory of Arcachon," won by both Mme de Montalembreuse and M. Tarde, that of the proper names like "Pont-au-bronc," used both in *Léocadia* and in *Le voyageur sans bagage,* and "Dupont-Dufort," applied to characters in *Le voyageur sans bagage* and in *Le bal des voleurs,* point up similarities between various characters, and suggest they are all inhabitants of the same universe.

The characters of Anouilh reveal broadly the various kinds of people who make up a world. Not richly, but surely quite clearly, they embody the characteristics of mankind as envisaged by the dramatist. Sometimes they are realistic; they come alive for us with all the complexity of human beings. At other times they are merely puppets, clearly moved by the author or by some *meneur de jeu* on stage—simple, grotesque creatures with no will of their own. But always they effectively serve their primary purpose in depicting for us Anouilh's concept of the human condition.

6

The Use of Myth

UNTIL 1941 Anouilh had shown no interest in classical themes as possible sources for his plays, but in
the next five years he produced three plays based upon
Greek myths. They are among his most significant plays
and are representative of a period during which the author was stressing in his theater the basic problems of
heroic man facing life. *Eurydice,* written in 1941, is
what Raymond Williams, in his suggestive study of the
use of myth as form, calls "legend recreated and modi-
fied into substantial contemporary terms."[1] The second
of these plays, *Antigone,* Williams calls "pure legend
used as an objective correlative"; that is, used to evoke
the particular emotion desired by the playwright. The
last play on classical themes, *Médée,* is similar to
Antigone in that it has analogies to contemporary life,
but unlike the earlier play, *Médée* is not "pure" legend,
and it is not presented in a neutral setting.

Anouilh's interest in the classical stories during this
period is further indicated by the fact that about 1942
he was writing an *Oreste,* which remains a fragment.
This piece suggests to a marked degree the themes to be
developed in Antigone.[2]

Anouilh has not been alone in reworking these ancient themes. The importance of myth in the contemporary theater has been stressed by several writers.
According to Sartre, the dramatist's mission is to pre-

192

sent to his audience myths they can understand and feel deeply, to speak to them in terms of their most general preoccupations, and to dispell their anxieties. The author must project for the audience an enlarged and enhanced image of its own sufferings, dealing with the great myths of death, exile, and love. In creating such a theater, Sartre says, the dramatic poet should remember that the greatness of the theater "derives from its social and, in a certain sense, religious functions: it must remain a rite."[3] Thus, Sartre seeks to lead the theater back to its beginnings as ritual, and to incorporate that function into those already accepted by contemporary authors:

> Theatre ought to be a great collective, religious phenomenon. . . . the playwright must fuse all the disparate elements in the auditorium into a single unity by awakening in the recesses of their spirits the things which all men of a given epoch and community care about.[4]

Let us note the words, "all men of a given epoch and community." For Sartre, the artist's first concern is with the world in which he is living now, and the writer ought, first, to say something valid for his contemporaries. This view tends to impose a certain restriction, particularly where myth is concerned, for, in the words of Jean Boorsch, "the myth is by its very nature ambiguous, polyvalent, susceptible of ever renewed, ever changing interpretations in all directions."[5] If we would give to a myth a reading that makes it particularly timely for today's audience, we take away from it just so much in timelessness, in the eternal and universal values which are inherent in the myth. This presentation of a partial perspective of reality is, as Francis Fergusson clearly points out, one of the distinguishing features of modern drama. In the works of Sophocles and Shakespeare, the world is there in its entirety, viewed from multiple perspectives. This approach provides what Mr. Fergusson calls an "embarrassment of riches," which is blended into unity by a single underlying theme. If Sophocles "succeeded in preserving the suggestive mystery of the Oedipus myth, while presenting it in a wonderfully unified dramatic form," it is because he was writing for a society whose theater was a central part of its life, and was based upon ritual. Sophocles, of course, was able to see deeper than the literal imitation of the ritual which is embodied in his plays, and to express the eternal truths he saw inherent in the ritual, and the tragic rhythm with which it beats.[6]

As Fergusson remarks, Euripides, who was writing for the same theater, does not have the comprehensive insight of Sophocles, and his plays tend to express partial perspectives. He fails to see the myth as a whole, and for this reason his use of myth or ritual is more nearly like that of a contemporary dramatist. He may express the epiphany in a more concrete form, by the physical appearance of the gods, but his intention is satirical, and his faith in Apollo is no greater than that of Sartre in his Jupiter.[7]

Shakespeare's theater also is conceived of as ritual, in its civic, military, religious, and political aspects, and owes the possibility of its development to the central place it occupied in Elizabethan life and to the antiquity of its roots in the Middle Ages. It is a return to this idea of theater as ritual which Sartre advocates in his article on the young playwrights of France. However, such a return is no longer possible, Fergusson suggests, because the social *point de repère* is lacking. The modern theater is "isolated from any common area of public awareness"; there exists no central idea of a theater.[8]

Giraudoux recognized a similar necessity for a great social background against which a great theater might exist. In his essay "L'auteur au théâtre" he states:

There is no author in the theater. The greatest names in literature are the names of dramatic authors, but this is true precisely because these bright names stand for an entire epoch and not for a man. . . . All great epochs are not necessarily great theatrical epochs, but there can be no theatrical epoch except in a great epoch.[9]

The restrictions imposed upon the contemporary author by the position the theater has assumed—or rather, failed to assume—in society, make it clear that any treatment of myths today will necessarily be a partial treatment. This is not to say that a partial treatment of myth is not desirable. It is only to state that the limited perspective resulting from a partial treatment fails to reflect the full richness and awareness of the complexity of the human situation which the myth itself possessed. The modern dramatist still has valid reasons for choosing such material as a basis for his plays. In a perceptive study on "The Reinterpretation of the Myths,"[10] Gilbert Highet points out what he considers to be the principal reasons: (1) modern playwrights "are in search of themes which can be treated with strong simplicity, themes which have enough authority to stand up without masses of realistic or 'impressionist' detail to make them convincing"; (2) these themes are "profoundly suggestive in content . . . every great myth carries a deep significance for men of every age, including our own"; (3) "by bringing myths nearer to humanity, they make them more real"; (4) they find in them "inexhaustible sources of poetry"; (5) most important of all: "myths are permanent. They deal with the greatest of all problems, the problems which do not change, because men and women do not change."

Eurydice

Anouilh's formal approach to the legend of Orpheus and Eurydice is very similar to Cocteau's handling of the Tristan myth in the film *L'Eternel Retour:* the characters of the older myth are put into a modern setting and relive, in somewhat different circumstances, but along the same general lines, their now legendary

195

story. The Cocteau film follows more closely the various elements of the old love story than does Anouilh's version of the Greek myth. But Cocteau had a richer and more varied tradition upon which to lean: the story of Tristan has been elaborated upon for centuries and is more complex and rife with adventure than the Orpheus myth. In its essentials the story of Orpheus and Eurydice as we find it in classical times is as follows: Orpheus, son of Calliope and Apollo (there are other versions of his lineage), sings so beautifully that he charms the animals, trees, and the very stones and mountains. Eurydice becomes enamored of him. One day, she is bitten by a snake as she is fleeing from the attentions of Aristaeus. She dies, and Orpheus, seeking her, goes to Hades, where he charms the guardians of the dead with his song, and wins back Eurydice, with the condition that he must not look at her until they come into the daylight. He violates the condition and loses her again, this time irretrievably. In solitude he nurses his sorrow, refusing food and drink, and is finally killed by a band of Bacchic worshippers who tear him limb from limb. There are several versions of the death of Orpheus. In some he is struck by a bolt of lightning; in others he commits suicide; but the version in which he is torn asunder by the Bacchantes is the most prevalent. There are variations in other elements of the story, also. Plato, in the *Symposium*, expresses the idea that Orpheus made a bad impression upon the gods of Hades because he refused to follow Eurydice in death, and came instead to bring her back to earth. In place of the real Eurydice, they gave him a phantom bride who, of course, disappears when he looks at her.[11]

The Orpheus legend is perhaps one of the most richly suggestive in Greek mythology.[12] It speaks to us of the mysteries of birth and death, the cycle of life and of the year in nature, the coming of life in spring and death in autumn; it tells of the poet, of love, of the real and the ideal, the conscious and the unconscious, the world of waking and of dreams. Of these and many other aspects of the *ur-myth*, Anouilh has chosen to emphasize one in particular—that of love. Eurydice develops the love theme perhaps more than any other of Anouilh's plays.

In the general outline, he has followed the myth, but there is a great deal of deviation in detail. Anouilh's Orphée is a musician, but he is a wandering violinist of no great talent. Eurydice, far from being a nymph, is the none-too-pure daughter of a traveling actress. She is pursued by (in fact she has succumbed to) an aging satyr, but it is not so much her flight from him which brings about her death as it is her flight from the impossible image that Orphée has created in his mind, and her realization that she can never be that Eurydice whom he loves. Her death is the result of an automobile accident.

It is not through his musical gifts that Orphée is allowed to resuscitate Eurydice. It is, rather, a free gift of Providence, who shows an interest in this couple who have been destined for each other, as their meeting would seem to indicate. Orphée never descends to the world of death to bring back his Eurydice. Instead, she is sent to him, and their interview takes place in the railway station where they first met, surrounded by an aura of the supernatural. Orphée is offered a living Eurydice if he can refrain from looking at her until dawn. The alteration here is significant, and changes the entire meaning of this crucial point in the myth. The fact of Orphée's inability to see Eurydice is no longer a problem of ideality or a dream taking place in the underworld or the subconscious, lying in the realm of the eternal. It is reduced to a definite temporal reality, and takes place on this side of death. And his breaking of the condition imposed upon him by Providence is not so much an indication that Orphée could have lived with Eurydice had he not looked at her as it is a demonstration of Orphée's inability to make the compromise demanded by love on earth. Had he been forced to refrain from looking at her for only a few moments, he would still have acted as he did, because his rebellion in this particular instance is not so much against the rule imposed by Providence as it is against the ugliness of life. In spite of his rejection of life's ugliness, Orphée is not eager to die, and he rebels against death as he does against life. But at last, convinced of the cheapness of a continued existence, he consents to go out and meet his death, and thus gain back Eurydice. She is not the Eurydice he knew in life, however, but the idealized Eurydice whose image he had tried to project over her, and in death their love becomes luminous and pure. There is no question here of frenzied Bacchantes tearing the musician apart, nor of a head singing as it floats down the Hebrus. Cocteau in his *Orphée* has adhered more closely to the details of the myth, although his surrealist "interpretation," which he claims[13] is free of symbols, contains but a partial perspective of the original. His theme is the poet and death. The complex overtones of the Greek version; its universality of meaning; the rich suggestiveness of the natural setting; the roles of animals, trees, and stones—all this is missing in the more modern treatments, which focus our attention on one or two particular facets of the story.

We cannot deny the value of these plays as contemporary theater, but in the perspective of many centuries their diversity of application pales beside the inherent richness of the simple myth. Perhaps this is precisely why a treatment in such modern terms appeals more to today's audience than would a treatment such as Sophocles might have given the story. The modern playwright tends to give his spectators a ready-made interpretation of the myth as Anouilh does, or, sometimes, as in the instance of Cocteau's *Orphée,* to confuse the observer even more by clothing his interpretation in words and forms that appeal to something other than the conscious intellect.

One kind of aesthetic pleasure afforded by Eurydice, as indeed by any modern treatment of a well-known tale, is that of discovering the parallels that the author establishes with his sources—at times obvious, and at others extremely subtle. This kind of pleasure, denied to those who are unwilling to take more than a passive attitude, arises, of course, from our realization that the author is treating a theme with which we are already familiar. The pleasure is greater as the subtlety is more refined. Slowly, as the story develops, we should become aware of the aspects of the Orpheus myth with which Anouilh is preoccupied.

But the play has its weaknesses. The names of the characters and an awareness of the myth are necessary in order to make the supernatural elements sound less discordant with regard to the original setting of the play. Had the author been able in some way to bring about the return of Eurydice, or suggest Orphée's search for her without having recourse to the other-worldly, a greater unity of tone would have resulted. As it is, the first two acts portray life in a manner that is realistic with a twist of caricature. A difference of tone results from the presence of M. Henri; but even he is not treated as an obviously hyperphysical being. In the third act we are suddenly plunged into a twilight world where life and death join hands. In Cocteau's play such an atmosphere would be in accord with the general tone of the rest of the play, but in Anouilh's work it strikes a discordant note, or would, at least, if we were not prepared for it by the play's title. If the original setting had been retained, the atmosphere would perhaps have seemed more plausible. Even a *deus ex machina* was not frowned upon in terms of realism in the Greek theater, however undesirable it may have been from the viewpoint of tragic effect.[14]

If the names of Orphée and Eurydice help on the one hand to explain what is happening and, on the other hand, to excuse the appearance of the supernatural, one is justified in suspecting that the very names force the play to take the direction it follows. One might rightly feel that with other names Orphée and Eurydice might have done something else. This is where we may perhaps see most clearly the contingency of the partial interpretation. Anouilh has apparently chosen these characters because they are to a certain extent symbols of fidelity and love; furthermore, he has given them a hope of understanding each other by giving them similar backgrounds. The resulting misfortunes prove all the more convincingly that true love is impossible on earth. From one point of view, at any rate, this is true, for the myth is often used as an illustration of fidelity unto death. From another point of view, it does not prove Anouilh's point at all, for we could say that the misfortune is part of the myth and was forced upon the characters by the myth itself rather than by life and its compromise. The only complete statement, from all points of view, and hence inexplicable in any one simple way, lies in the original myth.

Antigone

The story of Antigone is the story of the individual against the state, the eternal opposed to the temporal, the hero to the mass, purity to compromise, and absolute values to the merely expedient. Anouilh's Antigone represents many of these things for us, and in her we can see preserved much of the polyvalence of the original myth. The beginning of the play makes clear at once that we are neither in ancient Greece, nor in some modern country like that depicted in *Eurydice*. Instead we find ourselves before "a neutral setting," peopled by characters dressed in simple evening clothes —the most neutral costumes possible. If the cut of the costumes seems too modern and the card-playing of the guards has a note of contemporaneity, Prologue, who advances to the footlights, immediately reminds us that we are within a certain tradition, and that these characters are about to play the story of Antigone. His simple explanation of the characters and of the story they are going to enact establishes the conventional nature of the play. Chorus will enter several times to comment upon the action, and to converse with certain of the characters. His role is similar to that of the Greek Chorus, although his function is purely dramatic, never lyric. "Not the least of the achievements of this method," comments Raymond Williams, "is that it restores to the dramatist major control of the form of his play."[15] There is no suspense in the modern sense, for we know how the play will end; we have no doubt but that Antigone will die. Even if we did not know the myth, the Chorus is there to tell it to us and to remind us that tragedy is restful because there is nothing we can do but accept it. The interest of the play arises, as in the Greek theater, from something much more profound than the plot: the moral struggle between two wills, both of which are right, and the intensity of the heroine, which is reflected in every aspect of the play of which it is the dominant note.

Anouilh has made a liberal use of anachronism in his play. This serves several purposes: it furnishes a humor to contrast with the tension of the greater part of the play, and it reminds us that we are not in Greece, but in a timeless ground where antiquity and modernity can touch fingertips without becoming ridiculous. It is another indication of the neutrality of setting and the universality of application and appeal which the author attempts in his play.

Anouilh's *Antigone* is not a translation or an adaptation of Sophocles' play—it is a re-creation.[16] The general outline of the story is the same, but, as we found in *Eurydice,* there is considerable alteration and omis-

sion of details.) The seven parts of Sophocles' tragedy
are as follows: I Antigone invites Ismene to share with
her the "risk and toil" of burying Polynices. Ismene
decides to take the way of moderation, to follow Creon's
decree. II Creon explains his decree; the guard comes to
tell Creon that someone has cast the sacrificial burial
dust upon the body of Polynices. III The guard, having caught Antigone as she sprinkled the dust and performed the libations a second time, brings her to Creon.
She admits her guilt, and Creon, his pride hurt and his
authority challenged, condemns her to be buried alive.
IV Haemon tells his father that the citizens admire
Antigone, and begs him to reconsider. He refuses, and
Haemon leaves, his "mind distressed." V Antigone is led
to burial. VI Tiresias warns Creon that the gods are
angry at his pollution of Polynices' body, and Creon
consents, much against his will, to bury the body and
to release Antigone. VII The Messenger tells how
Creon, after burying the dead, arrived too late at the
cavern in which Antigone was immured. Tearing down
the stones, he discovered she had hanged herself. Haemon, by her side, looked loathingly at his father and
attempted to strike him, then stabbed himself. The
Queen, Eurydice, hearing the Messenger's report, retires to her palace, where, as a second Messenger re-
lates to Creon, she kills herself. Creon is left in hopeless
despair, realizing that he is the cause of his own suffering, and the Chorus sings a brief song in praise of wisdom and censuring "unholy pride."

Several of these scenes are repeated in Anouilh's play
—not word for word, but in their basic outlines, although Anouilh tends to add to those scenes that are
most important in relation to the Antigone-Créon struggle which is the central agon of his play, and to subtract
from those that have no direct bearing on their conflict. Both plays begin at sunrise with a conversation
between Antigone and her sister. (The Antigone-Nurse
scene in Anouilh's play is a preparation for the Anti-

gone-Ismène scene which is to follow.) It is in this first scene that we learn of Antigone's choice. Both authors depict her as a free being who chooses her way, but whereas in Sophocles' play she describes her choice and what she is about to do, in Anouilh's, she describes what she has already done, for she has just returned from burying Polynices. Ismène, in both plays, shrinks from any extravagant action, and chooses the way of obedience to Creon's decree. Later Antigone tells her: "Thou mad'st thy choice to live and I to die";[17] and in Anouilh: "Tu as choisi la vie et moi la mort."[18]

Anouilh has inserted here a scene between Antigone and Hémon. It not only serves to reveal the love between the couple and the heroism of Antigone in renouncing this love, but it heightens the pathos of her death, and prepares us for what is to happen later.

The story then continues along the same lines as in the Greek play, as the Guard brings Créon news of the burial of Polynices, leaves frightened by the King's threats, and returns later with Antigone who has been apprehended. Then ensues the central scene of Anouilh's play, in which Antigone and Créon come to grips over their problem. In the Greek original the scene is rather brief, and we learn from it that Antigone's reason for burying her brother was that divine immutable law demanded it. She represents the "unwritten laws of God which know not change." Creon, on the other hand, represents what is best for the state. His first duty is to the kingdom he rules. He conceives of himself as the symbol of the kingdom, and brooks no interference in his rule. In showing his concern that his pride has suffered and his authority been challenged to the point of humiliation, he becomes less sympathetic than Anouilh's Créon, but also more absolute. The French Créon is more humane: he would save Antigone if he could, for her sake and for Hémon's. He is also a more clearsighted monarch: he knows that what he is doing is in the best interests of state, but at the same time he realizes it is a compromise, and that Antigone is right to a certain extent. Actually, both protagonists are right, and Sophocles felt this as much as Anouilh, but the latter gives emphasis to the fact by making his Créon more humane and keenly intelligent, and his Antigone more desperately strong in her resistance to what Créon represents. We cannot say that Anouilh's Antigone has a stronger will than Sophocles', but she appears to, because she is heroic will personified. Her action rises not from a desire to satisfy the religious law, for she feels it is meaningless. Rather, it is an inner compulsion, a desire to be true to herself, that motivates her actions, and the only way she can be true to herself is by refusing the compromise of life represented by the policy of Créon. Her action is a symbol of her liberty. Créon with all his logic cannot batter down her defenses, and if she insists upon death even in the face of the absurdity of her reasoning, it is because she has the courage to be her truest self.

This conception of Antigone's struggle is an interpretation, and in that respect a reduction of the original myth to specific terms that reason can understand. If Anouilh found this perspective, it is because it lay inherent in Sophocles' play, suggested below the rational level—implicit there, but explicit here in the French version. Anouilh has helped us to see certain facets of Sophocles' play of which we might otherwise have been unaware because we lack the proper background for accepting any play we see as a treatment of man's ultimate problems—a celebration of the mystery of human life. The solitude of these heroic individuals, the compromise of life, the freedom of choice, problems of state, the meaning of happiness—all these lie behind or beneath Sophocles' drama. Anouilh has only brought them to the fore as any modern dramatist must do if today's audience is to be made aware of at least the partial meaning of myth. As Fergusson points out, the modern dramatist is almost compelled to preach, invent, and argue to accomplish what Sophocles or Shakespeare, writing for audiences with a certain awareness, could accomplish by "appealing in both cases to ancient and publicly accepted values and modes of understanding."[19]

The scene between Créon and Hémon which follows in Anouilh's play is brief and to the point. There is none of the expression of filial obedience and admiration we find in Sophocles. There is only the desperate cry of disappointment of the youth who has suddenly seen what growing up means, and sees his father as he really is. He can only refuse to accept the compromise, and follow Antigone.

The greater development of the scene between Haemon and Creon found in Sophocles is another example of the multiple aspects of reality to be found in the myth. If the scene were merely an additional one, unrelated to the central conflict, it would indeed be superfluous, but a feeling of unity is retained because the Creon-Haemon relationship—the admiration of son for father, the sense of obedience conflicting with the despair over loss of Antigone—is a reflection on another plane, in a different area, of the central conflict.

Anouilh remembers Sophocles, and his heroine, for a moment assuming the lyric tone of the Greek theater, cries out, "O tombeau! O lit nuptial! O ma demeure souterraine . . ."[20] But this is said in the midst of the ironic scene in which the Guard prates on about ranks, advancement, and salaries. As the heroine in the Greek play is led to her death, she greets the cavern, "O tomb, my bridal chamber, vaulted home . . ."[21] and she dies in the hope that she will join her loved one in Hades.

Anouilh's omission of the Tiresias section of the Greek play might be praised on the grounds that it avoids diversity in the play, which is not concerned with any conflict between Créon and the gods, or even between Créon and Tiresias as a representative of the people's opinion. The Créon-Antigone agon is the central experience of Anouilh's play, and since this is the partial perspective he wishes to emphasize, his tightening of the plot by this omission is to be commended. Such is not the case with the Greek *Antigone* where the Tiresias episode is another aspect of the complex reality whose multiple perspectives are suggested to us by Sophocles, or would be had we the requisite background to grasp the full significance of each character and each act.

At the end, Anouilh's Chorus comes again to remind us that tragedy is restful because the outcome is inevitable. Now all is over: "all who were to die are dead. . . . A great and sad calm falls over Thebes and over the empty palace where Créon must begin to wait for death."[22]

Into the mold of the *Antigone* of Sophocles, unified by certain omissions, Anouilh has poured a drama whose breadth of appeal is enhanced by a variety of themes and by neutrality of setting and characters—two characteristics shared by the ancient and the modern theaters. Although lacking the multiplicity of perspectives that Sophocles' play had for the people of his day, Anouilh's *Antigone* is still broad in its appeal and a richly suggestive treatment of myth for audiences of our age.

The absence of a ritual theater has not prevented Anouilh from presenting more than one aspect of the myth, for this modern *Antigone* contains much of the suggestiveness of myth, and at the same time says something to men today. The legend is pure and comprehensible, unobscured by surrealistic magic or by the complex overwrought language that makes of Giraudoux's beautiful *Electra* an enigma until it is studied thoroughly. The story and characters are treated with dignity; the audience is made to feel itself a part of the play insofar as it is directly addressed by Prologue and Chorus. A classic austerity reigns in the tightness of the plot, the tension achieved, and the simplicity of means.

The tortured irony of the scenes with the guards brings us into closer relationship with the characters in the play, as we are jarred to laughter by the contrast between the guards and Antigone, and immediately are filled with shame, realizing that we too are like the guards and incapable of making the sacrifice of an Antigone.

If Anouilh's *Antigone* comes closer to the universality of the Greeks than do most other modern re-creations of myths, it is not only because of the inherent expressiveness of the myth and the author's ability to see below the rationalized surface of the story. In addition to these important factors, we should remember that *Antigone* was written and produced during the Occupation. Even if we do not believe Anouilh intended it as a thrust at the occupiers and at Vichy, we must still recognize that he could rely on a heightened sensitivity in his audience, and a feeling of a collective religious kind of experience before a spectacle depicting the struggle for individual liberty and showing the physically vanquished as essentially free.

Médée

Médée is not played against a modern setting, nor is it set against the neutral grey of a cyclorama. We are in heroic Greece, among the contemporaries of Jason and Créon. Apart from one detail, there is no use of anachronism. The legend is presented as significant in itself. This is not to say that Anouilh is only telling a story, for without seeking to establish apparent parallels with contemporary life by change of setting, the costumes, or use of anachronism, he suggests them to us by his handling of the story and characters themselves. He highlights certain aspects that were already inherent in the myth. Euripides and Seneca, whose versions are the earliest and best-known ones to treat the story of Medea in dramatic form, had presented a Medea whose central interest is in revenge for the insult to her dignity which the ungrateful Jason has committed by treacherously abandoning her for Creusa. The handling of the characters changes from Euripides to Seneca. The latter shows a shift of sympathy toward Jason, whom Euripides had presented as an opportunist and a hypocritical cad. Both treat Medea as a woman whose actions are a result of her former love for Jason, but Seneca stresses her magical powers and recalls her earlier deeds; his portrayal of Medea is "more a study in criminal psychology than of human suffering, and so loses some of the emotional and psychological power of the Greek play."[23] The murder of her children is the culmination of Medea's revenge, and leaves Jason desolate, for he has already lost his bride and her father earlier through Medea's magic.

Both classical plays are effective from the standpoint of delineation of character. The conflict in Medea's mind, her love of her children, her passionate resentment, and her plans of revenge form the soul of the tragedy. "The tragedy of Medea is the tragedy of a woman to whom love is everything."[24]

To express the action of the classical *Medea*'s in the infinitive form advocated by the Moscow Art Theater,[25] we might say that it is: "To avenge myself." The action of Anouilh's *Médée* shows a sharp change in focus: "To become myself," defines Médée's action, which underlies the entire tragedy as Anouilh has expressed it. This is made clear when we see that the murder of Créuse and of her own children is not so much a result of Médée's desire for revenge as it is an outgrowth of her inherent hatred of *le bonheur* and the realization that to become her true self she must free herself first from Jason, from her past with him, and espouse the Evil that is her inherent nature. In a lyric outburst she evokes her new love:

> It is now, Médée, that you must be yourself . . .
> Oh evil! Great living beast who crawls upon me
> and licks me, take me! I am yours tonight, I am

your wife. Enter me, tear me apart, swell and burn within me. . . . I am alive at last! I suffer and am born. These are my nuptials. It is for this night of love with you that I have lived.[26]

When she drags her children toward her house wagon to slaughter them, it is not with thoughts of revenge, but with words of hatred for the compromises toward which they are heading in life: "Trap of children's eyes, crafty little brutes, heads of men. . . . little wills to live and be happy . . ."[27]

The central struggle of Euripides' play takes place within the heroine: it is the "study of a soul divided against itself."[28] In Anouilh's play this central struggle is retained, but it is represented on the exterior plane by Jason, or rather by that part of Médée which would cling to Jason, as opposed to Médée's wish to be true to herself and independent of Jason. Thus, the struggle is no longer between the desire for revenge and her love for her children; it is the conflict of every heroic person —the desire for peace and comfort opposed to the desire to be true to one's self. Médée chooses the latter course, and when she dies in the burning house wagon she can cry, "I am Médée at last, forever!"[29] It has been shown[30] that parts of this speech, as of other speeches in this play, are translated from Seneca, but the essential lines —those indicative of Médée's victory in destruction— are Anouilh's. Like all the heroic race, to be true to herself, Médée must die. Although this is a deviation from the myth, it avoids the appearance of a *deus ex machina* to save the protagonist at the last moment—a device often criticized for its appearance in the classical versions of this play.

In Euripides' play there is another distinguishing feature: the presence of a chorus. The chorus in the ancient theater had many important functions which in the modern theater have been taken over by individuals, especially by the *confident*. Anouilh follows the modern practice, better understood by a modern audience. The chorus, with its mythic characteristics, has been replaced by a matter-of-fact individual—the Nurse. The myth has not gained by this change.

In Anouilh's *Médée* we see the action shifted from vengeance to a search for the self. A sterner realism is maintained, and combined with a lyricism that is at times not unworthy of the Greek poet. There is no chorus; no attempt to represent the play in a form reminiscent of Greek drama other than in the use of the classical story itself. But the handling of that story is modern in its straightforwardness and in its appeal to reason. If there is any of the sense of mystery possessed by the primitive myth that directly or indirectly furnished Euripides with his story, it is only on the periphery, as it is in Euripides' and Seneca's treatments, for these two classical dramatists have also taken a rational approach to their plays, and have accentuated one aspect of the story: the revenge of a woman deserted by the man she has loved. Anouilh's perspective is also partial, but the facet he shows us is a different one: a woman returning to the "purity" of her truest self which has been obliterated but not destroyed by years of compromise with life, represented by her love for, and dependence upon, Jason. Anouilh's handling is meaningful for contemporary audiences insofar as it is suggestive in terms of the problems of man's purpose, fate, and freedom—problems that preoccupy us so much today.

Conclusion

ANOUILH, as we have seen, is interested primarily in revealing to us his view of man and man's place in the
universe. His principal theme is man himself as he
faces his destiny. The secondary themes of love and
money are but further illustrations of this theme, as
they reveal man in his aspirations and his compromises,
his greatness and his baseness. As the dramatist develops, we witness changes in the focus of his ideas. In
essence, however, his ideas remain the same. The hero,
opposed to compromise and imbued with a vision of
inner purity, attempts at first to escape from his past
and his immediate environment. Soon, the hero takes
on a more universal significance, and becomes representative of man's efforts to oppose the impurity and compromise of life itself, often expressed in terms of love
and of money. At a later period Anouilh shows us in
more detail the abhorred world of people who have
accepted life and lost their vision of purity. At the same
time, the hero's stature diminishes, and in the latest
plays he becomes a caricature of his former self.

This development in attitude is paralleled by an in-
creasing tendency to treat the play as a play rather than
as life itself. The earliest plays are of the realistic variety. Soon, however, the *Pièces roses*, with their game
of masks and the escape from reality which it affords,
give ample evidence of the author's gift for fancy.

Throughout the second period, the realistic and the fanciful strains remain separate, but during the third, they are blended together in the *Pièces brillantes* and the *Pièces grinçantes;* and in *L'alouette* the serious play is performed with the understanding that it is a play, and the major scenes, a kind of make-believe. The author's themes of heroic despair and happy compromise, represented by the *noir* and the *rose,* come together briefly.

Man's condition—the central preoccupation of this theater—is presented to us in a dynamic way; painted now in realistic, now in romantic, now in classical terms; sometimes grave, sometimes amusing, always absorbing. Our interest is kept alive by characters who are not only interesting as symbols but appealing as people, or meaningful as types who possess a certain reality given to them either by their complexity, by their very passion, or by their presentation as caricatures.

Moreover, the ideas Anouilh presents are embodied in the characters, in the structure of the plays, and in the situations that we behold. They are an integral part of each play—its very being—rather than any external lesson preached through the dialogue. For the sake of clarity, the dialogue is used as an additional means of elucidation. Anouilh has succeeded in formulating each play as a complete entity in which the action, the intrigue, the characters, and the dialogue all possess a unity of purpose and contribute to the same end. They fully embody Anouilh's concept of man's predicament. This is true of each play individually, and of the plays taken as a group. Each one is the expression of a gradually evolving attitude toward life, presenting a comprehensive picture of man's fate, with few contradictions or inconsistencies.

We have seen that there is a realistic core at the center of Anouilh's theater, apparent from the very beginning, and dominating the first period particularly. It is evidenced by the common, everyday type of settings chosen, by the low characters often depicted, by the so-called photographic style in dialogue, and by the attempt to present the characters as though they were real-life people, with no more exaggeration than that necessitated by theatrical convention. The realistic element decreases, however, and the elements of fancy increase, as Anouilh matures.

Often realistic in appearance, these plays are imbued with a romantic spirit. This spirit is seen most clearly in the feeling of revolt which is depicted as being so much a part of the heroic character, who is misunderstood, lonely, and opposed to most of what society stands for. The rebels take their stand against all society and against life itself. As Anouilh's thought ripens, the youthful revolt seems to fade into the background, where it remains during his third period (with the short-lived exception of *L'alouette*), dominated by a feeling of bitter disillusionment. Finally, in *Becket*, the heroic revolt returns once again to the fore, but grown wiser with the years.

The classical spirit is evidenced in the simplicity of action, the unity of plot, a harmony in the ideas expressed and their means of expression, and the use of myth. *Antigone* and *Médée* come to mind immediately as examples of these classic qualities. But all the *pièces noires* are built along similar unilinear designs, with the will of the hero giving the play its direction, and his character expressing in tangible form the themes of the play, while the secondary characters add contrast, commentary, and color. Each play presents implicitly the ideas of the author, not simply expressed through rational argumentation, but embodied in the entire complex of the piece. And these ideas, by their very nature, are of universal interest. They are also particularly dramatic, for they reveal life in terms of a fundamental and insoluble conflict, and they are translated with consummate skill into theatrical terms. Anouilh is undoubtedly one of the most finished craftsmen writing for the theater today. One has the impression that he could take almost any material, and through the magic of his vivid language, through the sorcery of his vision, transform it into effective theater.

If complete command of his difficult métier has made Anouilh one of the most popular dramatists in France today, it has not caused him to turn to that insubstantial kind of comedy which for many years we have considered typical of the French. On the contrary, within the framework of a theater that is largely oriented toward commercialism and pure entertainment, Anouilh continues to reflect a profound awareness of our anxious era when man, insecure in a universe that seems devoid of reason, has come to doubt the authenticity of those values he had always accepted. Anouilh has revealed to him more clearly his predicament. If this is scant consolation, it offers at any rate a heroic inspiration (be it valid or not) for man's facing of his destiny. And because man must always face his destiny, such a theater will always be of value and interest, for it helps make him aware, not only of those forces with which he must contend, but of those qualities within himself which may give him strength for the struggle.

Notes

INTRODUCTION

[1] Quoted in Edward Owen Marsh, *Jean Anouilh* (London: W. H. Allen, 1953), p. 9.

[2] These biographical details and those in the following three paragraphs are to be found in Marsh, *op. cit.*, pp. 19–24.

[3] *Ibid.*, p. 9.

[4] For dates pertaining to the writing, production, and publication of this play, as of all Anouilh's plays, see the Bibliography. For the sake of conformity, I shall use the French titles of the plays throughout, as well as the French names of the characters.

[5] Quoted by Harold Hobson, *The French Theatre Today* (London: Harrap, 1953), p. 43. See also the same author's *The Theatre Now* (London: Longmans, Green, 1953), p. 33.

[6] Hobson, *The Theatre Now*, p. 23.

[7] *Arts* (Paris), 7–13 octobre, 1959.

[8] *Ibid.*

[9] It is significant in this regard that three of the four plays of Anouilh which have enjoyed real success in this country—*Le bal des voleurs*, *Léocadia* and *L'alouette*—tend to an optimistic view of life, and the fourth, *La valse des toréadors*, may be dismissed by the thoughtless theatergoer as a typical French "sex comedy."

[10] Isolde Farrell, "Anouilh Returns," New York *Times*, Sunday, Jan. 3, 1954, "Drama," p. x3.

[11] *Ibid.*

CHAPTER 1.

The numbers following the titles of Anouilh's plays refer to pages in the edition marked by an asterisk in the Bibliography. All translations from the plays are mine.

[1] J.-P. Sartre, "Forgers of Myths," *Theatre Arts*, XXX (1946), 324 ff.

[2] *Nouvelles pièces noires*, pp. 96–97.

[3] *Ibid.*, p. 93.

[4] *Ibid.*, p. 125.

[5] *Ibid.*, p. 112.

[6] Gabriel Marcel, "De Jézabel à Médée," *Revue de Paris*, LVIᵉ année (juin, 1949), 98.

[7] *Pièces noires*, p. 170.

[8] *Ibid.*, p. 256.

[9] *Ibid.*

[10] *Illustration Théâtrale* (Paris), no. 370 (18 mai, 1935), 21.

[11] *Pièces noires*, p. 362.

[12] *Pièces roses*, pp. 330–331.

[13] *Ibid.*, p. 344.

[14] *Nouvelles pièces noires*, pp. 118–121.

[15] *Pièces noires*, pp. 207–210.

[16] *Ibid.*, pp. 49, 78, 111, 116, 143, 235.

[17] *Nouvelles pièces noires*, p. 17.

[18] *Ibid.*, p. 126.

[19] Marcel, *op. cit.*, p. 103.

[20] *Pièces noires*, pp. 422–423.

[21] *Ibid.*, p. 475. The similarity of this passage to Bergson's theory of time as duration is noteworthy: "Duration is the continuous progression of the past which gnaws into the future, and swells as it advances. . . . Undoubtedly we only think with a small part of our past; but it is with our entire past, including the fundamental contour of our soul, that we desire, will, act. . . . His [a living being's] past is prolonged in its totality in his present, and remains there actual and active" (*L'évolution créatrice* [31ᵉ éd.; Paris: Librairie Félix Alcan, 1927], pp. 5, 16).

[22] *Nouvelles pièces noires*, p. 195.

[23] Henri Perruchot, "Le Théâtre Rose et Noir de Jean Anouilh," *Synthèses*, no. 49 (juin, 1950), 62.

[24] Marcel, *op. cit.*, pp. 105–107.

[25] Oreste Pucciani, *The French Theater Since 1930* (Boston: Ginn, 1954), p. 146.

[26] *Ibid.*, p. 147.

[27] *Nouvelles pièces noires*, p. 178.

[28] *Ibid.*, p. 182.

[29] *Ibid.*, p. 193.

[30] *Ibid.*, p. 191.

[31] *Ibid.*

[32] *Ibid.*

[33] *Ibid.*, p. 211.

[34] *Ibid.*, p. 206.

[35] Marcel, *op. cit.*, p. 107.

[36] *Nouvelles pièces noires*, p. 212.

[37] *Ibid.*, p. 283.

[38] *Ibid.*, p. 354.

[39] *Ibid.*, p. 347.

[40] *Ibid.*

[41] *Ibid.*, pp. 344–345.

[42] *Ibid.*, p. 347.

[43] *Ibid.*

[44] *Ibid.*, p. 377.

[45] *Ibid.*, pp. 393–395.

[46] *Ibid.*, p. 400.

[47] *Ibid.*, p. 402.

[48] *Ibid.*, p. 403.

[49] *Pièces noires,* p. 440.

[50] Marcel, *op. cit.,* p. 106.

[51] *Pièces noires,* p. 491.

[52] *Ibid.*, p. 369. This passage recalls a similar description in Camus' *Mythe de Sisyphe.*

[53] *Ibid.*, p. 466.

[54] *Pièces roses,* p. 170.

[55] *Pièces noires,* p. 497.

[56] *L'alouette,* p. 132.

[57] *Ibid.*, p. 157.

[58] *Ibid.*, p. 175.

[59] *Ibid.*, pp. 176–177.

[60] *Ibid.*, p. 141.

[61] *Pièces grinçantes,* p. 471.

[62] *L'alouette,* pp. 214–215.

[63] *Ibid.*, p. 217.

[64] *Pièces brillantes,* p. 53.

[65] *Ibid.*, p. 126.

[66] *Ibid.*, p. 101.

[67] *Ibid.*, pp. 40–41.

[68] *Ibid.*, p. 56.

[69] *Ibid.*, p. 134.

[70] *Ibid.*, pp. 138–139. (It may be pointed out that, technically speaking, Capulat's penultimate line and Mme Desmermortes' last have thirteen syllables in French. When spoken, however, they result in "verse" of twelve syllables.)

[71] *Ardèle ou La marguerite,* p. 44.

[72] *Ibid.*, p. 64.

[73] Marcel, *op. cit.,* p. 109.

[74] Cf. Pierre de Boisdeffre, *Métamorphose de la littérature,* Vol. II (Paris: Ed. Alsatia, 1952), pp. 187–188; Serge Radine, *Anouilh–Lenormand–Salacrou* (Genève: Ed. des Trois Collines, 1951), pp. 49–52.

[75] *Pièces brillantes,* p. 411.

[76] *Ibid.*, p. 468.

[77] *Ibid.*, p. 471.

[78] *Ibid.*, p. 463.

[79] *Ibid.*, pp. 451, 455.

[80] *Ibid.*, p. 462.

[81] De Boisdeffre, *op. cit.,* p. 181.

[82] *Pièces brillantes,* pp. 188, 194.

[83] *Ibid.*, p. 289.

[84] *Ibid.*, p. 291.

[85] *Ibid.*, p. 182.

[86] This name is spelled Saint-Pé in *La valse des toréadors,* but for

the sake of conformity, and since the name is often mentioned with reference to *Ardèle* as well as to the later play, it will appear as Saintpé throughout.

[87] *La valse des toréadors*, pp. 106–107.

[88] *Ibid.*, pp. 107–108.

[89] *Ibid.*, p. 103.

[90] *Ibid.*, p. 105.

[91] *Ibid.*, p. 104.

[92] *Ibid.*, pp. 76–77.

[93] *Pièces grinçantes*, p. 443.

[94] *L'hurluberlu*, p. 47.

[95] *Ibid.*, p. 131.

[96] Radine, *op. cit.*, p. 48.

[97] *Ibid.*, p. 50.

[98] Marcel, *op. cit.*, p. 110.

[99] Karl Jaspers, *Tragedy Is Not Enough* (Boston: Beacon Press, 1952), p. 101.

[100] *Becket ou L'honneur de Dieu*, p. 209.

[101] *Ibid.*, p. 134.

[102] *Ibid.*, p. 65.

[103] *Ibid.*, p. 77.

[104] *Ibid.*, pp. 178–180.

[105] *Ibid.*, p. 182. The distance that separates Anouilh's Becket from Eliot's is immense, of course, although *Murder in the Cathedral*, a rather popular play in Paris, may very well have suggested this particular subject to Anouilh.

[106] *Ibid.*, p. 169.

[107] *Pièces noires*, p. 85.

[108] *Ibid.*, p. 197.

[109] *Ibid.*, p. 438.

[110] *Ibid.*, p. 496.

[111] *Ibid.*, p. 453.

[112] *Ibid.*, p. 326.

[113] *Nouvelles pièces noires*, p. 135.

[114] *Ibid.*, p. 166.

[115] Perruchot, *op. cit.*, p. 60.

[116] See Henri Bergson, *Essai sur les données immédiates de la conscience* (Paris: Presses Universitaires de France, 1948), p. 128.

[117] Perruchot, *loc. cit.*

[118] Marcel, *op. cit.*, p. 107.

[119] *Nouvelles pièces noires*, p. 281.

[120] *Ibid.*, p. 253.

[121] *Ibid.*, p. 402.

[122] *Ibid.*, p. 388.

[123] *Ibid.*, p. 378.

[124] *Ibid.*, pp. 400–401.

[125] Bergson, *op. cit.*, p. 125.

[126] *Ibid.*, p. 129.

[127] *Pièces brillantes*, p. 154.

[128] *Ibid.*, p. 191.

[129] *Ardèle*, pp. 6–7.
[130] *Pièces brillantes*, p. 436.
[131] *Ornifle ou Le courant d'air*, p. 82.
[132] *Ibid.*, p. 184.
[133] *Pièces grinçantes*, p. 494.
[134] *Ibid.*, p. 469.
[135] *Becket*, p. 191.
[136] *L'alouette*, p. 28.
[137] *Ibid.*, p. 121.
[138] *Ibid.*
[139] *Ibid.*, p. 144.
[140] *Ibid.*, p. 4.
[141] *Ibid.*, pp. 144–146.
[142] *Ibid.*, pp. 76–77.
[143] Such is the conclusion also of Giraudoux's *Electre*. When the heroine succeeds in establishing absolute justice, it brings about social chaos in the form of revolt, warfare, and destruction. The play ends on a hopeful note, however, as the beggar points to the dawn of a new day.
[144] *New York Times Book Review*, Jan. 15, 1950, p. 6.
[145] T. S. Eliot, *The Cocktail Party* (New York: Harcourt, Brace, 1950), p. 188.

Chapter 2.

[1] *La valse des toréadors*, p. 196.
[2] *Pièces noires*, p. 49.
[3] *Ibid.*, p. 75.
[4] *Nouvelles pièces noires*, pp. 125–126, 128.
[5] *Ibid.*, p. 83.
[6] *Pièces noires*, p. 464.
[7] *Ibid.*, p. 465.
[8] *Ibid.*
[9] *Ibid.*
[10] *Ibid.*, p. 477.
[11] *Ibid.*, p. 478.
[12] *Ibid.*, p. 433.
[13] *Ibid.*, p. 394.
[14] *Ibid.*, p. 411.
[15] *Ibid.*, p. 413.
[16] *Ibid.*
[17] *Ibid.*, p. 456.
[18] *Ibid.*, pp. 467–468.
[19] *Ibid.*, p. 498.
[20] *Ibid.*, pp. 499–500.
[21] *Ibid.*, p. 500.
[22] In the theater of Giraudoux, for example, although love is considered an ennobling sentiment, it is also made clear that Giraudoux considers fidelity impossible. Even Alcmène, the very symbol of love and fidelity, is tricked into being unfaithful to Amphitryon. Georges

219

May, in a study of the couple in Giraudoux's world, concludes that we may infer two workable compromises. The first is that of wisdom, which consists in agreeing to let love remain an ideal, and not to insist that it come true. It is interesting that May interprets this as one of the lessons of the Eurydice myth: "Orpheus may have his wife provided he never sees her" ("Love Versus Marriage in the World of Giraudoux," *Yale French Studies*, no. 11, p. 114). For Giraudoux, such a compromise was acceptable. For the Promethean heroes of Anouilh, it is impossible, and we must interpret the myth as meaning that since Orpheus cannot live without seeing Eurydice, while she cannot live being seen by him, death is the only solution. Giraudoux's second workable compromise, according to May, "consists in respecting the fickleness inherent in love; in considering love, as travelers do, as an adventure constantly to be renewed" (p. 114). Such a compromise is equally abhorrent to Anouilh's hero.

In *Patchouli*, Salacrou affirms that human love cannot fill the heart of man. The aged Countess Coralie disabuses Patchouli of any romantic beliefs he might have had. His love for Fernande Javot is not strong enough to hold her, and she becomes the mistress of a movie producer. His parents are no better off, and Mme Saint-Croix's conclusion is "L'amour, quelle saleté!" (Armand Salacrou, *Théâtre*, Vol. I [14ᵉ éd.; Paris: Gallimard, 1943], p. 271).

[23] *Nouvelles pièces noires*, p. 353.
[24] *Ibid.*, p. 398.
[25] *Ibid.*, p. 390.
[26] *Ibid.*, p. 385.
[27] *Ibid.*, pp. 383–384.
[28] *Ibid.*, p. 390.
[29] *Ibid.*, p. 386.
[30] *Ibid.*, p. 402.
[31] *Pièces brillantes*, p. 228.
[32] *Ibid.*, p. 221.
[33] *Ibid.*, p. 222.
[34] *Ibid.*
[35] Marsh, *op. cit.*, p. 157.
[36] *Pièces brillantes*, p. 364.
[37] *Ibid.*, p. 374.
[38] *Ibid.*, p. 418.
[39] *Ardèle*, p. 74.
[40] *Ibid.*, p. 9.
[41] *Ibid.*, p. 11.
[42] *Ibid.*, p. 54.
[43] *Pièces noires*, p. 465.
[44] *Ardèle*, pp. 61–62. Cf. similar phrases in *Colombe* and *Eurydice*.
[45] *Ibid.*, p. 79.
[46] *Ibid.*, pp. 79–80.
[47] *Ibid.*, p. 58.
[48] *Ibid.*, p. 115.
[49] *Ibid.*, p. 118.
[50] *Ibid.*, pp. 64–65.
[51] *Ibid.*, pp. 69–70.

[52] *Ibid.*, p. 83.
[53] *La valse des toréadors*, p. 25.
[54] *Ibid.*, p. 23.
[55] *Ibid.*, pp. 137–139.
[56] *Ibid.*, p. 172.
[57] *Ibid.*, p. 151.
[58] *Ibid.*, pp. 193–194.
[59] *Nouvelles pièces noires*, p. 184. Jeannette uses the word in a similar context when she says, "Quand je serai vieille, quand je comprendrai tout, comme les autres, je sais que je dirai cela moi aussi, que rien n'est de la faute de personne" (*Ibid.*, p. 253). *Thérèse:* "Je veux comprendre, tout comprendre. Avant je n'essayais jamais de comprendre. Je disais: je suis trop jeune, je comprendrai quand je serai vieille. Je voulais pouvoir me révolter de toutes mes forces" (*Pièces noires*, p. 233).
[60] *La valse des toréadors*, p. 70.
[61] *Ornifle*, p. 95.

Chapter 3.

[1] *Jézabel* and *La sauvage* are the only plays in which the rich are not definitely designated as belonging to the nobility. It is significant that these bourgeois rich show a greater sympathy, if not understanding, for the poor. In *L'invitation au château* the *nouveau-riche* Messerschmann is made to feel the nobles' scorn for his humble past.
[2] *Pièces noires*, pp. 67–68.
[3] *Ibid.*, p. 72.
[4] *Ibid.*, p. 76.
[5] *Ibid.*, pp. 168–170.
[6] *Ibid.*, p. 210.
[7] *Ibid.*, pp. 231–232.
[8] *Ibid.*, p. 224.
[9] *Ibid.*, p. 228.
[10] *Ibid.*, p. 229.
[11] *Ibid.*, p. 233.
[12] *Pièces brillantes*, p. 183.
[13] *L'alouette*, p. 214.
[14] *Pièces brillantes*, p. 58.
[15] *Ibid.*, pp. 133–134.
[16] *Ibid.*, pp. 62–63.
[17] *Ibid.*, pp. 84–85.
[18] *Ibid.*, p. 110.
[19] *Ibid.*, p. 117.

Chapter 4.

[1] *Pièces brillantes*, p. 387.
[2] Quoted by Francis Fergusson, *The Idea of a Theater* (Garden City, N.Y.: Doubleday, 1953), p. 160.

[3] This problem is discussed effectively by Fergusson, *ibid.*, pp. 156 ff. I am indebted to him for much of what follows in the introductory part of this chapter.

[4] *Pièces noires*, p. 127.

[5] *Nouvelles pièces noires*, p. 204.

[6] *Ibid.*, p. 193.

[7] *Ibid.*, p. 385.

[8] *Pièces noires*, p. 388.

[9] *Ibid.*, p. 128.

[10] Marcel Berger, *Le style au microscope*, Vol. III (Paris: Calmann-Lévy, 1952), p. 40.

[11] Hubert Gignoux, *Jean Anouilh* (Paris: Ed. du Temps Présent, 1946), p. 124.

[12] *La valse des toréadors*, pp. 158–159.

[13] *Pièces noires*, p. 500.

[14] *Pièces roses*, pp. 140–141.

[15] *Ibid.*, p. 186.

[16] *Ardèle*, p. 89.

[17] See, for example, Serge Radine, *Anouilh–Lenormand–Salacrou* (Genève: Ed. des Trois Collines, 1951), p. 44.

[18] Lester G. Crocker, "*Hamlet, Don Quijote, La Vida es Sueño:* The Quest for Values," *PMLA*, LXIX (March, 1954), 280.

[19] *Ibid.*, p. 306.

[20] José Ortega y Gasset, *Meditaciones del Quijote* (3ra ed.; Madrid: Calpe, 1922), p. 187.

[21] In an interview to Isolde Farrell in the New York *Times*, Sunday, Jan. 3, 1954, "Drama," p. x3.

[22] This is discussed brilliantly by Crocker, *op. cit.*, pp. 278–313.

[23] *La Vida de Don Quijote y Sancho* (Buenos Aires: Espasa-Calpe, 1949), p. 247.

[24] *Pièces noires*, p. 22.

[25] *Illustration Théâtrale* (Paris), no. 370 (18 mai, 1935), 33.

[26] Henri Perruchot, "Le Théâtre Rose et Noir de Jean Anouilh," *Synthèses*, no. 48 (juin, 1950), 58.

[27] Gignoux, *op. cit.*, p. 123.

[28] *Pièces roses*, p. 46.

[29] *Ibid.*, p. 109.

[30] *Ibid.*, p. 108.

[31] *Ibid.*, p. 137.

[32] Gignoux, *op. cit.*, p. 137.

[33] *Pièces roses*, p. 330.

[34] *Pièces noires*, p. 300.

[35] Quoted by Raymond Williams, *Drama from Ibsen to Eliot* (London: Chatto and Windus, 1952), pp. 190–191.

[36] *Pièces noires*, p. 378.

[37] *Ibid.*, p. 487.

[38] *Nouvelles pièces noires*, p. 177.

[39] *Ibid.*, p. 347.

[40] *Ibid.*, p. 394.

[41] *Pièces brillantes*, p. 10.

[42] *Ibid.*, p. 152.
[43] *Ibid.*
[44] Marsh, *op. cit.*, p. 156.
[45] *Pièces brillantes*, p. 396.
[46] *Ibid.*, p. 398.
[47] *Ibid.*, p. 438.
[48] *Ibid.*, p. 378.
[49] *Ibid.*, p. 448.
[50] P. C. de Marivaux, *Théâtre* (Paris: Laplace et Sanchez, 1879),
p. 240.
[51] *Pièces brillantes*, p. 516.
[52] *Ibid.*, p. 518.
[53] *Ibid.*, p. 533.
[54] *Ibid.*, p. 534.
[55] *La valse des toréadors*, pp. 158–159.
[56] *Ibid.*, p. 189.
[57] *L'alouette*, pp. 9–12.
[58] *Ibid.*, p. 131.
[59] *Ibid.*, p. 29.
[60] *Ibid.*, p. 176.
[61] *Ibid.*, p. 229.
[62] *Ibid.*, p. 227.
[63] *Ibid.*
[64] *Ornifle*, p. 196.
[65] *Pièces grinçantes*, p. 443.
[66] *L'hurluberlu*, pp. 207–208.
[67] *Nouvelles pièces noires*, p. 72.
[68] *Ibid.*, p. 73.
[69] *Pièces noires*, p. 330.
[70] *Ibid.*, p. 468.
[71] *Ibid.*, p. 497.
[72] *Ibid.*, p. 48.
[73] *Pièces brillantes*, pp. 315–316.
[74] *Ibid.*, pp. 318, 320.

Chapter 5.

[1] J.-P. Sartre, "Forgers of Myths," *Theatre Arts*, XXX (1946), 326.
[2] René-Marill Albérès, *La révolte des écrivains d'aujourd'hui* (Paris:
Ed. Corrêa, 1949), p. 141.
[3] James de Coquet, in *Les annales politiques et littéraires*, 10 avril,
1935, p. 351. Coquet seems to exclude the possibility that Frantz's
actions represent a confusion in the dramatist's mind.
[4] Marcel Berger, *Le style au microscope*, Vol. III (Paris: Calman-
Lévy, 1952), p. 58.
[5] Jean Didier, *A la rencontre de Jean Anouilh* (Liège: La Sixaine,
1946), p. 21.
[6] *Pièces noires*, p. 300.
[7] *Pièces roses*, p. 195.
[8] *Ibid.*, p. 140.

[9] Marsh, *op. cit.*, p. 85.
[10] *Pièces roses*, pp. 143–144.
[11] *Ibid.*, p. 147.
[12] *Ibid.*
[13] *Ibid.*, pp. 141–142.
[14] *Pièces noires*, pp. 176–177.
[15] *Ibid.*, p. 187.
[16] *Nouvelles pièces noires*, p. 234.
[17] *Becket*, p. 65.
[18] *Pièces noires*, p. 65.
[19] *Ibid.*, p. 221.
[20] *Pièces roses*, p. 23.
[21] *Pièces brillantes*, p. 53.
[22] *Ibid.*, p. 54.
[23] *Pièces roses*, pp. 129–130.
[24] *Pièces noires*, p. 373.
[25] *Ibid.*, p. 372.
[26] *Ibid.*, p. 374.
[27] *Ibid.*
[28] *Pièces brillantes*, p. 146.
[29] *La valse des toréadors*, p. 189.
[30] *Nouvelles pièces noires*, p. 25.
[31] *Ibid.*, p. 354.
[32] *La valse des toréadors*, p. 179.

CHAPTER 6.

[1] Raymond Williams, *Drama from Ibsen to Eliot* (London: Chatto and Windus, 1952), pp. 196–201.
[2] *Oreste* was published in its fragmentary form in *La Table Ronde*, 3ᵉ cahier, 1945. Most of it appears as an appendix to Robert de Luppé's *Jean Anouilh*.
[3] J.-P. Sartre, "Forgers of Myths," *Theatre Arts*, XXX (1946), 332.
[4] *Ibid.*, p. 330.
[5] Jean Boorsch, "The Use of Myth in Cocteau's Theatre," *Yale French Studies*, V (1950), 78.
[6] Francis Fergusson, *The Idea of a Theater* (Garden City, N.Y.: Doubleday, 1953), p. 28.
[7] *Ibid.*, pp. 46–47.
[8] *Ibid.*, pp. 124–139. Such is, of course, the thesis of Fergusson's book. Needless to say, all scholars are not in agreement with this thesis.
[9] Jean Giraudoux, "L'auteur au Théâtre," in his *Littérature* (Montreal: Ed. Variétés, 1946), pp. 209–210.
[10] Gilbert Highet, "The Reinterpretation of the Myths," *Virginia Quarterly Review*, XXV (1949), 99–115.
[11] In Ivan M. Linforth, *The Arts of Orpheus* (Berkeley: University of California Press, 1941), pp. 11, 19.
[12] *Ibid.*
[13] Jean Cocteau, *Orphée* (Paris: Librairie Stock, 1927), p. 129, note.

[14] Samuel H. Butcher, *Aristotle's Theory of Poetry and Fine Art with a Critical Text and Translation of the Poetics* (London: Macmillan, 1920), chap. xv, pp. 55–57.

[15] Williams, *op. cit.*, p. 198.

[16] Sophocles' play is used as the basis of comparison here because it is the first and best-known treatment of the story of Antigone. In the plays of Aeschylus, Euripides, and Seneca, Antigone is not one of the major characters in the struggle, nor is she depicted as the same proud and fearless woman we see in the plays of Sophocles and Anouilh. Anouilh has clearly followed Sophocles' development of the plot and has even borrowed certain speeches from him (see below). This chapter is concerned with Anouilh's treatment of myth, and the question of influences is not taken into consideration. What we hope to see is what Anouilh offers us through the medium of myth as compared to what is offered by the primitive myth itself, or its earliest literary representation.

[17] Sophocles, *Antigone,* Plumptre translation (New York: Putnam, n.d.), p. 33.

[18] *Nouvelles pièces noires,* p. 195.

[19] Fergusson, *op. cit.*, p. 130.

[20] *Nouvelles pièces noires,* p. 204.

[21] Sophocles, *Antigone,* p. 49.

[22] *Nouvelles pièces noires,* p. 211.

[23] George E. Duckworth, ed., *The Complete Roman Drama,* Vol. II (New York: Random House, 1942), p. 528.

[24] *Ibid.,* p. 529.

[25] Fergusson, *op. cit.*, p. 244.

[26] *Nouvelles pièces noires,* p. 397.

[27] *Ibid.,* p. 400.

[28] Gilbert Norwood, *Greek Tragedy* (London, 1920), p. 196.

[29] *Nouvelles pièces noires,* p. 402.

[30] John C. Lapp, "Anouilh's 'Médée': A Debt to Seneca," *Mod. Lang. Notes,* LXIX (March, 1954), 183–187.

Appendix:
French Texts of Quotations
from the Plays of Anouilh

PAGE 7
La Mère. Je veux bien être une vieille, mais pas une vieille seule dans une maison, qui vit avec ses idées. ... Il ne faut plus chercher. Il ne faut plus rien se demander. ... Que veux-tu donc apprendre pour que nous souffrions tous les deux?
Marc. La vérité! Et je la connaîtrai: dût-elle être la plus horrible. ...
La Mère. Marc, non! Marc, tu es jeune, tu es bon; ... Sois heureux et laisse-moi finir tranquillement, sans rien me demander d'autre. A quoi bon, maintenant? Dis, à quoi bon?

PAGE 7
C'est honteux à dire, mais vous verriez comme avec un peu d'argent tout devient facile. Marc m'aime, je l'aime et nous vous aimerons.

PAGE 10
A genoux, à genoux. Je dois les ramasser à genoux pour ne pas mentir, je suis de cette race.

PAGE 11
Marcellin. Ça passe plus vite que tu ne le crois et tous les jours se ressemblent. ...
Ludovic. Mais la vie se réduit donc à des mots pour des

hommes libres? ... Mais tu as tout de même fait d'autres voyages, j'imagine, sans bouger ta peau. Des voyages au fond d'un être, au fond d'une foule ... Tu as vécu libre au milieu des autres, c'est un voyage pour chaque jour, ça? ... Pas un amour, pas une haine? Pas un enthousiasme pour une idée ou pour un être?

Marcellin. Ce sort te paraît, peut-être, médiocre, j'en suis content, moi. J'estime avoir rempli mon temps, joyeusement, mais honnêtement aussi, sans faire de mal à personne.

PAGE 17

Je vous admire avec haine. Vous êtes tellement belle, tout est si sale ici, si pauvre, si raté. ... Quelle bonté, quelle clarté sur ton visage! ... Oui, je le sais que je peux tout te dire! que tu comprendras tout, que tu excuseras tout! ... Vous allez être admirable comme toujours.

PAGE 18

Tu ne sais rien d'humain, Florent ... (*Elle le regarde.*) Ces rides, quelles peines les ont donc tracées? Tu n'as jamais eu une vraie douleur, une douleur honteuse comme un mal qui suppure ... Tu n'as jamais haï personne, cela se voit à tes yeux, même ceux qui t'ont fait du mal. ... Comme tu es sûr de toi! ... Comme tu es fort! ... Tu es un riche. C'est pire [qu'un vainqueur.] Un vainqueur qui n'a pas combattu.

PAGE 23

Orphée. Ils sont passés maintenant, les bons comme les mauvais. Ils ont fait leur petite pirouette, dit leurs trois mots dans ta vie ... Ils sont comme cela dans toi, pour toujours. (*Il y a un silence.*)

Eurydice (*demande soudain*). Alors, une supposition, si on a vu beaucoup de choses laides dans sa vie, elles restent toutes dans vous?

Orphée. Oui.

Eurydice. Bien rangées les unes à côté des autres, toutes les images sales, tous les gens, même ceux qu'on a haïs, même ceux qu'on a fuis? Tous les tristes mots entendus, tu crois qu'on les garde au fond de soi? Et tous les gestes qu'on a faits, la main se les rappelle encore, tu crois?

Orphée. Oui. ...

Eurydice. Mais on n'est jamais seule alors, avec tout cela autour de soi. On n'est jamais sincère même quand on le veut de toutes ses forces ... Si tous les mots sont là, tous les sales éclats de rire, si toutes les mains qui vous ont touchée sont encore collées à votre peau, alors on ne peut jamais devenir un autre.

PAGE 24

Orphée. C'est trop difficile; tous les gens qui t'ont connue sont autour de toi; toutes les mains qui t'ont touchée sont là, qui rampent sur toi. Et tous les mots que tu as dits sont sur tes lèvres ...

PAGE 26

Moi, je peux dire "non" encore à tout ce que je n'aime pas et je suis seul juge. Et vous, avec votre couronne, avec vos gardes, avec votre attirail, vous pouvez seulement me faire mourir, parce que vous avez dit "oui."

PAGE 26

Vous me dégoûtez tous avec votre bonheur! Avec votre vie qu'il faut aimer coûte que coûte. On dirait des chiens qui lèchent tout ce qu'ils trouvent. Et cette petite chance, pour tous les jours si on n'est pas trop exigeant. Moi, je veux tout, tout de suite,—et que ce soit entier,—ou alors je refuse! Je ne veux pas être modeste, moi, et me contenter d'un petit morceau si j'ai été bien sage. Je veux être sûre de tout aujourd'hui, et que cela soit aussi beau que quand j'étais petite—ou mourir.

PAGE 27

C'est un livre qu'on aime, c'est un enfant qui joue à vos pieds, un outil qu'on tient bien dans sa main, un banc pour se reposer le soir devant sa maison.

PAGE 27

Quel sera-t-il mon bonheur? Quelle femme heureuse deviendra-t-elle, la petite Antigone? Quelles pauvretés faudra-t-il qu'elle fasse elle aussi, jour par jour, pour arracher avec ses dents son petit lambeau de bonheur? Dites, à qui devra-t-elle mentir, à qui sourire, à qui se vendre? Qui devra-t-elle laisser mourir en détournant le regard?

PAGE 28

Eux, tout ça, cela leur est égal. C'est pas leurs oignons. Ils continuent à jouer aux cartes ...

PAGE 29

Il a un nez, un terrible odorat, et l'odeur, rien que l'odeur de l'amour, il la sent. Et il n'aime pas ça, pas ça du tout, l'amour.

PAGE 29

Tu es satisfait? C'est bien ainsi que tout devait se passer. Je leur avais pourtant dit que tu n'aimais pas cela.

PAGE 29

Je ne veux pas devenir grande. Je ne veux pas apprendre à dire oui. Tout est trop laid.

PAGE 30

Ah! si j'avais pu ne jamais vous connaître! Le monde avait une forme avant, bonne ou mauvaise. Les choses autour de moi avaient une place et un nom et tout était si simple.

PAGE 30

Cette horreur et tous ces gestes pour rien, cette aventure grotesque, c'est la nôtre. Il faut la vivre. La mort aussi est absurde.

PAGE 30

Sous ce ciel de raison, au bord de cette mer égale, qui n'a que faire de ta passion désordonnée et de tes cris.

PAGE 30

Médée. Race d'Abel, race des justes, race des riches, comme vous parlez tranquillement. C'est bon, n'est-ce pas, d'avoir le ciel pour soi et aussi les gendarmes. C'est bon de penser un jour comme son père et le père de son père, comme tous ceux qui ont eu raison depuis toujours. ... Joue le jeu, Jason, fais le geste, dis oui! Tu te prépares une belle vieillesse, toi!

Jason. Poursuis ta course. Tourne en rond, déchire-toi, bats-toi, méprise, insulte, tue, refuse tout ce qui n'est pas toi. Moi, je m'arrête. Je me contente. J'accepte ces apparences aussi durement, aussi résolument que je les ai refusées autrefois avec toi. Et s'il faut continuer à se battre, c'est pour elles maintenant que je me battrai, humblement, adossé à ce mur dérisoire, construit de mes mains, entre le néant absurde et moi. ... Et c'est cela, sans doute, en fin de compte—et pas autre chose—être un homme.

Médée. N'en doute pas, Jason. Tu es un homme maintenant.

Jason. Adieu, Médée. Je ne peux pas te dire: sois heureuse ... Sois toi-même.

PAGE 32

J'ai retrouvé ma patrie et ma virginité que tu m'avais ravies: Je suis Médée, enfin, pour toujours!

PAGE 32

La Nourrice. Après la nuit vient le matin et il y a le café à faire et puis les lits. Et quand on a balayé, on a un petit moment tranquille au soleil avant d'éplucher les légumes. C'est alors que c'est bon, si on a pu grappiner quelques sous, la petite goutte chaude au creux du ventre. ... Ce sera une bonne année. Il y aura du soleil et du vin. ...

Le Garde. Faut pas se plaindre. Il y aura encore du pain pour tout le monde cette année-ci.

PAGE 33

Mon cher, il y a deux races d'êtres. Une race nombreuse, féconde, heureuse, une grosse pâte à pétrir, qui mange son saucisson, fait ses enfants, pousse ses outils, compte ses sous, bon an mal an, malgré les épidémies et les guerres, jusqu'à la limite d'âge; des gens pour vivre, des gens pour tous les jours, des gens qu'on n'imagine pas morts. Et puis il y a les autres, les nobles, les héros. Ceux qu'on imagine très bien étendus, pâles, un trou rouge dans la tête, une minute triomphants avec une garde d'honneur ou entre deux gendarmes selon: le gratin.

PAGE 35

Nous étions jeunes, quoi, nous étions gais. Nous avions compris la vie, nous autres.

PAGE 36

Je pense que depuis que maman est morte, je te suis aux terrasses des cafés avec mon violon, je te regarde te débattre avec tes additions le soir. Je t'écoute parler du menu du prix fixe et puis je me couche et je me relève le lendemain.

PAGE 36

L'argent, l'amour: on ne peut plus rien vouloir. C'est pourtant simple, sacrebleu, la vie!

PAGE 38

Cette petite alouette chantant dans le ciel de France, au-dessus de la tête des fantassins ...

PAGE 38

Et tout cela finit par s'éteindre et se noyer tranquillement dans les eaux de vaisselle. ... et au deuxième moutard pendu, hurlant, à ses jupes, nous sommes tranquilles sur les voix qu'elle entendra.

PAGE 38

Après tout, c'est un ancien ange, il est de chez nous.

PAGE 39

L'Inquisiteur. Si puissants que nous devenions un jour, sous une forme ou sous une autre, si lourde que se fasse l'Idée sur le monde, si dures, si précises, si subtiles que soient son organisation et sa police; il y aura toujours un homme à chasser quelque part qui lui aura échappé, qu'on prendra enfin, qu'on tuera et qui humiliera encore une fois l'Idée au comble de sa puissance, simplement parce qu'il dira "non" sans baisser les yeux. (*Il siffle entre ses dents, haineux, regardant Jeanne.*) L'insolente race!

PAGE 39

Quand quelque chose est noir, je ne peux pas dire que c'est blanc, voilà tout.

PAGE 39

Il faut supprimer autant que possible les hommes.

PAGE 40

Mais je ne veux pas que les choses s'arrangent ... Je ne veux pas le vivre, votre temps ... Vous voyez Jeanne ayant vécu, les choses s'étant arrangées ... Jeanne délivrée, peut-être, végétant à la Cour de France d'une petite pension? ... Jeanne acceptant tout, Jeanne avec un ventre. Jeanne devenue gourmande ... Vous voyez Jeanne fardée, en hennin, empêtrée dans ses robes, s'occupant de son petit chien ou avec un homme à ses trousses, qui sait, Jeanne mariée?

PAGE 40

Il n'y a rien à faire, on n'est pas de la même race, tous les deux.

PAGE 43

Je trouve l'homme trop modeste. Il se laisse mener alors que c'est presque toujours à lui de décider et qu'il est pratiquement indomptable. L'amour, la maladie, la bêtise, il a trouvé commode d'appeler tout: fatalité. Moi, je ne connais que la mort, ma chère. ... je ne me sens pas d'humeur à supporter l'ordre normal des choses aujourd'hui ... Alors tant pis pour la fatalité!

PAGE 43

Ah! que ce bal est donc bête ... Regardez-les tourner. Ils croient qu'ils s'amusent et ils ne pensent qu'à leur petite vanité et à leurs petites affaires.

PAGE 44

Capulat. Les voilà revenus de leur sombre baptême,
      Le flot noir et glacé va les rendre à l'amour.
      Enfant tu te taisais et peut-être qu'il t'aime!
Mme Desmermortes. Capulat! Capulat! Ne rimez pas toujours!
Capulat. Hélas! je ne peux plus, je ne peux plus, Madame ...
      Tous ces événements ont bouleversé mon âme,
      Et c'est plus fort que moi, elle s'exprime en vers!
Mme Desmermortes. Alors sortez les faire hors du jardin d'hiver!

PAGE 45

Il y a autre chose que l'amour. Il y a le monde. Il y a le scandale. ... Vous savez bien qu'il ne s'agit que de respecter les apparences. De ne pas offrir le scandale en pâture au monde.

PAGE 46

Nous avons vécu comme on danse, en musique, sur des pas réglés, et avec grâce. ... Tout cela continuera à me paraître, toujours, la seule façon intelligente de vivre, d'échapper au désordre et à la vulgarité. Seulement. ... Cette ligne de ma vie si gracieuse et si nette, depuis mon premier cotillon réussi jusqu'à ma présidence probable au

Jockey, dans vingt ans et à mes obsèques, avec tout Paris en haut de forme à la Madeleine, je viens de m'apercevoir que ce serait sans doute un joli souvenir pour les autres, un joli thème d'article pour "le Figaro"—et rien pour moi. Je ne savais pas pourquoi j'étais si gai toujours: je m'ennuyais.

PAGE 48

Julien. Je sais que ton coeur est bon et que tu fais des efforts pour comprendre ce que je t'explique [la corruption du monde théâtral]; mais tu es toute petite encore et la facilité a des pièges terribles. ...
Colombe. Mais c'est si vilain la facilité?
Julien. Oui, Colombe.
Colombe. C'est pourtant bon les choses qui se font sans peine et qui vous font plaisir.
Julien (crie). Non, ce n'est pas bon ...
Colombe. Comme tout est compliqué avec toi, mon chéri. ... Et pour moi tout est tellement plus simple ... Tout le monde est gentil, il n'y a rien de laid et j'ai seulement envie d'être heureuse.

PAGE 49

Moi je suis faible, c'est entendu. Quand quelque chose me fait plaisir: claquer de l'argent au poker, boire un verre de trop, lever une jupe; j'ai beau me dire non, c'est plus fort que moi, je dis oui.

PAGE 51

Quand on fait quelque chose de contraire à l'honneur, l'honneur c'est de ne jamais en convenir. ... Passons, vous comprendrez quand vous serez plus grand. Retenez seulement de tout ceci qu'il faut respecter les apparences.

PAGE 53

Il y a en vous quelque chose d'un peu dogmatique, d'un peu pédant, d'un peu guindé, disons le mot, d'un peu ennuyeux, qui indispose.

PAGE 53

Ce n'est pas de la haine, mon Père. C'est de la peine. Il y a un demi-siècle que j'ai de la peine. Cela commence à

234

devenir long. Petit garçon, j'avais vu ça tout autrement. Je ne m'en suis pas remis.

PAGE 58

Tant que Becket sera obligé d'improviser son honneur, il te servira. Et si un jour, il le rencontre ... Mais où est l'honneur de Becket?

PAGE 58

J'aime au moins une chose, mon prince, et cela j'en suis sûr. Bien faire ce que j'ai à faire.

PAGE 59

Becket. Je n'ai pas à vous convaincre. J'ai seulement à vous dire non.

Le Roi. Il faut pourtant être logique, Becket!

Becket. Non. Cela n'est pas nécessaire, mon roi. Il faut seulement faire, absurdement, ce dont on a été chargé— jusqu'au bout.

Le Roi. Je t'ai bien connu tout de même! ... Absurdement. Voilà un mot qui ne te ressemble pas.

Becket. Peut-être. Je ne me ressemble plus.

Le Roi (*ricane*). Tu as été touché par la grâce?

Becket (*grave*). Pas par celle que vous croyez. J'en suis indigne.

Le Roi. Tu t'es senti redevenir saxon, malgré les bons sentiments collaborateurs du papa?

Becket. Même pas.

Le Roi. Alors?

Becket. Je me suis senti chargé de quelque chose tout simplement, pour la première fois, dans cette cathédrale vide, quelque part en France, où vous m'avez ordonné de prendre ce fardeau. J'étais un homme sans honneur. Et, tout d'un coup, j'en ai eu un, celui que je n'aurais jamais imaginé devoir devenir mien, celui de Dieu. Un honneur incompréhensible et fragile, comme un enfant-roi poursuivi.

PAGE 60

Becket a une tendresse protectrice pour le roi. Mais il n'aime au monde que l'idée qu'il s'est forgée de son honneur.

PAGE 61

N'essayez pas de vous duper vous-même avec l'honnêteté et la morale.

PAGE 62

Ces courts instants où l'on surprend le destin en train de poser ses pions sont troublants, n'est-ce pas?

PAGE 62

Quel besoin de mettre un pronom possessif devant chacune de vos petites ficelles.

PAGE 63

Je ne sais pas. C'est la première fois. Quelque chose d'étranger qui s'est mis à faiblir en moi. Et si tu pleurais, si tu souffrais encore, cela allait saigner comme une plaie ... J'étais en train de quitter l'hôtel. J'ai reposé mes valises et je suis entré pour te calmer. Et comme rien ne te calmait, alors je t'ai fait cette promesse pour que tu te taises.

PAGE 63

Notre chère liberté, cela consiste en fin de compte à nous accepter tels que nous sommes ...

PAGE 63

Il n'y a rien à faire. Elle s'appelle Antigone et il va falloir qu'elle joue son rôle jusqu'au bout. ... C'est une question de distribution.

PAGE 64

Tout ce qui est bon est défendu. ... l'autre là-haut. Chaque fois qu'on est heureux, cela le met épouvantablement en colère. Il n'aime pas ça.

PAGE 65

Je ne peux pas t'empêcher d'être toi. Je ne peux pas t'empêcher de faire le mal que tu portes en toi. Les dés sont jetés, d'ailleurs. Ces conflits insolubles se dénouent, comme les autres, et quelqu'un sait sans doute déjà comme tout cela finira. Je ne peux rien empêcher. Tout juste jouer le rôle qui m'est dévolu, depuis toujours.

PAGE 69

Il n'avait qu'à me laisser garder mes moutons et à filer près de ma mère, je ne serais jamais devenue orgueilleuse ...

PAGE 69

Charles. Il n'avait qu'à m'en donner du courage. Je ne demandais pas mieux, moi!

Jeanne (*sévère*). Tu crois donc que c'est ta nourrice et qu'Il n'a que toi à s'occuper? Tu ne pourrais pas essayer de te débrouiller un peu toi-même avec ce que tu as?

PAGE 70

Tu peux en faire un bon ou un mauvais usage, Charles, pour cela, Il te laisse libre, Dieu.

PAGE 70

Les vrais miracles, ceux qui font sourire Dieu de plaisir dans le Ciel, ce doit être ceux que les hommes font tout seuls, avec le courage et l'intelligence qu'Il leur a donnés.

PAGE 70

Nous ne pouvons que jouer nos rôles. Chacun le sien, bon ou mauvais, tel qu'il est écrit, et à son tour.

PAGE 71

Dieu s'était tu depuis l'arrestation de Jeanne. Ni elle, quoi qu'elle en ait dit, ni nous bien sûr, ne l'entendions plus. Nous, nous avons continué avec notre routine; il fallait défendre la vieille maison d'abord, cette grande et raisonnable construction humaine qui est en somme tout ce qui nous reste, dans le désert, les jours où Dieu s'absente. ... Mais c'est dans cette solitude, dans ce silence d'un Dieu disparu, dans ce dénuement et cette misère de bête, que l'homme qui continue à redresser la tête est bien grand. Grand tout seul.

PAGE 76

On est mieux comme ça. Ce n'est pas que cela veuille dire grand-chose, mais tout de même, on se sent moins seul, dans le noir.

PAGE 77

Je veux que mon amour soit une chose immaculée, je veux que nous soyons des amants sans calculs, sans craintes, sans honte.

PAGE 78

Oh! mon Dieu. Pourquoi m'avez-vous donné cet amour puisque vous ne m'avez pas donné avec lui toutes les crédulités nécessaires?

237

PAGE 80

Jamais. Je cherchais mon homme parmi tous ces hommes, mais ce n'était sans doute pas parmi eux que je pouvais le rencontrer.

PAGE 82

Deux peaux, deux enveloppes, bien imperméables autour de nous, chacun pour soi avec son oxygène, avec son propre sang quoi qu'on fasse, bien enfermé, bien seul dans son sac de peau.

PAGE 82

Son foie, sa rate, ses tripes, ses seuls amis. ... Deux prisonniers qui ne se verront jamais. Ah! on est seul, tu ne trouves pas qu'on est trop seul?

PAGE 83

La Mère. Moi, ce que je ne comprends pas, c'est que tout leur paraisse si triste à ces enfants! Enfin, mon gros chat, nous aussi, nous avons été des amants passionnés, est-ce que cela nous a rendus tristes?

Vincent. Mais pas du tout! pas du tout! d'abord, moi, je l'ai toujours dit: un peu d'amour, un peu d'argent, un peu de succès, la vie est belle!

La Mère. Un peu d'amour? Beaucoup d'amour! cette gamine se figure qu'elle a tout inventé avec son petit violoniste. Nous aussi, nous nous sommes adorés. Nous aussi nous avons voulu nous tuer l'un pour l'autre. Tu te souviens à Biarritz en 1913 quand j'ai voulu me jeter du haut du rocher de la Vierge?

Vincent. Heureusement que je t'ai retenue par ta cape, mon aimée.

PAGE 84

Je ne croyais pas que c'était possible de rencontrer un jour le camarade qui vous accompagne, dur et vif, porte son sac et n'aime pas non plus faire de sourires. Le petit copain muet qu'on met à toutes les sauces et qui, le soir, est belle et chaude contre vous.

PAGE 84

Orphée. Cela va être une vie de chien!

Eurydice. C'est cela, l'amour! ...

238

PAGE 85

Un beau jeune homme et une belle jeune fille! et prêts à jouer le jeu sans tricher, jusqu'au bout. Sans ces petites concessions au confort ou à la facilité qui font les amants vieillissants et prospères.

PAGE 85

Deux petites bêtes courageuses, aux membres souples, aux dents longues, prêtes à se battre jusqu'au matin, comme il se doit, et à tomber, blessées ensemble.

PAGE 86

Vivre, vivre! Comme ta mère et son amant, peut-être, avec des attendrissements, des sourires, des indulgences et puis des bons repas, après lesquels on fait l'amour et tout s'arrange. Ah! non. Je t'aime trop pour vivre!

PAGE 88

Amour, triste amour, tu es content? Cher coeur, cher corps, chère romance. Est-ce qu'on n'a pas des métiers à faire, des livres à lire, des maisons à bâtir? Est-ce que ce n'est pas bon, aussi, le soleil sur la peau, le vin frais dans le verre, l'eau du ruisseau, l'ombre à midi, le feu l'hiver, la neige et la pluie même, et le vent, et les arbres, et les nuages, et les bêtes, toutes les bêtes innocentes, et les enfants avant qu'ils ne deviennent trop laids? Triste amour, dis, est-ce que tout aussi n'est pas bon?

PAGE 89

Et le soir, à la halte, le soldat et le capitaine se deshabillaient côte à côte, tout surpris de se retrouver un homme et une femme sous leurs deux blouses et de s'aimer.

PAGE 89

Il a fallu que je me recolle à ta haine, comme une mouche, que je reprenne mon chemin avec toi; que je me recouche le lendemain contre ton corps ennuyé pour pouvoir enfin m'endormir.

PAGE 90

J'ai essayé, Jason, tu ne l'as pas su? J'ai essayé encore avec d'autres, depuis. Je n'ai pas pu!

PAGE 90

Regarde-les, ton petit frère et ta femme, c'est moi. C'est moi! C'est l'horrible Médée! Et essaie maintenant de l'oublier!

PAGE 91

La Surette. Et finalement qu'est-ce que je leur dis sur l'Amour, Madame-Chérie?
Madame Alexandra. Vous nous embêtez avec votre Amour, imbécile! Vous voyez bien que nous parlons de choses sérieuses.

PAGE 91

Poète-Chéri. "Pour que le véritable amour fleurisse, il faut avoir arraché au préalable de son coeur les mauvaises herbes du désir et de la passion."
Madame Alexandra. Mais, Poète-Chéri, grand poète! qu'est-ce que vous nous chantez? L'amour n'est que passion voyons! Comment pouvez-vous dire cela? Mais moi à l'âge de cette petite, je m'étais déjà suicidée quatre fois par amour.

PAGE 93

Imagine, Héro, qu'un jour tout se mette en place autour de toi. Que tout devienne simple et paisible; mais en même temps, inaccessible.

PAGE 94

Le Comte. Liliane, ce n'est pas ton procès, ni le mien, ni celui du général ou d'Ardèle ou de Villardieu. Nous faisons le procès de l'amour. Tante Ardèle a l'amour caché dans sa bosse comme un diable, l'amour tout nu et éclatant dans son corps difforme, sous sa vieille peau. Et nous qui trichons tous avec l'amour depuis je ne sais combien de temps, nous voilà nez à nez avec lui maintenant. Quelle rencontre!

PAGE 95

Si Dieu avait voulu que l'amour soit éternel, je suis sûr qu'il se serait arrangé pour que les conditions du désir le demeurent. En faisant ce que je fais, j'ai conscience d'obéir obscurément à ses desseins.

PAGE 95

Mourir! Mourir par désespoir d'amour! Moi aussi, j'ai été désespéré à en mourir une bonne demi-douzaine de fois. Est-ce que je suis mort, sacrebleu? Non.

240

Vous croyez cela, vous aussi. Et je me dépouille, et je me déchire et je me tue pour l'être aimé? C'est vrai. Tant que l'être aimé est cette projection idéale de moi-même, tant qu'il est mon bien, ma chose, tant qu'il est moi. C'est si bon de sortir de l'immonde solitude. A soi-même, sincèrement on n'oserait pas. Mais tout donner à cet autre qui est vous, quelle bonne pluie d'été sur un coeur racorni. Jusqu'au moment où, caprice, hasard, l'autre redevient un autre, sans plus. Alors on arrête les frais, naturellement. Que voulez-vous donc qu'on donne à un autre sur cette terre? Ce serait de la philanthropie, ce ne serait plus de l'amour. ... Si nous persuadons à tante Ardèle de renoncer à tout donner à son bossu, c'est-à-dire à elle-même, c'est que nous pouvons tous guérir.

Villardieu. Et la nuit, pendant que je surveille sa porte, elle surveille la sienne. Le comte est le seul d'entre nous qui pourrait dormir. Je dis: "qui pourrait," car sa petite amie, qu'il ne peut jamais voir, lui fait des scènes, et je suis persuadé qu'il ne dort non plus.

Le Comte. Pourquoi ne voulez-vous pas lui reconnaître les droits que vous vous reconnaissez? ...
La Comtesse. Vous savez bien qu'il ne s'agit que de respecter les apparences. ... Malgré son âge, nous sommes obligés de considérer Ardèle comme une enfant irresponsable. Que peut-elle savoir de l'amour?
Le Comte (calmement). De l'amour comme vous l'entendez, comme je l'entends, comme l'entendent le général, Villardieu et Nathalie, rien peut-être. Mais de l'amour comme l'entend Ardèle, tout, surement ... Et qui peut dire si ce n'est pas précisément cela, l'amour?

La vie est faite de pièces de deux sous et il y en a une fortune pour ceux qui savent les amasser.

Lorsqu'on trouve un billet de mille, il ne faut pas le laisser filer.

PAGE 100

Il faut aimer contre eux, tante Ardèle! Il faut aimer contre tout. Il faut aimer de toutes vos forces pour ne pas devenir comme eux.

PAGE 102

Et sous ce déguisement de carnaval un coeur de vieux jeune homme qui attend toujours de tout donner. Mais comment se faire reconnaître sous ce masque? C'est ce qu'on appelle une belle carrière.

PAGE 103

La Générale. Nous fermions les yeux tous les deux dans le lit. Mais pendant que tu faisais ta petite besogne en imaginant Dieu sait qui—tu ne te figures pas tout de même que c'est à toi que je pensais?
Le Général. Comme vous êtes vulgaire, madame et impudique! Mais passons. Si nous en étions là l'un et l'autre, pourquoi tant de larmes, de reproches, pourquoi tant de cris depuis si longtemps?
La Générale (s'est dressée, terrible). Parce que tu es à moi, Léon. Tu es à moi, tu entends?—pour toujours—si lamentable que tu sois. Tu es à moi comme ma maison, comme mes bijoux, comme mes meubles, comme ton nom. Et je n'accepterai jamais, jamais quoi qu'il arrive, que ce qui est à moi soit à d'autres!
Le Général. Et vous croyez que c'est cela, madame, l'amour?
La Générale (dans un grand cri effroyable debout sur son lit, en chemise, cauchemardesque). Oui!
Le Général. Foutre, madame! Je refuse. Je ne suis pas à vous.
La Générale. A qui alors?
Le Général. A personne, madame. A moi peut-être.
La Générale. Non! Tu ne t'appartiens plus. Je suis ta femme. ... Tu m'appartiens.

PAGE 105

Pauvre ami, voulez-vous que je vous dise la moralité de cette histoire? Il ne faut jamais comprendre son ennemi—ni sa femme... Il ne faut jamais comprendre personne, d'ailleurs, ou on en meurt.

242

PAGE 106

Personne n'aime, ma chère, que dans le romans de bibliothèque de gares ... On joue le petit ballet du désir comme les toutous.

PAGE 112

Vous seriez mon fils, je vous pardonnerais de ne pas avoir le sens des affaires ni le goût de l'étude. Mais vous ne possédez ni la fortune qui vous permette, ni le nom qui vous oblige à vivre en oisif. ... Il faut travailler, mon petit; pour les gens de votre monde, il n'y a que cela.

PAGE 112

La drôlesse prétend qu'elle l'aime! C'est magnifique. Qu'ont-elles toutes? Qu'elles songent à servir et à être honnêtes d'abord, et qu'elles laissent le reste aux cocottes.

PAGE 113

Tu ne connais pas son travail de chaque jour, son ingéniosité, sa patience. Depuis vingt ans, moi, je l'ai à mes trousses comme une chienne hargneuse. Je sais que rien ne lui résiste, même pas la jeunesse, qui pourtant est aussi vivante et aussi forte que l'amour ... J'ai peur d'elle ...

PAGE 115

Oh! rien, Florent. Tu aurais beau le jeter tout entier au vent, par la fenêtre, en riant, comme l'autre jour, que ma peine ne s'envolerait pas avec lui ... Tu n'es pas seulement riche d'argent, comprends-le, tu es riche aussi de ta maison de petit garçon, de ta longue tranquillité et de celle de tes grands-pères ... Tu es riche de ta joie de vivre qui n'a jamais eu à attaquer ni à se défendre, et puis de ton talent aussi. Tu vois qu'il y a vraiment trop de choses à jeter par la fenêtre ... Et ne crois pas que tu es un monstre, surtout. Hartman t'a trompé en employant ce mot. Tu m'as torturée et tu es bon, tu sais, et ce n'est pas de ta faute, parce que tu ne sais rien.

PAGE 116

Je mets longtemps à les faire, ces tricots; et je saute des mailles par-ci par-là—je n'ai jamais été bonne ouvrière.

Mais les pauvres vous sont si reconnaissants quand ils savent qu'on les a faits soi-même.

. . . .

Je ne suis pas de ces oisives qui pourraient rester les mains vides. J'ai deux jardiniers, mais il m'arrive de tailler mes rosiers moi-même.

PAGE 116

Au fond, les midinettes et les dactylos nous envient; elles ne savent pas leur bonheur. La liberté que donne l'argent en travaillant, l'argent bien à soi. Si elles savaient comme sous prétexte de bonne éducation on est pingre, au fond, avec les jeunes filles, dans les meilleures familles françaises...

PAGE 118

J'ai une particularité, monsieur Julien, comme tous les ânes, je broute. Deux fois par jour. Et comme c'est elle qui me fait brouter, j'avale le reste avec le picotin.

PAGE 118

Warwick. Cela aurait même été, je vous l'ai dit, un peu vulgaire, un peu peuple, un peu bête, de vouloir mourir coûte que coûte, pour braver tout le monde et crier des insultes sur le bûcher.
Jeanne (doucement, comme pour elle). Mais je suis du peuple, moi, je suis bête... Et puis ma vie n'est pas ornée comme la vôtre, Monseigneur, toute lisse, toute droite, entre la guerre, la chasse, les plaisirs et votre belle fiancée... Qu'est-ce qui va me rester, à moi, quand je ne serai plus Jeanne?

PAGE 120

J'ai eu des pauvres bien entendu, comme j'ai eu des chevaux et des faces-à-main. On vit avec sa classe qu'on le veuille ou non.

PAGE 121

Moi, j'adorerais être pauvre! Seulement, je voudrais être vraiment pauvre. Tout ce qui est excessif m'enchante. Et puis, il doit certainement y avoir une grande poésie dans la misère, ... Comme cela serait amusant! Je te ferais ta vaisselle. Je cuirais, mon cher, pour toi. Je demanderais à Roeséda Soeurs de me faire des petits tabliers très drôles. (Il n'y a qu'elle, tu sais, qui pourrait réussir ça). Oh! rien

244

qu'un bout d'étoffe, une fronce, mais son chic! Nous aurions
des petites casseroles, des petits balais. Tu travaillerais dans
une usine. (Avec mes relations au Comité des Forges, tu
penses que je te trouverais tout de suite une place de
métallo). Tu rentrerais le soir harassé de fatigue et sentant
très mauvais. Ce serait délicieux! Je vous laverais, cher, avec
une petite éponge. Ah! que c'est beau, que c'est beau
d'être pauvre!

PAGE 122

L'argent ne peut rien! Tu auras beau en amasser encore dix
fois comme tu en as, tu n'en auras jamais assez pour t'éviter
d'être humilié et empêcher ta fille de souffrir. Ils sont plus
forts que nous papa, avec leurs portraits pleins de poussière
et leurs maisons qui ne tiennent plus debout. Ils veulent
bien prendre notre argent pour payer les réparations, mais
c'est tout. Ah! je te hais, je te hais d'être ta fille! J'aurais
tant voulu être comme eux!

PAGE 129

Le naturel, le vrai, celui du théâtre, est la chose la moins
naturelle du monde, ma chère. N'allez pas croire qu'il suffit
de retrouver le ton de la vie. D'abord dans la vie le texte
est toujours si mauvais! Nous vivons dans un monde qui a
complètement perdu l'usage du point-virgule, nous parlons
tous par phrases inachevées, avec trois petits points sous-
entendus, parce que nous ne trouvons jamais le mot juste.
Et puis le naturel de la conversation, que les comédiens
prétendent retrouver: ces balbutiements, ces hoquets, ces
hésitations, ces bavures, ce n'est vraiment pas la peine de
réunir cinq ou six cents personnes dans une salle et de
leur demander de l'argent, pour leur en donner le spectacle.
Ils adorent cela, je le sais, ils s'y reconnaissent. Il n'empêche
qu'il faut écrire et jouer la comédie mieux qu'eux. C'est très
joli la vie, mais cela n'a pas de forme. L'art a pour objet
de lui en donner une précisément et de faire par tous les
artifices possibles—plus vrai que le vrai.

PAGE 132

Une salle de café de ville d'eaux. Décor médiocre et
prétentieux. La scène est presque entièrement occupée par
l'estrade de l'orchestre. D'un côté la porte de l'office, que

les garçons poussent du pied, les bras chargés de leur plateau.

Trois tables en scène. La première, près de l'estrade, sert aux musiciens; elle est couverte de musique, de boîtes d'instrument; les deux autres sont vides; l'une d'elles a ses chaises renversées pour marquer qu'elle est retenue.

Le reste de la salle est invisible. Au mur un système de glaces qui multiplie l'orchestre et donne la profondeur du café.

L'orchestre se compose du pianiste: Gosta; du contre-bassiste: M. Tarde; de la violoncelliste: Mme Tarde; des premier et second violons: Thérèse et Jeannette.

Quand le rideau se lève, l'orchestre est en train d'achever un morceau très brillant. Le garçon écoute près de l'estrade; à la fin du morceau quelqu'un appelle le garçon au fond. Il se précipite, essuyant une table au passage.

PAGE 134

Vous avez toute juste le poids qu'il fallait ajouter au mien pour que je tienne sur la terre. Jusqu'à tout à l'heure, j'étais trop léger, je flottais, je me cognais aux meubles, aux gens.

PAGE 136

Comme dans la vie, ou comme au théâtre, du temps qu'il était encore bon. Un dénouement arrangé, pas trop triste en apparence, et dont personne n'est vraiment dupe—et quelque temps après: rideau.

PAGE 138

Vous qui êtes habitués à un théâtre où l'on ne mélange pas les genres, vous devez regarder avec étonnement ce jeune homme qui vous entraîne vers un vaudeville avec des traits tirés, des mains qui tremblent ... D'autres ont la tragédie tout naturellement à leur disposition; au moindre départ, à la plus petite peine, ils peuvent agiter leur mouchoir ou y aller de leur larme entourés de l'émotion unanime. Il se trouve que, moi, j'ai à jouer ma vie sur un vaudeville. Voilà.

PAGE 138

Isabelle. Vous jouez le drame ou le vaudeville?

Philémon. Je joue tout, Mademoiselle. Le classique et le moderne, le tragique et le comique.

Isabelle. Et vous ne mélangez jamais les genres?

246

Philémon. De mon temps cela ne se faisait pas, Mademoiselle! Mais avec les pièces qu'on nous sert maintenant, évidemment ...

PAGE 142

Oh! mon Dieu, je suis un monstre. Les autres amoureux croient à l'éternité, à la chaumière et à l'eau fraîche. Pourquoi m'avez-vous donné cet amour puisque vous ne m'avez pas donné avec lui toutes les crédulités nécessaires?

PAGE 150

Vincent. Je portais encore des pattes à cette époque. ...
La Mère. Les moustaches cirées des tziganes, les grands iris mauves et les renoncules vert pâle qui décoraient les murs. ... C'était l'époque de la broderie anglaise ... J'avais une robe toute blanche.

PAGE 152

Sorties de leur propre représentation, cela ne les amuse plus.

PAGE 152

Il faut que je dégoûte un peu. C'est dans mon rôle. Pas celui de la pièce de Marivaux, dans l'autre—celle que je joue vraiment.

PAGE 152

Héro (*déclame*). "Et que m'ordonnez-vous seigneur, présentement?
    De plaire à cette femme et d'être son amant?"
La Comtesse. Vous le pouvez Héro, si vous le voulez. Cette petite est une folle, une romanesque, une midinette, si ce n'est pas pis. Tout Paris sait que vous êtes irrésistible. Séduisez-la. Tant pis si nous jouons *Ruy Blas!*

PAGE 153

Rien que d'être bien une minute dans ses bras comme je l'ai été tout de suite. ... Après, s'il faut vivre l'autre vie, la vraie, celle qu'on doit gagner. ... cela ne fait rien.

PAGE 153

Ah! Ah! la plaisanterie est drôle! Vous me prenez donc pour un benêt? Pour un père de comédie? Vous imaginez que

je vais mettre un manteau sombre et prendre un rhume
dans le jardin pour voir si je n'y trouve point d'échelle?

PAGE 154

Il se peut qu'il y prenne un rhume, il se peut qu'il y trouve
l'amour ... Ou bien les deux. On verra bien! L'auteur ne sait
pas lui-même.

PAGE 155

Warwick. Nous sommes tous là? Bon. Alors le procès, tout
de suite. Plus vite elle sera jugée et brûlée, mieux cela sera.
Pour tout le monde.
Cauchon. Mais, Monseigneur, il y a toute l'histoire à jouer.
Domrémy, les Voix, Vaucouleurs, Chinon, le Sacre ...
Warwick. Mascarades! Cela, c'est l'histoire pour les enfants.
La belle armure blanche, l'étendard, la tendre et dure
vierge guerrière. C'est comme cela qu'on lui fera ses statues,
plus tard, pour les nécessités d'une autre politique. ... Vous
n'allez pas vous amuser à refaire toutes les batailles tout de
même? Orléans, Patay, Beaugency ... Ce serait extrêmement
désagréable pour moi.
Cauchon (*sourit*). Rassurez-vous, Monseigneur, nous ne
sommes pas assez nombreux pour jouer les batailles ...

PAGE 156

A quel moment, Messire? On ne sait plus où on en est. On
mélange tout. Au commencement quand j'entends mes Voix
ou à la fin du procès quand j'ai compris que mon roi et
mes compagnons aussi m'abandonnaient, quand j'ai douté,
quand j'ai abjuré et que je me suis reprise?

PAGE 157

La vraie fin de l'histoire de Jeanne, la vraie fin qui n'en
finira plus, celle qu'on se redira toujours, quand on aura
oublié ou confondu tous nos noms, ce n'est pas dans sa
misère de bête traquée à Rouen, c'est l'alouette en plein
ciel, c'est Jeanne à Reims dans toute sa gloire ... La vraie
fin de l'histoire de Jeanne est joyeuse. Jeanne d'Arc, c'est
une histoire qui finit bien!

PAGE 159

Il faut gaiement jouer la comédie. L'homme est un animal
inconsolable et gai. ... Tu verras, en grandissant, Toto, que
dans la vie, même quand ça a l'air d'être sérieux, ce n'est

tout de même que du guignol. Et qu'on joue toujours la même pièce.

PAGE 160

(*Elle la caresse du doigt, s'arrange les cheveux, se tire les yeux, lui sourit.*) Marc, tu l'as gardée? Tu l'as gardée cette photographie! Je l'ai pourtant cherchée, tu ne voulais pas me dire que tu l'avais ici, avec tes lettres de jeune homme, comme la photographie d'une petite amie... (*Un temps*). Une petite amie en manches à gigot. Tu m'aimes donc un peu, mon petit? (*Un silence*). Celle-là peut-être, mais moi? (*Elle va à la glace, se regarde sans un geste, sans que rien ne bouge sur son visage. Soudain, elle déchire la photographie sans la regarder*).
La Mère. J'en avais le droit. C'était une photographie de moi, n'est-ce pas?
Marc (*crie*). Non!
(*Un silence, ils se regardent*).
La Mère (*lentement*). C'est pour cela que je l'ai déchirée.

PAGE 162

Julien. Ne dis pas de mal de cette Colombe d'il y a deux ans. Je la garde celle-là! Elle est à moi!
Colombe. À toi, pauvre homme? Parce que tu l'as connue celle-là aussi! Un ange n'est-ce pas, tu l'as cru?... Garde-la si tu veux, ta Colombe en sucre d'orge, mais cette Sainte-Nitouche-là, je peux bien te dire que tu l'as rêvée tout éveillé comme le reste, mon pauvre biquet.
Julien (*l'a prise par les deux bras, il la secoue comme un fou*). Je te défends, tu entends, je te défends, celle-là, de la salir!
Colombe. J'ai bien le droit. C'est de moi qu'il s'agit tout de même?
Julien. Non!

PAGE 168

Mais, entre des milliers de souvenirs possibles, c'est justement le souvenir d'un ami que j'appelais avec le plus de tendresse. J'ai tout échafaudé sur le souvenir de cet ami imaginaire. Nos promenades passionnées, les livres que nous avions découverts ensemble, une jeune fille qu'il avait aimée en même temps que moi et que je lui avais sacrifiée, et

249

même—vous allez rire—que je lui avais sauvé la vie un jour en barque.

PAGE 168

Isabelle. C'est vrai que vous lui avez sauvé la vie en barque, autrefois?

Robert. En barque? Non, Mademoiselle, je regrette, mais je ne sais pas nager.

Isabelle (après un silence). Ah! Et cette jeune fille que vous lui avez sacrifiée?

Robert. Une jeune fille sacrifiée? Non, je ne me souviens pas. Je suis confus, Mademoiselle, mais je n'ai jamais entendu parler de cette jeune fille.

PAGE 174

Georges. Le rôle de la mère ... C'est le plus difficile. Quelle gamme de l'ennemie à perruque grise, qui défend chèrement son héritage, à la mère inquiétante qui frémit et perd le fil de la conversation comme une amoureuse quand son fils entre ou sort du salon!

Mme de Montalembreuse. Un bon rôle de mère doit contenir toutes les mères, c'est bien simple!

Georges. Non, je voudrais que celui-ci soit tout simple. Evident. La mère telle qu'on la décrit dans les livres d'enfants. Telle que les petits garçons la rêvent dans les cuisines, à côté des bonnes, en attendant que leur vraie maman rentre—trop parfumée—de ses éternelles courses de l'après-midi. Une mère qui n'aurait pas de courses à faire dans les magasins, pas d'amis à voir. Une mère admirable en somme.

Mme de Montalembreuse. Toutes les mères sont admirables cher Monsieur, l'instinct parle!

Georges. Il suffit d'une si légère négligence. Un sourire à un homme étranger qu'on laisse surprendre. Un seul mot trop dur, un jour d'exaspération, quand on n'a plus devant soi qu'un petit ennemi désarmé, mais irréductible. Un seul baiser oublié. Et un enfant, c'est là à vous épier, à tout exiger de vous chaque jour aussi tyranniquement, aussi minutieusement qu'un sergent de semaine. Oh! je sais bien que ce n'est pas un rôle facile, celui de la mère. C'est un rôle où l'on ne peut pas se faire doubler et qu'il ne faudrait pas accepter à la légère.

PAGE 175
Vous pensez! C'était une petite violiniste ... une petite putain de rien du tout ... Je lui ai flanqué une paire de gifles, oui!

PAGE 177
Georges. Tu es un vieux monsieur charmant, très jeune encore, d'une jeunesse contre laquelle le temps ne peut rien. Tu es le papa idéal, celui qui, avec la barbe, a renoncé aussi au genre "biblique," celui qui a su à temps se transformer en un grand frère. Un grand frère qui ne jouerait même pas les frères aînés, mais les camarades; tu es mon camarade, papa. D'ailleurs, tu t'habilles comme moi, et même—mais, c'est si naturel à ton âge—en plus jeune.
Philemon. Mais tout de même ... un père, n'est-ce pas?
Georges (sourit). Bien sûr, papa ... les jours où, précisément, un grand frère ordinaire aurait le droit de penser d'abord à lui; les jours où il faut se dévouer, pardonner, donner de l'argent aussi ... Ces jours-là tu redeviens un vrai papa, fort et rassurant, avec lequel on peut se permettre d'être une minute un petit garçon.

PAGE 182
Mme Desmermortes. Vous êtes laide. Quand on est laid, on n'a jamais vingt ans.
Capulat. On n'en a pas moins un coeur!
Mme Desmermortes. Ah! ma tout bonne. Cet instrument-là sans les autres ne sert à rien. Mais ne me faites pas dire de bêtises ... Vous avez tout de même été heureuse, Capulat, digne et respectée. Pour une fille comme vous, c'est la meilleure part. ... Il vous reste le bon Dieu à vous. Une vie d'ennui, c'est un placement.

PAGE 186
Philémon. Elle me pince le bras: "Ferdinand, nous avons joué dans cette ville!"
Mme de Montalembreuse. Quelque chose me le disait!
Philémon. Alors, moi, sceptique: "Des Places Clemenceau, il y en a partout, ma bonne amie." "Je te dis que quelque chose me le dit!" Et soudain elle s'écrie: "Regarde la statue!"
Mme de Montalembreuse (avec un geste). Ah! cette statue.
Philémon. Je regarde la statue; je m'arrête cloué sur place ...

251

Georges (*coupant court*). Et vous aviez vraiment joué ici autrefois?

Philémon. (*très simplement*). Non, c'était une erreur.

PAGE 187

Paris ne se toque plus que de petites imbéciles qui n'ont pas de seins et sont incapables de dire trois mots sans bafouiller ...

PAGE 187

La mère d'Eurydice fait une entrée triomphale. Boa, chapeau à plume. Elle n'a pas cessé de rajeunir depuis 1920. ... [Vincent est] argenté, beau et mou sous des dehors très énergiques. Le geste large, le sourire amer, l'oeil vague. Baise-main.

PAGE 206

Tous ceux qui avaient à mourir sont morts. ... Un grand apaisement triste tombe sur Thèbes et sur le palais vide où Créon va commencer à attendre la mort.

PAGE 208

C'est maintenant, Médée, qu'il faut être toi-même ... O mal! Grande bête vivante qui rampe sur moi et me lèche, prends-moi. Je suis à toi cette nuit, je suis ta femme. Pénètre-moi, déchire-moi, gonfle et brûle au milieu de moi. ... Je vis enfin! Je souffre et je nais. Ce sont mes noces. C'est pour cette nuit d'amour avec toi que j'ai vécu.

PAGE 209

Piège des yeux d'enfants, petites brutes sournoises, têtes d'hommes. ... petites volontés de vivre et d'être heureux ...

Bibliography

I: PLAYS OF ANOUILH IN FRENCH

The date in parentheses indicates the year in which the play was written. The edition used in the present study is preceded by an asterisk.

Humulus le muet (1929). Written in collaboration with Jean Aurenche. Grenoble, Ed. Françaises Nouvelles, n.d.; in *Pièces roses*, Paris, La Table Ronde, 1958.
Frequently performed by amateur companies.

Mandarine (1929). Unpublished.
Performed in February, 1933, at l'Athénée; 13 performances.

Attile le Magnifique (1930). Never published or produced.

L'hermine (1931). Published in *Les oeuvres libres*, Paris, 1934; in *Pièces noires*, Paris, Ed. Balzac, 1942; in *Pièces noires*, Paris, Calmann-Lévy, 1945; in *Pièces noires*, Bruxelles-Paris, Ed. du Sablon, 1945; in *Pièces noires*, Calmann-Lévy, 1945, 1949, 1950, *1952; in *Pièces noires*, Paris, La Table Ronde, 1958.
First performed in April, 1932, at the Théâtre de l'Oeuvre; 37 performances; produced and acted in by Paulette Pax.

Jézabel (1932). Published in *Nouvelles pièces noires*, Paris, La Table Ronde, *1946, 1947, 1949, 1953. Never performed.

Le bal des voleurs (1932). Published in *Les oeuvres libres*, Paris, 1938; in *Pièces roses*, Paris, Ed. Balzac, 1942; Grenoble, Ed. Françaises Nouvelles, 1945; in *Pièces roses*, Paris, Calmann-Lévy, 1945; in *Pièces roses*, Bruxelles-Paris, Ed. du Sablon, 1945; in *Pièces roses*, Calmann-Lévy, 1949, 1950, *1952; Paris, Le Bélier, 1952; in *Pièces roses*,

Paris, La Table Ronde, 1958; Coll. Théâtre de Notre Temps, Grenoble, Ed. Borda, n.d.

First performed in 1938 at the Théâtre des Arts, by André Barsacq; 200 performances. Revived at the Atelier during the Second World War.

La sauvage (1934). Published in *Les oeuvres libres*, Paris, 1938; in *Pièces noires*, Paris, Ed. Balzac, 1942; in *Pièces noires*, Paris, Calmann-Lévy, 1945, 1949, 1950, *1952; in *Pièces noires*, Paris, La Table Ronde, 1958.

First performed in January, 1938, at Les Mathurins; more than 100 performances; with Ludmilla Pitoëff and Georges Pitoëff. Revived at the Théâtre des Champs-Elysées, 1944.

Y avait un prisonnier (1934). Published in *L'Illustration* (Paris), 18 mai, 1935, Théâtre, nouvelle série, no. 370.

First performed in March, 1935, at the Théâtre des Ambassadeurs; ran approximately two and a half months; with Marie Bell.

Le petit bonheur (1935). Never published or performed.

Le voyageur sans bagage (1936). Published in *L'Illustration* (Paris), 10 avril, 1937, Théâtre, nouvelle série, no. 411; in *Pièces noires*, Paris, Ed. Balzac, 1942; in *Pièces noires*, Paris, Calmann-Lévy, 1945, 1949, 1950, *1952; in *Pièces noires*, Paris, La Table Ronde, 1958.

First performed in February, 1937, at Les Mathurins; 190 performances; with Georges Pitoëff and Ludmilla Pitoëff. Revived at the Atelier during the Second World War; also at the Michodière, with Pierre Fresnay, in 1944. Has also been made into a film.

Le rendez-vous de Senlis (1937). Published in *Pièces roses*, Paris, Ed. Balzac, 1942; in *Pièces roses*, Bruxelles-Paris, Ed. du Sablon, 1945; in *Pièces roses*, Paris, Calmann-Lévy, 1945, 1949, 1950, *1952; in *Pièces roses*, Paris, La Table Ronde, 1958.

First performed in 1938 at the Atelier. Revived at the Atelier in 1941 for 167 performances.

Léocadia (1939). Published in *Pièces roses*, Paris, Ed. Balzac, 1942; in *Pièces roses*, Bruxelles-Paris, Ed. du Sablon, 1945; in *Pièces roses*, Paris, Calmann-Lévy, 1945, 1949, 1950, *1952; in *Pièces roses*, Paris, La Table Ronde, 1958.

First performed in 1939 at the Atelier. Revived in 1940 at the Michodière for 150 performances; with Yvonne Printemps, Pierre Fresnay, and Victor Boucher.

Eurydice (1941). Published in *Pièces noires*, Paris, Calmann-Lévy, 1945, 1949, 1950, *1952; in *Pièces noires*, Paris, La Table Ronde, 1958.

First performed in 1941 at the Atelier; 90 performances.

Oreste (fragment, 1942?). Published in *La Table Ronde*, 3e cahier, 1945; in Robert de Luppé, *Jean Anouilh*, Paris, Ed. Universitaires, 1959. Never performed.

Antigone (1942). Paris, La Table Ronde, 1946 (édition de luxe); La Table Ronde, 1946; in *Nouvelles pièces noires*, La Table Ronde, 1946; La Table Ronde, 1947; in *Nouvelles pièces noires*, La Table Ronde, *1947; Coll. le Club Français du livre, *Théâtre*, vol. 2, Paris, Le Club Français du Livre, 1948 (with *Médée*); in *Nouvelles pièces noires*, La Table Ronde, 1949, 1953.

First performed in February, 1944, at the Atelier; more than 500 performances; with Monelle Valentin and Jean Davy. Revived frequently.

Roméo et Jeannette (1945). Published in *Nouvelles pièces noires*, Paris, La Table Ronde, 1946, *1947, 1949, 1953.

First performed in November, 1946, at the Atelier; 140 performances.

Médée (1946). Published in *Nouvelles pièces noires*, Paris, La Table Ronde, 1946, *1947; Paris, Le Club Français du Livre (with *Antigone*), 1948; in *Nouvelles pièces noires*, La Table Ronde, 1949, 1953; La Table Ronde, 1953.

First performed in April, 1953, at the Atelier; with Michèle Alfa.

L'invitation au château (1947). Paris, La Table Ronde, 1948; in *Pièces brillantes*, La Table Ronde, *1951.

First performed in 1947 at the Atelier; 334 performances.

Ardèle ou La marguerite (1948). Paris, La Table Ronde, *1949; in *Réalités Littéraires*, no. 29, sept., 1949; in *Pièces grinçantes*, La Table Ronde, 1956, 1957.

First performed in 1949 at the Comédie des Champs-Elysées; with Claude Sainval, Marcel Pérès, Jacques Castelot, and Marie Morgan.

Episode de la vie d'un auteur (1948). Published in *Cahiers de la Compagnie Madeleine Renaud–Jean-Louis Barrault,* no. 26, mai, 1959.

Presented as a curtain raiser with *Ardèle* in 1949.

Cécile ou L'école des pères (1949). Published in *Pièces brillantes,* Paris, La Table Ronde, *1951; La Table Ronde, 1954.

First performed in 1949.

La répétition ou L'amour puni (1950). Genève, La Palatine, 1950; in *Pièces brillantes,* Paris, La Table Ronde, *1951; Classiques Larousse, 1957.

First performed in November, 1950, at the Théâtre Marigny; with Jean-Louis Barrault, Madeleine Renaud, Jean Servais, Simone Valère, and Elina Labourdette.

Colombe (1950). Published in *Pièces brillantes,* Paris, La Table Ronde, *1951.

First performed in February, 1951; with Danièle Delorme, Yves Robert, and Marie Ventura.

La valse des toréadors (1951). Paris, La Table Ronde, *1952; in *Pièces grinçantes,* La Table Ronde, 1956, 1957.

First performed in January, 1952, at the Comédie des Champs-Elysées; with Claude Sainval, Marie Ventura, and Madeleine Barbulée.

L'alouette (1952?). Paris, La Table Ronde, *1953.

First performed in November, 1953, at the Théâtre Montparnasse; with Suzanne Flon and Michel Etcheverry.

Ornifle ou Le courant d'air (1955). Paris, La Table Ronde, *1956; in *Pièces grinçantes,* La Table Ronde, 1956, 1957.

First performed in November, 1955, at the Comédie des Champs-Elysées; with Pierre Brasseur.

Pauvre Bitos ou Le dîner de têtes (1956). Published in *Pièces grinçantes,* Paris, La Table Ronde, *1956, 1957.

First performed in October, 1956, at the Théâtre Montparnasse.

L'hurluberlu ou Le réactionnaire amoureux (1958). Paris, La Table Ronde, *1959.

First performed in February, 1959, at the Comédie des Champs-Elysées.

Becket ou L'honneur de Dieu (1959). Paris, La Table Ronde, *1959.

256

First performed in October, 1959, at the Théâtre Montparnasse-Gaston Baty; with Daniel Ivernel and Bruno Crémer.

II: PLAYS OF ANOUILH IN ENGLISH TRANSLATION

Dates of the first London and New York productions follow the listings of the translations.

Thieves' Carnival (*Le bal des voleurs*), translated by Lucienne Hill. London: Methuen, 1952, 1959; New York: Samuel French, 1956. In E. R. Bentley, *The Modern Theatre*, vol. 3 (New York: Doubleday).
London, 1951. New York, 1955.

Restless Heart (*La sauvage*), translated by Lucienne Hill. London: Methuen, 1957, 1958.
London, 1957.

Traveller Without Luggage (*Le voyageur sans bagage*), translated by John Whiting. London: Methuen, 1959.

Dinner with the Family (*Le rendez-vous de Senlis*), translated by Edward Owen Marsh. London: Methuen, 1958; London: Samuel French, 1958.
London, 1957.

Time Remembered (*Léocadia*), translated by Patricia Moyes. London: Methuen, 1955, 1956; New York: Coward-McCann, 1958; New York: Samuel French, 1959.
London, 1954. New York, 1957.

Point of Departure (*Eurydice*), translated by Kitty Black. London: Samuel French, 1951. Same translation published as *Legend of Lovers*, New York: Coward-McCann, 1952.

Eurydice, translated by Lothian Small. In *Two Plays* (with *Antigone*), London: Methuen, 1951.
London, 1950 (Kitty Black translation). New York, 1951 (Black).

Antigone, translated by Lewis Galantière. New York: Random House, 1946; New York: Samuel French, 1947; London: Methuen, 1951, 1957; in *Two Plays* (with *Eurydice*), London: Methuen, 1951.
London, 1948. New York, 1945.

Fading Mansions (*Roméo et Jeannette*), translated by

257

Donogh Macdonogh. This translation was presented in Great Britain in 1949, but, so far as I have been able to ascertain, has not been published.

Medea, translated by Luce and Arthur Klein. In E. R. Bentley, *The Modern Theatre,* vol. 5 (Doubleday).

Ring Round the Moon (*L'invitation au château*), adapted by Christopher Fry. London: Methuen, 1950, 1952; New York: Oxford, 1950; New York: Dramatists Play Service, 1952; in *Three European Plays* (Penguin Books, 1958).

Ardèle, translated by Lucienne Hill. London: Methuen, 1951; in *Ardèle and Colombe* (Methuen, 1959).

London, 1951. New York, 1950, under the title *The Cry of the Peacock,* an unpublished adaptation.

Colombe, adapted by Denis Cannan. London: Methuen, 1952; in *Ardèle and Colombe* (Methuen, 1959). Adapted as *Mademoiselle Colombe* by Louis Kronenberger. New York: Coward-McCann, 1954.

London, 1951 (Cannan). New York, 1954 (Kronenberger).

Waltz of the Toreadors, translated by Lucienne Hill. London: Elek Books, 1956; London: Samuel French, 1958; New York: Coward-McCann, 1957; New York: Samuel French, 1958.

London, 1956. New York, 1957.

The Lark, translated by Christopher Fry. London: Methuen, 1955; 1956; 1959; London: Samuel French, 1957; New York: Oxford, 1956. Adapted by Lillian Hellman, New York: Random House, 1956.

London, 1955 (Fry). New York, 1955 (Hellman).

The Fighting Cock (*L'hurluberlu*) was translated by Lucienne Hill for the New York production in December, 1959, but has not been published.

Mermaid Dramabooks, Hill and Wang, New York, have published the following two volumes of Anouilh's plays:

Volume I: *Antigone* (Lewis Galantière), *Eurydice* (Kitty Black), *The Ermine* (Miriam John), *The Rehearsal* (Lucienne Hill), *Romeo and Jeannette* (Miriam John).

Volume II: *Restless Heart* (Lucienne Hill), *Time Remembered* (Patricia Moyes), *Ardèle* (Lucienne Hill), *Mademoiselle Colombe* (Louis Kronenberger), *The Lark* (Lillian Hellman).

258

III: Articles by Anouilh

"Mon cher Pitoëff," *Aujourd'hui,* 11 septembre, 1940.
"Propos déplacés," *La Gerbe,* 14 novembre, 1940.
"Hommage à Giraudoux," *Chronique de Paris,* février, 1944.
"Hommage à Georges Pitoëff," *Opéra,* 4 mai, 1949.
"Ludmilla Pitoëff," *Opéra,* 19 septembre, 1951.
" 'La Valse des Toréadors?' Que voilà une bonne pièce," *Le Figaro,* 3 janvier, 1952.
"Lettre à une jeune fille qui veut faire du théâtre," *Elle,* 21 janvier, 1955.
"Du chapitre des 'Chaises,' " *Le Figaro,* 23 avril, 1956.

IV: Studies of Anouilh

Including works that contain sections devoted to the theater of Anouilh.

Albérès, René-Marill. *La Révolte des Ecrivains d'Aujourd'hui.* Paris: Ed. Corrêa, 1949.

Ambrière, Francis. *La Galerie Dramatique: 1945–1948. Le Théâtre Français Depuis la Libération.* Paris: Ed. Corrêa, 1949.

Barsacq, Henri. "Jean Anouilh," *Opéra,* 20 décembre, 1946.

Berger, Marcel. *Le Style au Microscope:* Vol. III. Paris: Calmann-Lévy, 1952.

Blanchart, Paul. "Jean Anouilh ou le Sauvage," *Théâtre,* 3e cahier. Paris: Ed. du Pavois, 1945.

Boisdeffre, Pierre de. *Métamorphose de la Littérature: Vol. II, De Proust à Sartre.* Paris: Ed. Alsatia, 1952.

———. *Des Vivants et des Morts.* Paris: Ed. Universitaires, 1954.

———. *Une Histoire Vivante de la Littérature d'Aujourd'hui.* Paris: Le Livre Contemporain, 1958.

Bonnes, Jean-Paul. "L'Antigone de Jean Anouilh," *La Revue Nouvelle,* III (1 juin, 1946), 662 ff.

Brasillach, Robert. "Jean Anouilh ou le Mythe du Baptême," in *Les Quatre Jeudis.* Paris: Ed. Balzac, 1944.

Brodin, Pierre. *Présences contemporaines:* Vol. I. Paris: Ed. Debresse, 1954.

Brown, John Mason. *Seeing Things*. New York: McGraw-Hill, 1946.

Cahiers de la Compagnie Madeleine Renaud–Jean-Louis Barrault, no. 26. Articles by Marguerite Jamois, André Barsacq, Roland Pietri and Jean-Denis Malclès, Roland Laudenbach, Jean-Louis Barrault, and A. Frank.

Carat, Jacques. "Délivrance d'Anouilh," *Paru*, no. 29 (avril, 1947), 40–43.

Champigny, Robert. "Theatre in a Mirror: Anouilh," *Yale French Studies*, no. 14 (Winter, 1954–55), 57–64.

Chastaing, Maxime. "Jean Anouilh," *Esprit*, XVI, no. 131 (mars, 1947), 499–504.

———. "Jean Anouilh ou le Théâtre de la pureté," *Jeux et Poésie* (3e série). Lyon: Ed. de l'Abeille, 1945.

———. "Théâtre et jugement chez Jean Anouilh," *La Vie Intellectuelle*, mars, 1948.

Chiari, Joseph. *The Contemporary French Theatre, The Flight From Naturalism*. New York: Macmillan, 1959.

Clouard, Henri. *Histoire de la Littérature française:* Vol. II. Paris: Albin Michel, 1949.

Coquet, James de. "Le Théâtre: L'Hermine," *Les Annales Politiques et Littéraires*, LII (10 avril, 1935), 350–351.

———. "Le Théâtre: La Sauvage," *ibid.*, LV (25 janvier, 1938), 71–72.

Curtis, Anthony. *New Developments in the French Theatre*. London: Curtain Press, 1948. "The Masques," VIII.

Didier, Jean. *A la Rencontre de Jean Anouilh*. Liège: La Sixaine, 1946.

Duvignaud, Jean. "La Vierge et le mousquetaire," *Nouvelle Revue Française*, (janvier, 1954), 128–130.

Farrell, Isolde. "Anouilh Returns," New York *Times*, Sunday, Jan. 8, 1954, "Drama," p. x3.

Gignoux, Hubert. *Jean Anouilh*. Paris: Ed. du Temps Présent, 1946.

Grossvogel, David I. *The Self-Conscious Stage in Modern French Drama*. New York: Columbia University Press, 1958.

Heiney, Donald. "Jean Anouilh, the Revival of Tragedy," *College English*, March, 1955.

Hobson, Harold. *The French Theatre of Today: An English View*. London: Harrap, 1953.

Jamet, Claude de. *Images mêlées*. Paris: Ed. de l'Elan, 1948.

John, S. "Obsession and Technique in the Plays of Jean Anouilh," *French Studies*, XI (April, 1957), 97–116.

Lapp, John C. "Anouilh's 'Médée': A Debt to Seneca," *Modern Language Notes*, LXIX (March, 1954), 183–187.

Lerminier, Georges. "Les tentations de Jean Anouilh," *Age Nouveau*, avril, 1951.

———. "Anouilh et la chasse à l'âme," *Terre Humaine*, mars, 1952.

Luppé, Robert de. *Jean Anouilh*. Paris: Ed. Universitaires, 1959.

Marcel, Gabriel. "De 'Jézabel' à 'Médée,'" *Revue de Paris*, LVIe année (juin, 1949), 96–110.

Marchant, William. "Pièces Roses," *Theatre Arts*, XXXIV (Nov., 1950), 36–39.

Marsh, Edward Owen. *Jean Anouilh: Poet of Pierrot and Pantaloon*. London: W. H. Allen, 1953.

Mury, Gilbert. "Anouilh devant l'action," *Poésie 47*, no. 36.

Perruchot, Henri. "Le Théâtre Rose et Noir de Jean Anouilh," *Synthèses*, no. 49 (juin, 1950), 49–63.

Pillement, Georges. *Anthologie du Théâtre Français Contemporain*: Vol. II, "Le Théâtre d'Avant-garde." Paris: Ed. du Bélier, 1945.

Pope-Hennessy, James. "The Theatre," *The Spectator*, Feb., 18, 1949, p. 218.

Poujol, Jacques. "Tendresse et Cruauté dans le Théâtre de Jean Anouilh," *French Review*, XXV, 337–347.

Pucciani, Oreste F. *The French Theater Since 1930*. Boston: Ginn, 1954.

Radine, Serge. *Anouilh–Lenormand–Salacrou: Trois Dramaturges à la Recherche de leur Vérité*. Genève: Ed. des Trois Collines, 1951.

Sartre, Jean-Paul. "Forgers of Myths: The Young Playwrights of France," *Theatre Arts*, XXX (1946), 324–335.

Saurel, René. "L'Alouette de Jean Anouilh," *Les Temps Modernes*, no. 96 (novembre, 1953), 955–956.

Scott-James, Paul. "The Theatre of Anouilh," *Contemporary Review*, no. 1025 (May, 1951), 302–308.

Truc, Gonzague. *Ecrits de Paris*, juillet, 1948.

Valency, Maurice. "The World of Anouilh," *Theatre Arts*, XLI (July, 1957), 31 ff.

V: GENERAL BIBLIOGRAPHY

Including all works quoted and cited, and a selected list of those consulted.

Beigbeder, Marc. *L'Homme Sartre*. Paris: Ed. Bordas, 1947.

Bentley, Eric. *The Modern Theatre: A Study of Dramatists and the Drama*. London: Robert Hale, 1950.

————. *In Search of Theater*. New York: Vintage Books, 1954.

Bergson, Henri. *Essai sur les Données Immédiates de la Conscience*. Paris: Presses Universitaires de France, 1948.

————. *L'Evolution Créatrice*. 31e éd.; Paris: Librairie Félix Alcan, 1927.

Boorsch, Jean. "The Use of Myth in Cocteau's Theatre," *Yale French Studies*, V, 75–81.

Boutang, Pierre. *Sartre est-il un "Possédé"?* Paris: La Table Ronde, 1946.

Brooks, Cleanth, and Robert B. Heilman. *Understanding Drama*. New York: Henry Holt, 1948.

Butcher, Samuel H. *Aristotle's Theory of Poetry and Fine Art, with a critical text and translation of the Poetics*. London: Macmillan, 1920.

Campbell, Lewis. *Tragic Drama in Aeschylus, Sophocles and Shakespeare*. New York: Longmans, Green, 1904.

Camus, Albert. *L'Homme Révolté*. Paris: Gallimard, 1951.

Cocteau, Jean. *Orphée*. Paris: Librairie Stock, 1927.

Coindreau, Maurice. "The Evolution of the Contemporary French Theatre," *Yale French Studies*, V, 27–33.

Courtney, William L. *The Idea of Tragedy in Ancient and Modern Drama*. Westminster: A. Constable, 1900.

Crocker, Lester G. *"Hamlet, Don Quijote, La Vida es Sueño,* the Quest for Values," *Publications of the Modern Language Association,* LXIX (1954), 278–313.

Drucker, Peter F. "The Unfashionable Kierkegaard," *Sewanee Review,* LVII (Oct.–Dec., 1949), 587–602.

Duckworth, George E., ed. *The Complete Roman Drama.* New York: Random House, 1942.

Eliot, T. S. *The Cocktail Party.* New York: Harcourt, Brace, 1950.

————. *A Dialogue on Poetic Drama, Preface to Of Dramatick Poesie: An Essay 1668, by John Dryden.* London: Frederick Etchells and Hugh Macdonald, 1928.

Euripides. *The Plays of Euripides.* "Everyman's Library," Vol. II. Edited by Ernest Rhys. New York: Dutton, 1917.

Fergusson, Francis. *The Idea of a Theater.* Garden City, N.Y.: Doubleday Anchor Books, 1953.

Filon, Auguste, *De Dumas à Rostand.* Paris: Armand Colin, 1898.

Giraudoux, Jean. *Littérature.* Montréal: Les Editions Variétés, 1946.

Greene, William Chase. *Moira, Fate, Good and Evil in Greek Thought.* Cambridge, Mass.: Harvard University Press, 1944.

Highet, Gilbert. "The Reinterpretation of the Myths," *Virginia Quarterly Review,* XXV (1949), 99–115.

Hook, Sidney. "Jaspers' 'Perennial Scope of Philosophy,'" *New York Times Book Review,* Jan. 15, 1950, p. 6.

Jaspers, Karl. *Tragedy is Not Enough.* Boston: Beacon Press, 1952.

Jones, Frank. "Scenes from the Life of Antigone," *Yale French Studies,* VI, 91–100.

Leavitt, Walter. "Sartre's Theatre," *Yale French Studies,* I, 102–105.

Linforth, Ivan M. *The Arts of Orpheus.* Berkeley: University of California Press, 1941.

Marivaux, P. C. de. *Théâtre.* Paris: Laplace, Sanchez, 1879.

May, Georges. "Marriage versus Love in the World of Giraudoux," *Yale French Studies,* XI, 106–115.

Mounier, Emmanuel. *Existentialist Philosophies: An Introduction.* New York: Macmillan, 1949.

Norwood, Gilbert. *Greek Tragedy.* London, 1920.

O'Connor, William Van. *Climates of Tragedy.* Baton Rouge, La.: Louisiana State University Press, 1943.

Ortega y Gasset, José. *Meditaciones del Quijote.* Madrid: Calpe, 1922.

Peyre, Henri. *Qu'est-ce que le Classicisme?* Paris: Librairie E. Droz, 1933.

——. "What Greece Means to Modern France," *Yale French Studies*, VI, 53–62.

Salacrou, Armand. *Théâtre,* Vol. I. Paris: Gallimard, 1943.

Simon, Pierre-Henri. *Témoins de l'Homme: La Condition Humaine dans la Littérature Contemporaine.* Paris: Librairie Armand Colin, 1951.

Slochower, Harry. "The Function of Myth in Existentialism," *Yale French Studies*, I, 42–52.

Sophocles. *Antigone,* translated by E. H. Plumptre. New York: Putnam, n.d.

Unamuno, Miguel de. *El Otro: Misterio en tres Jornadas y un Epílogo.* Bilbao: Espasa-Calpe, 1932.

——. *Del Sentimiento Trágico de la Vida.* Buenos Aires: Espasa-Calpe, 1947.

——. *Tres Novelas Ejemplares y un Prólogo.* Quinta edición; Buenos Aires: Espasa-Calpe, 1945.

——. *La Vida de Don Quijote y Sancho.* Octava edición; Buenos Aires: Espasa-Calpe, 1949.

Van den Esch, Jose. *Armand Salacrou: Dramaturge de l'Angoisse.* Paris: Ed. du Temps Présent, 1947.

Vittorini, Domenico. *The Drama of Luigi Pirandello.* Philadelphia: University of Pennsylvania Press, 1935.

Williams, Raymond. *Drama from Ibsen to Eliot.* London: Chatto and Windus, 1952.